POST
KEYNESIAN
ECONOMIC
THEORY

POST KEYNESIAN ECONOMIC THEORY

A Challenge to Neo Classical Economics

Edited by

PHILIP ARESTIS

Head of Economics Division
Thames Polytechnic

THANOS SKOURAS

Head of Department of Applied Economics
North-East London Polytechnic

WHEATSHEAF BOOKS · SUSSEX

M. E. SHARPE, INC. · ARMONK, NEW YORK

First published in Great Britain in 1985 by
WHEATSHEAF BOOKS LTD
A MEMBER OF THE HARVESTER PRESS PUBLISHING GROUP
Publisher: John Spiers
Director of Publications: Edward Elgar
16 Ship Street, Brighton, Sussex
and in the USA by
M. E. SHARPE, INC.
80 Business Park Drive, Armonk, New York, 10504

British Library Cataloguing in Publication Data

Post-Keynesian economic theory: a challenge to
  neo-classical economics.
  1. Economics — History — 20th century
  I. Arestis, P.   II. Skouras, Thanos
  330.1   HB87
  ISBN 0-7450-0027-4

Library of Congress Cataloging in Publication Data
Main entry under title:
Post-Keynesian economic theory.

  Bibliography: p
  Includes index.
  1. Economics — History — 20th century — Addresses,
essays, lectures.   2. Keynesian economics — Addresses,
essays, lectures.   3. Neoclassical school of economics —
Addresses, essays, lectures.   I. Arestis, Philip,
1941-   . II. Skouras, Thanos, 1943-
HB87.P62   1985   330′.09′04   84-23615
ISBN 0-87332-318-1
ISBN 0-87332-319-X (pbk.)

Typeset in 11/12 point Times Roman by
Alacrity Phototypesetters, Banwell Castle, Weston-super-Mare
Printed in Great Britain by Whitstable Litho Ltd., Whitstable, Kent

THE HARVESTER PRESS PUBLISHING GROUP
The Harvester Press Publishing Group comprises Harvester Press
Limited (chiefly publishing literature, fiction, philosophy,
psychology, and science and trade books), Harvester Press
Microform Publications Limited (publishing in microform
unpublished archives, scarce printed sources, and indexes to these
collections) and Wheatsheaf Books Limited (a wholly
independent company chiefly publishing in economics,
international politics, sociology and related social sciences),
whose books are distributed by The Harvester Press Limited and
its agencies throughout the world.

To the memory of the first post-Keynesians:
Michal Kalecki, Joan Robinson, Piero Sraffa
and Sidney Weintraub.

Contents

Foreword

A. S. Eichner

One frequently sees reference in the post-Keynesian literature to an important article which has appeared as one of the *Thames Papers in Political Economy*, and yet even post-Keynesians may have trouble identifying the source. Were they to surmise that it is merely another journal, housed at some university, they would lack an important clue as to why the *Papers* have played so conspicuous a role in the development of post-Keynesian theory, for the explanation may well lie in the fact that the *Thames Papers* are not a typical journal housed at a major university — or indeed, not even a journal at all.

The *Thames Papers* are published three times a year by Thames Polytechnic, in south-east London, close to Greenwich. While most British readers will be familiar with the polytechnics, other readers may need to be told something about them. The nearest equivalent in the United States would be an institution of higher education with the local ties and technical focus of a community college, the academic standards of a state college and the degree-granting powers of a university. The faculty members in the polytechnics are expected to serve primarily as teachers, rather than as researchers, and this emphasis has had the effect of creating an environment, at least in so far as economics is concerned, which is especially conducive to the type of free inquiry in which institutions of higher education are supposed to engage (the pressure to 'publish or perish' under which academics at more prestigious institutions find themselves, whatever its effect on scholarly output in quantitative terms, does not appear to encourage the same openness to new ideas). While there are only a few economists in the faculty at any one polytechnic, together they constitute a considerable number who, as a practice not always observed elsewhere, attend each others' seminars and conferences. It was in this environment that the *Thames Papers* were founded a decade ago as a means of enabling the larger group of polytechnic lecturers to become more familiar with the ideas of post-Keynesian economics.

The *Papers* were originally the idea of Thanos Skouras, who was then Head of Economics at Thames Polytechnic, but has since transferred to North-East London Polytechnic. Skouras had received an initial exposure to post-Keynesian theory while doing his graduate work at London University and hoped not only to introduce these ideas to the larger group of polytechnic lecturers but also to learn more himself about post-Keynesian theory. He was subsequently joined, as the co-editor of the *Thames Papers*, by Philip Arestis who succeeded him as the Head of Economics at Thames Polytechnic, and who was no less interested in some alternative to the standard economic theory.

The advantage of the *Papers* is that they avoid the formal selection process which, in the case of so many journals, defeats the very purpose of their publication. Some of the papers are the result of an invitation to a well-known post-Keynesian or other critic of conventional economics to address a meeting of the polytechnic's economists. Others are papers which Skouras and Arestis have either heard given at a conference, or have heard about from others. In this way, the editors can determine the content of the *Papers* rather than depend on a chance submission: indeed, articles are not normally submitted for publication. The editors thus retain the initiative in this as well as in other matters, and the result, as can be seen from the collection which follows, is an unusually high proportion of important contributions to the post-Keynesian literature.

This volume illustrates several important themes in the post-Keynesian literature, perhaps the most important of which is the need for economic theory to be policy-relevant. Indeed, this is one way to distinguish post-Keynesian work from that of other economists.

The primary purpose of the conventional theory is to

demonstrate that the market economy is a self-regulating mechanism and that, consequently, there is little need for government intervention. This has been the purpose of economic theory ever since Adam Smith provided the first systematic exposition. Today, this purpose is reflected in the central place of honour which is given to general equilibrium models by the majority of economists. In contrast, post-Keynesians are unwilling to assume that a market economy is self-regulating. At the very least, they believe that continuing active government intervention is essential to avoid some of the worst possibilities which are inherent in a decentralised system of production, one in which business firms as the principal actors face an unknown, and unknowable future. Prices cannot be counted on to correct any deviation from the desired growth path for, in the view of post-Keynesians, markets are as likely to be destabilising as stabilising. Hence the need, not just for an economic policy by the government but also, and even more important, for a sufficient understanding of how the economic system actually works so that effective policies for avoiding the worst of economic possibilities can be devised.

The papers included in this volume are all in this spirit. Minsky explains why a breakdown of the monetary-financial system is possible; Chick, how the introduction of new funds into the system occurs; Arestis, why the reliance on fiscal policy to stimulate the economy need not 'crowd out' non-governmental borrowers; and Bhaduri and Steindl, why a restrictive monetary policy — and hence monetarism — has become the favourite nostrum of international banking interests in the post-1971 era. Most important of all, Kitromilides explains why economists have so much trouble persuading government to follow their advice. In this set of papers — and indeed in the collection as a whole — you will find none of the arid formalism which seems to distinguish most of the work presently being done in economics. Rather, you will find a series of papers which, as well as relevant to the major policy questions of the day, are not beyond the comprehension of a non-professional audience.

Another important characteristic of post-Keynesian theory

is the tension, not fully resolved, between those who draw their inspiration from Keynes himself, and those who base their work instead on the ideas of the Polish economist, Michal Kalecki. It is this difference — between those who place a greater emphasis on monetary factors and those who see real factors as being more important — which still remains to be resolved to the full satisfaction of the leading figures within both groups. Thus, paralleling the papers by Minsky, Chick and Arestis which build on the work of Keynes, are the papers by Harcourt, Sawyer and Skouras calling attention to Kalecki's no less important role as one of the key figures in the development of a distinctly different post-Keynesian body of theory. This is only a difference in emphasis however, and not a manifestation of two irreconcilable theories, as is the case with the micro and macro halves of the 'neoclassical synthesis'.

There is a further point of tension within post-Keynesian theory though, and one which, even if not reflected in this volume, still deserves to be mentioned. This is the difference between those who, following Harrod and Sraffa, are primarily interested in the long period and those who, drawing upon Keynes and Kalecki for their inspiration, are more concerned with the short period. Again, it is principally a matter of emphasis, or rather, of what types of question are being asked. In this volume, the focus is on the short period and the types of policy questions which arise within that time scale. This means that it is largely the followers of Keynes and Kalecki among the post-Keynesians, and not the Sraffians, who are represented. However, within these parameters and, more importantly, within the limits of what can be included in a single volume, one can see the contribution of the *Thames Papers* to the growing body of post-Keynesian literature.

Introduction

P. Arestis and Thanos Skouras

This book is a selection from *Thames Papers in Political Economy*, a series which has appeared three times a year for over a decade and has enjoyed a small but increasing circulation amongst interested readers, mainly in British universities and polytechnics. The character of the series was firmly set by Joan Robinson in the very first paper, 'History versus Equilibrium' (Robinson, 1974). Subsequently, *Thames Papers in Political Economy* have investigated theoretical and policy questions in political economy always from a non-neoclassical perspective. Indeed, since its instigation, the series has aimed to broaden the discussion of economic problems beyond the confines of neoclassical analysis and to contribute to the construction and development of an alternative to the dominant paradigm of neoclassical theory.

The alternative, to the development of which this series has mainly contributed, is that of post-Keynesianism. It is true that post-Keynesianism is not a homogeneous body of thought; nevertheless, there are two important characteristics which distinguish it from others. First, there is the critical and theoretical, in contrast to merely empirical,[1] opposition that it has presented to neoclassical economics; second, the continuing search for a consistent theoretical construction that will complete the largely aborted Keynesian revolution (Eichner and Kregel, 1975). The various theoretical contributions that are brought together in this construction derive from a large and often disparate variety of authors.[2] Amongst them the most pre-eminent are those post-Keynesian economists to whose memory this book is dedicated: the Polish Michal

Kalecki, the English Joan Robinson, the Italian Piero Sraffa and the American Sidney Weintraub.

It has not been easy to compile this selection. The strict constraint on length, dictated by publishing considerations, made it impossible to include all the papers of merit that we would have liked. Having drastically cut the number of papers in repeated drafts, the final selection could only be made by further excisions on the grounds of accessibility and length, as well as on the requirements of continuity with respect to the book. However, we hope we have offered the reader a balanced selection, that reflects the advances that have been made in the development of post-Keynesian economics and is indicative of the calibre of the *Thames Papers in Political Economy* series.

The first chapter, by Yiannis Kitromilides, raises the crucial question of policy-making in the real world and asserts the need for a relevant theory of political economy. Kitromilides challenges the traditional justification for strictly separating the economist's formulation and assessment of economic policy from the political process of policy-formation and implementation. He argues that the common distinction be-tween the 'politics' and 'economics' of economic policy is logically and practically inadequate and he finds a need for an integrated 'political economy' approach to policy-making.

In the following chapter, Hyman Minsky provides a succinct critique of the neoclassical synthesis and develops a novel theory of the operation of capitalist economies. In his view, the financial structures and interrelations which are essential to the capitalist system result inevitably in pronounced volatility and even fragility of the system. The financial aspects of advanced capitalism, which are closely linked to expectations about future profitability with the latter crucially affecting investment decisions, far from reinforcing equilibrating mar-ket mechanisms, necessarily cause the system to be unstable. Minsky's 'financial instability hypothesis', in essence, is that certain financial aspects of a capitalist economy, which are indissociable from its capitalist nature, make such an economy inherently unstable.

The importance of the financial aspects of capitalism, and of the banking system in particular, is also emphasised in Chapter

3 by Amit Bhaduri and Josef Steindl, who are concerned with the question of the rise of monetarism and the interests that are favoured by the pursuit of restrictive monetary and fiscal policies. They argue that it is the banking and *rentier* interests which are primarily served by such policies, and that it is the shift of economic power from industry to banking and the increase in the banks' international operations and influence in the last quarter century which have made the monetarist episode possible. They conclude that monetarist policies are short-sighted, that the advantage they afford to the banking interests is fraught with danger, and that monetarism is not a sustainable policy doctrine.

Monetarist theory and its fundamental similarity with the 'Keynesian' position, in contrast to Keynes' method, is the topic of Victoria Chick's chapter. Chick focuses on the *mode* of introducing new money into the system and analyses this question, not in terms of neoclassical comparative statics, but by means of a much more interesting and policy-relevant process analysis. She concludes that the apparent differences between neo(classical)-Keynesians and monetarists, as to the relative efficacy of fiscal and monetary policy, are due to their shared neglect of the way in which monetary change originates, demonstrating well their common distance from Keynes' style of analysis.

The efficacy and monetary implications of fiscal policy is also the theme of Philip Arestis's chapter. Fiscal policy has been questioned as an effective policy instrument not only by monetarists but also by other neoclassical economists — notably the advocates of 'rational expectations theory' — on the grounds that government spending is competitive to, and crowds out, private expenditure. Arestis reviews both the theoretical foundations of the crowding-out argument and the empirical evidence for it. His conclusion is that although it is important to distinguish between the different ways governments finance budget deficits, it is, nevertheless, the case that complete crowding-out is extremely implausible and that, for all practical purposes, fiscal policy is of great importance in terms of its impact on the level and pace of economic activity.

Whilst the relative efficacy of monetary and fiscal policy has been at the heart of the debate between monetarists and neo(classical)-Keynesians, a similar concern has not been the sole or even the main preoccupation of post-Keynesian economists. Geoff Harcourt provides a 'guided tour', at an admirably brisk pace, of most of the body of thought of post-Keynesianism. After presenting the main contributors and indicating their considerable differences, he begins to untangle the various analytical strands which come under the umbrella of post-Keynesianism. In presenting the main characteristics of post-Keynesianism, Harcourt recognises the importance of Kalecki's original contributions, and makes clear that Kalecki, as much as Keynes, provides the inspiration for many of the strands of post-Keynesianism.

A further consideration of Kalecki's contribution is provided by Malcolm Sawyer, in a chapter which might seem provocative to many post-Keynesians, especially in the US. Sawyer maintains that Kalecki's work provides a superior starting-point to that of Keynes for the development of macroeconomics. He shows that Kalecki differs from Keynes in four important respects: on the nature of competition in a developed capitalist economy; on the nature of the financial system; on the usefulness of equilibrium analysis; and on the relative importance of political factors, institutions and ideas. Sawyer concludes that Kalecki's position on all these is more realistic, and goes on to outline the key features of a post-Kaleckian macroeconomic theory.

Kalecki also provides the starting-point for the final chapter in this volume, by Thanos Skouras. Skouras outlines a Kaleckian approach to development and, in particular, to the problem of rapid industrialisation. His analysis distinguishes between different types of political regimes which are combined with different types of property relations in the backward agricultural sector in order to explore the role and importance of political conditions in the development process. He concludes that political factors cannot be abstracted from the analysis of development and that rapid industrialisation is rare, under any kind of political regime, mainly because of the sociopolitical stresses that it inevitably gives rise to.

In conclusion, we would like to take the opportunity to

thank all the contributors to the series over the years as well as our colleagues S. Daniel, G. Hadjimatheou, J. Harrison, K. Heidensohn, Y. Kitromilides, G. Koolman, P. Nore and P. Oxlade, who have served for various periods on the editorial board. To C. Driver for initially suggesting the possibility of such a book and for making useful and helpful comments; and to the other members of the Division of Economics (Thames Polytechnic) for their help and encouragement. We also wish to acknowledge with gratitude the financial and other support that the *Thames Papers in Political Economy* have been given by Thames Polytechnic from the beginning, and by North-East Polytechnic since 1978. Finally, but by no means least, special thanks are due to Edward Elgar of Wheatsheaf for encouragement and constructive suggestions at the various stages this volume has gone through.

NOTES

1   This does not mean, of course, that post-Keynesians have not attempted empirical investigation. For a recent attempt to verify empirically some aspects of post-Keynesianism, the reader is referred to the work of A.S. Eichner and his associates at Rutgers University (Forman and Eichner, 1981, is a very good example).

2   Eichner (1983) offers a detailed view of what constitutes the theoretical core of post-Keynesianism (see also Robinson, 1979a). Indeed, the paper by Harcourt in this volume (Chapter 6) throws considerable light on the differences and common ground among post-Keynesian economists.

1. The Formation of Economic Policy: A Question for Economists?

Y. Kitromilides

INTRODUCTION*

Economics is often described as a 'policy science'. What is normally meant by such a statement is that the implications of economic theory or the information generated by economic research can be applied and utilised in tackling problems of public policy. Although economists consider their subject to have relevance for policy, the process of policy-formation itself has not been of immediate interest to economists. The conventional justification for neglecting the study of the process of policy-formation in economics is based on the principle of intellectual division of labour: the economic policy of any government is part of the general policy-making process. In order to understand how the policy-making machine operates and why certain policy options are adopted or rejected, it is necessary to examine a wide set of factors — political, administrative, cultural (in addition to economic theory) — which affect the formation of policy. The study of these wider influences on policy falls outside the scope of the discipline of economics. According to this conventional view, the type of questions raised in the discussion of how economic policy is actually being formulated are best analysed by specialists in other fields, such as political science, public administration, sociology, etc. This leaves economists free to

7

concentrate on what is their major task, that of understanding how the economic system works. Naturally, on the basis of this understanding, economists may recommend policies on how society can achieve predetermined objectives, but it is not their job to study either the way the objectives themselves are established, or the actual design and implementation of policy.

In economics, therefore, policy questions are approached within a framework of a 'given' policy-making system, in the sense that the workings of the system itself is not the object of study. Discussions of economic policy in economic textbooks usually begin with a description of the various 'objectives of economic policy', followed by an examination of the various 'instruments of policy'. The formation of economic policy is seen as essentially political in that policy-makers determine the objectives of policy. The application of economic theory, however, is not seen as political but rather as a purely technical exercise of providing information on the best instruments to achieve given ends. An important distinction is, therefore, drawn between those aspects of policy which require values and are 'political', and those that do not and are purely technical.[1] Ultimately, all policies are inevitably based on values, but it is claimed that these are not the values of the technical expert, but of the political decision-makers. The economist's claim for participation in policy-making is based on his/her ability to provide 'dispassionate', 'neutral' and 'objective' scientific advice, which although by itself insufficient to determine policy, nevertheless helps policy-makers to assess the consequences of pursuing alternative objectives or select the best instruments to achieve predetermined ends. This view of policy-making and the relationship between scientific knowledge and public policy is usually referred to as the technocratic model.

THE TECHNOCRATIC MODEL: DESCRIPTIVE OR PRESCRIPTIVE?

The main features of the technocratic approach are (i) the insistence upon the separation of 'facts' from 'values', and (ii) the 'rational' nature of policy-making. We shall return to these features shortly, but first let us examine whether the technocratic model is a positive description of how economic policy is made, or a normative prescription of how economic policy should be made, or indeed both, as this is not always made clear. Most economists would readily admit that the descriptive dimension is not the most relevant and would emphasise the prescriptive or normative dimensions of the model: policy-makers should have clear objectives; values should be confined to the selection of ends; technical experts should be 'neutral', i.e. not invoke their own value judgements in making policy recommendations. Nevertheless, many economists, especially when giving empirical accounts and assessments of economic policy, recognise that this textbook technocratic view is inadequate, not only as a descriptive account of how economic policy is made, but also as a prescriptive – normative model of how economic policy-making should be made. As Blackaby (1979) explains:

The clear distinction between 'instruments' and 'objectives' which appears in most models of economic policy is at variance with what happens in practice. In most models whereas the valuations put on different objectives are for the politicians to decide, the choice of instruments is assumed to be a purely technical matter. In real life, instruments are not neutral in this way, but are value-loaded and both Chancellors and Parties have shown preference from time to time for particular types of instruments ... Indeed most of the most strongly expressed disagreements about economic policy have not been about objectives but about instruments. (p. 7)

Blackaby goes on to argue that the reason why instruments are 'value-loaded' is due to 'uncertainty' and 'immaturity' in the present state of positive economic science.

Economic policy models tend to assume that the workings of the economic system is known. If this had been so, actual economic policy in Britain would have been very different. If there were an agreed body of economic knowledge ... there might be little reason for disagreement about policy. Such a state of knowledge did not and does not exist. (p.8)

Thus, economists simply do not possess sufficiently precise knowledge about the workings of the economy to be able to offer the kind of positive, instrumental and neutral advice envisaged by the textbook technocratic model. An obvious manifestation of the immaturity of the subject is the frequent coexistence of rival theories, offering competing explanations about the causes of 'economic ills' and therefore competing 'cures' or policy prescriptions. This state of affairs allows economists, or indeed policy advisers in all the 'immature' sciences, a much more active political role in policy formation.

The technocratic approach, therefore, according to this view has serious shortcomings not only as a descriptive but also and more significantly as a prescriptive model of policy-making: economic policy-making cannot be as prescribed by the model, because economic knowledge is not as precise and therefore as value-free as the model assumes.

This criticism might be accepted, but it can still be argued that there is nothing *in principle* wrong with the technocratic model. A defender of the technocratic approach might respond to this criticism as follows: although it is useful to be reminded that the claims of the 'textbook' model are premature and exaggerated and that the present ability of economists to provide objective, value-free instrumental advice is over-estimated, it does not follow that the technocratic approach as *a normative model* must be rejected. Although policy disagreements are not confined to the selection of ends but also relate to the choice of means, this is only due to limitations in the *current* state of knowledge. As the discipline of economics advances and matures, and as the statistical tools and techniques of testing are refined and perfected, then the technocratic ideal can be approximated even further because essentially factual disagreements about instruments will be reduced and eventually eliminated. As Lindbeck (1977, p. 27) points out, such advances have already narrowed down the scope for subjectivity and increased considerably the 'death risk' of erroneous theories, thus making it increasingly possible for the technocratic application of economic knowledge to public policy problems.

IS THE TECHNOCRATIC MODEL A SOUND ONE IN PRINCIPLE?

There are two claims implicit in the above argument. First, that the social sciences in general, and economics in particular, can (and should) achieve the status of the natural sciences; and secondly, that such status will enable knowledge gained in the social sciences to be applied 'technocratically' in public policy-making. Even if the first claim was true, which is doubtful, the second claim is certainly false. All knowledge, whether in the natural or social sciences, cannot be entirely value-free. It may be easier in the natural sciences to have more conclusive tests of competing hypotheses and therefore reduce the element of subjective bias in the selection of theories, but it does not mean that the theories themselves are value-free. Whether scientific theories contain values does not depend solely on the extent of 'maturity' or 'sophistication' in testing techniques attained by a scientific discipline. Even in the most mature and precise sciences, knowledge is not completely free of subjective value and Katouzian (1980) provides a number of reasons why this must be so:

First, facts in general and scientific facts in particular are not randomly observed. The observer — especially the scientific observer — is *looking for* them even before he succeeds in locating them. In other words, he uses certain criteria for *selecting* the *relevant* facts; and these criteria are themselves subjective, *a priori*, prior to the observation. Second, once selected, such facts on their own normally reveal or prove nothing as they stand. They are *processed* by certain procedures which are not part of that, or any other observation; that is by analytical and/or empirical *methods* which are entirely products of the human mind. Third, the so-called observer would even have to *select* the *appropriate* analytical and empirical methods — including laboratory tests — from a wide range of possibilities. (p.139)

However mature and precise economic knowledge becomes, it will still be 'value-loaded'. One of the central features of the technocratic model, the insistence upon the separation of facts from values and the identification of questions about means

with factual questions and those about ends with value questions, is in principle untenable. In other words, not only *in
practice* economists are not in a position to provide value-free
advice — chiefly because of limitations and uncertainties in the
current state of knowledge — but also *in principle* value-free
knowledge and therefore value-free advice is not possible. This
is equally true of the 'mature' natural sciences and the 'immature' social sciences. In any case, Gouldner (1976), among
others, has forcefully argued that, even if it was possible to
have value-free knowledge, it will be undesirable for scientists,
in advising policy-makers, to be ethically neutral. Similarly,
Easlea (1973) questions whether value neutrality should be a
legitimate goal of social science:

Of course, if a social scientist has transformed himself through
mutilation into a computer, then clearly he no longer has values —
or, rather, his 'values' are, in each run, those of his programmer.
However such a being would be regarded by all his fellows as a
psychopath — hardly a state to be desired. Yet it would appear that
some social scientists do desire this state. For this insistence that
scientific advice be called 'value-free' suggests that social scientists
should aim at achieving an attitude of moral indifference to the
human situation (learning, in other words, to regard the rest of the
human race as biologists learn to regard the greenfly) with the
ultimate aim of being prepared to place their expertise unreservedly
at the service of whoever commands or pays. (p.173)

Completely value-free scientific knowledge may be impossible, or even undesirable, but there is still another line of
defence of the technocratic approach that might be attempted:
if rationality in public decision-making is considered desirable,
then the technocratic approach, by insisting on the specification and clarification of objectives and the search of efficient
instruments, offers a method of rational decision-making.
Policy recommendations by scientists, although admittedly
based on less than 100 per cent 'objective' knowledge, can
contribute towards the formation of a more rational public
policy. In fact, most economists would consider this as the
most valuable contribution of economics to public policy —
i.e. that the information provided by economists *could* be used

to enhance the rationality and consistency of economic policy, provided that policy-makers have clear objectives and they seek advice on the best way of achieving them.

CAN ECONOMIC KNOWLEDGE ENHANCE THE RATIONALITY OF POLICY?

The major contentious issue here centres on the meaning to be attached to the term 'rational policy'. The concept of rationality implicit in the technocratic approach is closely linked with the fact-value dichotomy: according to the textbook technocratic model, public policy issues are capable of 'rational' resolution when an issue can be settled by an appeal to facts. Disputes about values cannot be rationally settled. As one chief exponent of this position puts it:

differences about economic policy ... derive predominantly from different predictions about the economic consequences of taking action — differences that in principle can be eliminated by the progress of positive economics — rather than from fundamental differences in basic values, differences about which men can ultimately only fight. (Friedman, 1953, ch. 1)

Thus, according to this view of rationality, science in general and positive economic science in particular, by providing policy-makers with value-free, instrumental information narrows down the area of 'irrational' controversy in public policy-making to the selection of ends. Rational individuals may fight over differences about values, but it is irrational to fight over differences about facts. Once a consensus is established over values, a positive science offers the opportunity for people to reason rather than fight over policy. Clearly, the science of economics, as practised now, cannot contribute towards the formation of a more rational policy, because — as Blackaby reminds us — instruments, as well as objectives of policy, are 'value-loaded', and therefore cannot be selected on a rational basis. Furthermore, since values, as we have argued above, are *inherent* in instruments, 'irrationality' will always be present in policy-making. Rational policy in this sense seems unattainable. Of course, the technocratic conception of rationality is not the only possible interpretation of the term 'rational policy'. Often the term simply means that policies are consistent with objectives. More generally, rational policy is one which follows certain ideal steps or meets certain ideal conditions. According to Carley (1980), the following five steps constitute the basic activities of rational policy:

(1) A problem which requires action is identified and goals, values and objectives related to the problem are classified and organised.
(2) All important possible ways of solving the problem or achieving goals and objectives are listed — these are alternative strategies, courses of action or policies.
(3) The important consequences which will follow from each alternative strategy are predicted and the probability of those consequences occurring is estimated.
(4) The consequences of each strategy are then compared to the goals and objectives identified above.
(5) Finally, a policy or strategy is selected in which consequences most closely match goals and objectives, or the problem is most nearly solved, or most benefit is got from equal cost, or equal benefit at least cost. (p.11)

Actual policy can be judged according to the extent to which it approximates this 'ideal'. Clearly, rational policy requires information, but the rationality of policy does not depend on the nature of this information. Policies which are based on 'poor' or 'inadequate' information will be 'poor' and 'inadequate' policies, but they will still be rational if they follow rational procedures. Similarly, even subjective and 'value-loaded' information can contribute towards the formation of a rational policy in this sense. Scientific knowledge, whether in the 'mature' natural sciences or 'immature' social sciences, can 'enlighten' or 'illuminate' policy decisions, but it cannot neutrally (i.e. without taking a moral position) determine in all circumstances what are the best instruments to achieve given objectives.[2] Scientific knowledge therefore, can enhance the rationality of policy without the scientists being detached from the policy-making process.

If the assumption of value neutrality is abandoned, then the relationship between economic knowledge and economic policy must be redefined. Also the whole basis of the intellectual division of labour needs to be re-examined. Since the distinction between the 'purely technical' and the 'purely political' aspects of economic policy is rejected, the separate treatment of questions relating to the 'politics of economic policy' from the discussion of 'technical questions' involving instruments of policy must also be rejected.[3] The consequence of this separation has been, on the one hand, an inadequate treatment of the state and its economic behaviour in orthodox economic theory and, on the other hand, a certain compartmentalism of knowledge, a process whereby the results of analysis of problems demarcated as 'political', 'sociological', 'psychological', etc. do not influence the analysis of economic problems, and vice versa. This condition is nowhere better illustrated than in the treatment of the state in orthodox economic theory.

TOWARDS A THEORY OF ECONOMIC POLICY FORMATION

We have emphasised in this chapter that due to the commitment to the technocratic ideal, economists have not been concerned with descriptive–explanatory theories of state economic behaviour and economic policy formation. Their major preoccupation has been with normative models attempting to define the 'legitimate' areas of state intervention on the economy, given the overall objective of social welfare maximisation. However, comparatively recently there has been an attempt to provide a positive explanation of the actual behaviour of the state in terms of an economic theory of democracy on the one hand, and an economic theory of bureaucracy on the other (Breton, 1974). Two points are worth making in connection with these theoretical developments.

First, the economic theory of government has had no significant impact on the core of economic theory and it still remains a peripheral subject. Second, the theory is based on a number of rather dubious assumptions. For example, the various agents in the political and bureaucratic process are assumed to be engaged in optimising behaviour: politicians aim at maximising the probability of their re-election, and bureaucrats the size of their bureaux. The more realistic concepts of 'incrementalism' and 'satisficing' behaviour are completely left out. It should be noted that, Simon (1976), the author of the 'rational comprehensive' theory of decision-making, argues that the rationalist ideal of optimising behaviour is utopian. Instead, in his descriptive work on organisational behaviour, he introduces the notion of 'satisficing' (the idea that people and organisations do not seek to optimise or maximise anything, but rather to reach a 'satisfactory' or 'acceptable' outcome). Decision-makers, typically, go through alternatives until a satisfactory or adequate one is found and there the search ends, even though superior alternatives may exist. Similarly, Lindblom (1959) has argued that 'muddling through' and 'partisan mutual adjustment' are more accurate descriptions of the actual behaviour of policy-makers than constrained optimisation.[4] Finally, the assumption that the political system is one of representative government in which the private citizen has direct influence on policy through his/her voting behaviour is also patently unrealistic. Since this is a positive theory attempting to explain actual policy-making behaviour, one cannot defend these assumptions on the ground that 'policy-makers do not actually behave like this, but they ought to'. Clearly, there has been little 'intellectual trade' here, and there is a conflict between the political assumptions of economic theory and those of political science.[5]

Orthodox economics has, quite wrongly in our view, ignored questions of economic policy formation. Even when some economists attempt to investigate this, they tend to ignore the work of specialists in other fields (e.g. political science). This is contrary to the whole spirit of the principle of intellectual division of labour. We believe, however, that the explanations of public policy formation that exist within political science, although an improvement on the naive political assumption of orthodox economic theory, are nevertheless inadequate to fill the gaps in our knowledge of what determines the formation of economic policy.

The dominant tradition in western political science views the political process as democratic and pluralist: democratic because political power is widely dispersed, and pluralist because a variety of different and competing interests have access to and influence on policy. Democracy guarantees pluralism, and vice versa. It is not possible here to do full justice to the variety of viewpoints and perspectives that exist within the pluralist tradition, but its essential elements may be summarised as follows.

In a pluralist society public policies tend to result from and reflect the compromise and bargaining necessary to resolve the conflicting interests of the various participants in the policy process. Although only a relatively small group has formal authority to make public policy decisions (e.g. elected politicians and full-time administrators), nevertheless, at any given time, a much larger and more diverse number of individuals, groups and institutions influence the initiation and modification of public policy. Pluralists make two important claims. First, there is no evidence that public policies reflect consistently the interest of one dominant group in society or a ruling élite. This is because élites are mutually restrained by competitive interaction and because the unorganised and inarticulate masses possess sufficient 'potential power' so that policy-makers keep their interests constantly in mind. Second, conflicts of interest are dealt with in a way that does not threaten the stability of society as a whole. This is because, on the one hand, the wide diffusion of political power itself promotes the resolution of conflict and, on the other hand, the nature of conflict is seen as multilateral among a large number of groups, some of which can be bought off as a result of economic growth. Thus, irreconcilable conflicts, such as those concerned with the redistribution of income and wealth, can easily be managed in an affluent society with surplus resources.

A variety of criticisms have been directed against these pluralist claims. Here, we only give a brief summary of the major objections. Even if it is granted that a plurality of interests has access to policy-making, this does not necessarily guarantee either stability or democracy. On the contrary. To the extent that the various partisans have roughly equal power, this may result in stalemate rather than compromise, more conflict rather than less; to the extent that 'compromise' solutions are found, this may be at the expense of the weakest interest. In fact the treatment of power and influence in the pluralist model ignores many other aspects of the problem. By concentrating on the exercise of *visible* power, it fails to take notice of how élites exercise *covert* influence (e.g. through anticipatory consideration of élite interests by policy-makers, or through the power of non-decision). Also, the values and the general cultural or ideological environment are, in fact, overwhelmingly biased in favour of the ruling dominant class, so that even the disadvantaged themselves may subscribe to these values. Finally, pluralists use double standards in their attitude towards indirect or covert influence. Parenti (1970) elaborates further on these double standards:

(1) Despite the fact that large corporation leaders and other economic notables control vast resources of wealth and property that affect the livelihoods, living standards and welfare of the community, it cannot be presumed that they exercise indirect, or potential influence over political leaders. Furthermore, it is unscientific to speak of political leaders as having anticipatory reactions to the interests of these economic élites. There must be discernible evidence of upper-class participation and victory in specific conflicts. But

(2) it may be presumed that the unorganised, less educated, lower-income voters exercise an indirect influence over decisions to which they have no easy access and about which they often have no direct knowledge. They accomplish this by evoking in the minds of political leaders a set of 'constant' but unspecified anticipatory reactions to the voters' policy preferences, preferences that are themselves frequently unspecified and unarticulated. (p.506)

It must be concluded that pluralist explanations of policy-formation present a rather distorted picture of the structure of power and influence in capitalist societies. Thus if one relies on the principle of intellectual division of labour for illumination on the issue of economic policy formation, there are no satisfactory answers either within orthodox economics or orthodox political science.

THE THEORY OF THE CAPITALIST STATE

There is, of course, an alternative approach based on the Marxist tradition of political economy, which has been ignored both by orthodox economics and political science. There has recently been a proliferation of Marxist writings on the theory of the capitalist state and, although there are significant individual differences, they nevertheless share considerable common ground to form a coherent alternative approach. According to Gough (1979):

The common element in all Marxists' theories of the state which distinguishes them from all other theories, is the subordination of the state to the particular mode of production and to the dominant class or classes within that mode. In other words, the economically dominant class is also the politically dominant or *ruling* class. (p.39)

It is in the elaboration of this theme that the major difference both among Marxist writers and between them and the rival pluralist school is to be found.

The well-known orthodox Marxist proposition that the behaviour of the state (superstructure) in a capitalist society is a reflection of and is determined by the economic base, has been challenged by more recent Marxists' works on the state as a crude over-simplification. There have been a number of modifications and qualifications to the simple economistic or reductionist view of the capitalist state. One significant departure is the development of the concept of the 'relative autonomy' of the state. The essential argument can be summarised as follows.

The capitalist class is not a monolithic entity with a single interest, but instead consists of several distinct elements or factions which may have common but also conflicting interests. The state therefore cannot be conceived of as a mere instrument promoting the interest of the capitalist class, since at any given time there are contradictory interests to be satisfied. The capitalist class has simultaneously short-term sectional interests and long-term general interests. The latter can only be promoted if the state is independent of the former. This is so because the nature of competition among individual capitalists is such that the emergence of spontaneous cooperative action to further their collective interest is impossible. If the general interest of capital is to be served at all, it must be served by the state, and if it is to be served effectively, the state must be autonomous (i.e. not in alliance with any sectional interests). It is this relative autonomy that gives the appearance of a 'neutral' state, responding to the demands and pressures of a variety of groups in society. Indeed, some policies may even favour the working class, if it is calculated to be in the long-term interests of capital.

Establishing the necessity of an autonomous state under capitalism is one thing; demonstrating that such an autonomous state must be a capitalist state (i.e. it must necessarily act in the long-term interest of capital) is another matter altogether. Put differently: What is the mechanism that ensures that the 'autonomous' state is not also a neutral arbiter in line with the pluralist conception of the state, but instead one that promotes the long-term interest of the economically dominant class? Why is the appearance of neutrality only on the surface and not in essence? Once the simple 'economic reductionism' is abandoned, the answers to these questions assume crucial importance.

One possibility is to show that state personnel are drawn overwhelmingly from the economically dominant class with a fairly homogeneous ideological, cultural and political position. This, however, does not establish that the state would necessarily act in the interest of capital. Would the state's policies be radically different if the only thing that changed was the class background of its personnel? Another possibility is to demonstrate empirically the enormous indirect influence the whole of the capitalist class exerts. This is also subject to the same criticism as before: it does not show, as the theory requires, the necessity of the state acting in the interest of the capitalist class. Would a shift in the balance of power in favour of the working class by itself cause a change in the nature of the state's policies? If that is so, then the theory would be virtually indistinguishable from pluralism.

Finally, it is possible to consider the operations of the capitalist economy, in particular the problems of capital accumulation in a world capitalist economic system, and examine whether it imposes certain imperatives on the policies of the nation-state, imperatives which ensure that the policies adopted must serve the long-term interests of capital. It may, of course, appear that with such an approach we have come back full circle to 'economic reductionism', a view rejected earlier as an over-simplification of a far more complex relation between the state and the economy. This is not quite so, however. Gough (1979), utilising the idea of 'structural constraints' presents a more flexible and less mechanistic view of why the state is a capitalist state:

What distinguishes Marxist theory is not the view that a particular class dominates the institution of the state (though this is the normal state of affairs) but that whoever occupies these positions is constrained by the imperatives of the capital accumulation process. But at the same time, separation and relative autonomy of the state permits numerous reforms to be won, and it in no way acts as the passive tool of one class. Within these constraints there is room for manoeuvre for competing strategies and policies. There is scope for the various organs of the state to initiate policies to reverse them, to make choices and to make mistakes. (p.44)

There are still significant problems to be resolved within the alternative approach. For example, Crouch (1979) has criticised among other things 'the complete assymetry' in Marxist literature between the treatment of the interest of the capitalist class and the interest of the working class and the inadequate answer to the question of whether working-class gains or 'concessions' are in the long-term interest of capital or labour.

Also Longstreth (1979) has persuasively argued that, in the case of Britain, the determination of economic policy this century has been dominated by one faction of British capital, the finance sector, possibly to the detriment of the long-term interests of capital as a whole.

CONCLUSION

It has not been our aim to provide a full assessment and evaluation of the Marxist and pluralist theories of policy-making. The main aim has been to challenge the traditional justification for excluding questions of policy-formation from economic discussions of economic policy. We argue that the traditional case for such exclusion is based on the technocratic model, which distinguishes between the 'technical' and 'political' aspects of policy and on the principle of intellectual division of labour which insists that the two aspects must be studied separately. We believe there are logical and practical grounds for rejecting the technocratic approach to the study of public policy in general, and economic policy in particular, and therefore for abandoning the distinction between the 'politics' and 'economics' of economic policy. In the real world of policy-making no such distinction exists and economists now, as always, function as *political economists*. It is time that they stopped aspiring (and often pretending) to be anything else.

NOTES

* 　I would like to thank P. Arestis, C. Driver, G. Hadjimatheou, J. Harrison, P. Schlesinger, A. Skouras and N. Zafiris for valuable comments on an earlier draft.

1 　Professor Peston (1979) draws a distinction between technical and political 'concepts of solution' to a policy problem: 'Economists, as would be expected, do place considerable emphasis on the technical solution to a problem. They are aware, however, that all policy-making takes place within a political and administrative context. It follows that another kind of solution concept would be a political one which, while it may be

dependent on the technical economic one, is not identical to it.' (p.14).

2 Atkinson and Stiglitz (1980) come closer to this view than the techno-cratic position when they state that the purpose of their normative analysis 'is not to provide definite policy recommendations but rather to examine the structure of arguments. It is a misunderstanding of the purpose of this literature to suppose that it can yield answers such as the optimum tax rate is 35 per cent ... The intention is to illuminate debate about policy rather than contribute to the formulation of policy itself' (p.12).

3 Similarly, the issue of the communication of economic theories to policy-makers has been treated as a non-economic question and largely ignored by economists. For an attempt to discuss this issue, see Kitromilides and Skouras (1979).

4 Simon (1976) considers satisficing behaviour as an undesirable property of actual decision-making systems and considers the achievement of greater rationality both desirable and possible. Lindblom (1959), on the other hand, takes a diametrically opposite view. He argues that not only is it inevitable but also highly desirable that public policies are not and cannot be rational in the sense envisaged by the 'rational comprehensive' theory. In a pluralist society, where almost every conceivable public policy involves some conflict of interest, there is no single rational decision or 'correct' solution for a problem. Social science 'solutions' to public policy problems are not necessarily superior to incremental, pragmatic solutions arrived at through the process of 'muddling through'. Whatever the disagreements between 'rationalist' and 'incre-mentalists' at the normative level, both schools agree that rational optimism does not in fact take place in actual policy-making.

5 The familiar reply to this criticism is that a theory should be judged by the success of its prediction and not by the realism of its assumptions. The economic theory of government can generate certain predictions. This theory should be judged in accordance with the success of its predictions in relation to those of any rival theory, rather than the realism of its assumptions. For a penetrating critique of this methodological position, see Katouzian (1980).

2 The Financial Instability Hypothesis: A Restatement

H. P. Minsky

INTRODUCTION*

It is trite to acknowledge that the capitalist economies are 'not behaving the way they are supposed to'. However, most economists — especially the policy-advising establishment in the United States — refuse to accept that at least part of the fault lies in the 'supposed to'. As a result, one cause of the troubles of the capitalist economies is that the economic theory that underlies economic policy (which defines the 'supposed to') just won't do for these economies at this time.

In this chapter the salient features of an economic theory that is an alternative to today's standard theory are put forth. Within this theory, which I call the *financial* instability hypothesis, the recent behaviour of the capitalist economies is not an anomaly: these economies have been behaving the way capitalist economies with sophisticated financial institutions are supposed to behave once economic intervention prevents fragile financial relations from leading to debt deflations and deep depressions. Because the financial instability hypothesis leads to a different view of the normal functioning of capitalist economies it has implications for economic policy that differ from those of the standard economic theory of our time.

We are in the midst of three closely related crises in economics: in performance, policy and theory. The crisis in performance is that inflation, financial disturbances, chronically high unemployment rates and instability of international exchanges are not desirable attributes of an economy and yet they now characterise not only the US economy but also well nigh all the more affluent capitalist economies.

The crisis in policy is that both monetary and fiscal policy seem to be ineffective, not only because of the trade-off between inflation and unemployment that is summarised by the Phillips curve, but more significantly because of a strong tendency for an expansion to become an inflationary expansion which, in turn, leads to an incipient financial crisis. With the current structure of the economy and policy reactions an incipient financial crisis leads to an inflationary recession: what is now called stagnation. In the years since the mid-1960s financial crises have emerged as clear and present, though intermittent, dangers. In the present structure of the economy and policy an inflationary 'floating-off' of inherited debt has become part of the process that has enabled capitalist economies to avoid deep and prolonged depressions.

The crisis in economic theory has two aspects: one is that 'devasting logical holes' have appeared in conventional theory; the other is that conventional theory has no explanation for financial crises. The logical flaw in standard economic theory is that it is unable to assimilate capital assets and money of the kind we have, which is created by banks as they finance capital asset production and ownership. The major propositions of neoclassical theory, which are that a *multi-market full employment equilibrium exists* and that *this equilibrium will be sought out by market processes*, has not been shown to be true for an economy with capital assets and capitalist financial institutions and practices. Furthermore, the financing of investment and capital asset holdings within a modern banking environment makes the effective money supply endogenous; endogenous money implies that there is a great deal of deviation amplifying complementarity among markets. Furthermore, 'too much' complementarity means that no equilibrium exists for multi-market interdependent systems. From time to time, especially during strong economic expansions and contractions, complementarity due to financial interactions becomes a dominant though transitory trait of our economy. Monetary theory cannot assume that monetary

changes occur within an economy that always has strong
equilibrium tendencies. The very definition of equilibrium that
is relevant for a capitalist economy with money differs from
the definition used in standard Walrasian theory.[1]

The second failure of standard theory is that it has no
explanation of financial instability. Three times in recent
decades (1966, 1969–70 and 1974–75) financial instability
loomed large in the United States. From the point of view of
standard theory, that which was happening in, let us say,
1974–75 just could not happen as a normal functioning result
of the economic process.

The financial instability hypothesis is an alternative to the
neoclassical synthesis (i.e. to today's standard economic
theory). It is designed to explain instability as a result of the
normal functioning of a capitalist economy. Instability of
financial markets — the periodic crunches, squeezes and
débâcles — is the observation. The theory is constructed so
that financial instability is a normal functioning, internally-
generated result of the behaviour of a capitalist economy.

The financial instability hypothesis is rich. It not only offers
an explanation of serious business cycles but it also offers
explanations of stagflation that goes beyond the money
supply, the fiscal posture of the government, or trade union
misbehaviour. It integrates the formation of relative prices wth
the composition of aggregate demand. In the financial
instability hypothesis, the pervasive role of profits in the
functioning of a capitalist economy is made clear. Profits are
that part of prices that support the financial system and the
structure of financial relations by providing the cash flows that
validate past financial commitments. Profits are also the
signals for investments and current financial commitments.
Furthermore, because they differ in how they generate profits,
the weighting of competition and monopoly markets in the
economy affects the system's reactions to monetary and fiscal
policy measures. But more important than these detailed
results is the 'big theorem' that emerges: this theorem is that *a
capitalist economy with sophisticated financial institutions is
capable of a number of modes of behaviour and the mode that
actually rules at any time depends upon institutional relations,*

the structure of financial linkages and the history of the economy.

The financial instability hypothesis has policy implications that go beyond the simple rules for monetary and fiscal policy that are derived from the neoclassical synthesis. In particular, the hypothesis leads to the conclusion that the maintenance of a robust financial structure is a precondition for effective anti-inflation and full employment policies without a need to hazard deep depressions. This implies that policies to control and guide the evolution of finance are necessary.

THE PLACE OF THE FINANCIAL INSTABILITY HYPOTHESIS IN ECONOMIC THEORY

The financial instability hypothesis is a variant of post-Keynesian economics. The interpretation of Keynes that has descended from the formalisations by Hicks, Hansen, Modigliani and Patinkin of *The General Theory* has always been of questionable legitimacy.[2] The interpretation of Keynes that is developing under the rather unfortunate label of post-Keynesian economics emphasises the importance of time and uncertainty, especially as they relate to capital asset pricing, investment and the liability asset structures of households, business and financial institutions, to an understanding of Keynes. One focal point of the emerging post-Keynesian theory is the proposition that the liquidity preference functions of the neoclassical synthesis is both a poor representation of Keynes' thought and an inept way to examine how money and finance affect the behaviour of a capitalist economy.[3]

In the interpretation of Keynes used in the neoclassical synthesis the liquidity preference function is interpreted as a demand for money function. In the rebuttal to Viner's (1936) outstanding review of *The General Theory*, Keynes (1937a) denied the validity of such an interpretation. Keynes argued that with a given set of long-run expectations (and with given institutional arrangements and conventions in finance) the supply and demand for money affects the price level of capital assets. In particular, Keynes argued against any view that the effect of the quantity of money was mainly on the price level of output or even the money value of output. Keynes argued that the supply and demand for money determines the price level of capital assets. His objection has been ignored, and the neoclassical model-builder continues to interpret liquidity preference as a demand equation for money. The revival of the quantity theory by Professor Friedman rests upon a stable demand for money function which permits the money supply to be the main determinant of the money value of total output (Friedman, 1956). It is but a small step from Friedman's construct to the pre-Keynesian view that the supply and demand for labour yields output and the quantity of money yields the price level.

The current dominant thrust in economic theory, which holds that the Walrasian theoretical scheme of a system of interdependent equations in which relative prices are the only argument, is valid and that the main proposition of this theory, which is that the economy will follow a full employment growth path, is valid, has taken economic theory full circle back to the 1920s and 1930s. This time, however, the neoclassical theory is buttressed against the objections raised by Keynes by what specialists in the philosophy of science characterise as degenerative and *ad hoc* assumptions. In the light of the current state of capital theory it is known that the proposition, that an investing economy with money and capital assets generates a growth equilibrium rests upon a prior assumption that investment goods and capital-asset prices are always equal.[4] This equality assumption is equivalent to assuming that the economy is now, and always will be, in equilibrium. Assuming the 'result' that a theory is 'designed' to prove is clearly not admissible. The buttressing of neoclassical theory by the assumption that capital asset prices are equal to investment goods prices reduces neoclassical theory to a tautology.

The view that Keynes advanced in his rebuttal to Viner (a view which appears in *The General Theory*) is that money, along with liability structure preferences, the mix of available capital assets, and the supply of financial assets, generates the prices of capital assets. In Keynes' view, each capital and financial asset is a combination of quick cash and future income. Furthermore, each liability is a dated demand or contingent commitment to pay cash. As a result of the nature of debts and contracts there will always be a subjective return from holding quick cash. The quantity of money determines the amount of quick cash that will be held and thus the subjective returns from holding money. The money prices of those assets which can be exchanged or pledged for quick cash only at a cost, and with varying degrees of certainty, but which yield cash income streams will have prices that adjust to the standard set by the subjective return on money. In contrast to the way in which the price system for capital assets is set the price system of current output (both consumption and investment output) is set by the short-run profit expectations of firms, demand conditions and the cost of producing output.

In aggregate, and in a closed economy, the cost of using capital assets to produce current output are mainly labour costs. The price system of current output is keyed to the money wage rate as the main determinant of relative unit costs of different outputs.

A capitalist economy, therefore, is characterised by two sets of relative prices, one of current output and the other of capital assets. Prices of capital assets depend upon current views of future profit (quasi-rent) flows and the current subjective value placed upon the insurance against uncertainty embodied in money or quick cash: these current views depend upon the expectations that are held about the longer-run development of the economy. The prices of current output are based upon current views of near-term demand conditions and current knowledge of money wage rates. Thus the prices of current output — and the employment offered in producing output — depend upon shorter-run expectations. Capital asset and current output prices are based upon expectations over quite different time horizons: capital asset prices reflect long-run expectations and current output prices reflect short-run expectations.

The alignment of these two sets of prices, which are based upon quite different time horizons and quite different

proximate variables, along with financing conditions, determines investment. Furthermore current investment demand,
along with other factors, such as consumption out of profit
income, savings out of wages income, the way government
taxes and spending respond to income, and the foreign trade
balance yield aggregate effective demand. The aggregate
effective demand for consumption, investment, government,
and export output yields employment.

The financial instability hypothesis starts with the determinants of each period's effective demand. It takes into
account the financial residue or legacy from past financing
activity and how this legacy both imposes requirements upon
the current functioning of the economy and conditions the
future behaviour of the economy. The financial instability
hypothesis forces us to look beyond the simple accounting
relations of the gross national product tables to the flow of
funds in a capitalist economy where cash payment commitments exist because they are a legacy from past financing
decisions.

The financial instability hypothesis which is rooted in
Keynes differs from what is explicit in Keynes and other post-
Keynesian economists in that financial institutions and usages
are integrated into the analysis. Furthermore, because of the
emphasis upon finance, and the way in which changes in
relative prices of current output and capital assets are brought
about, the hypothesis is more clearly a theory of the cyclical
behaviour of a capitalist economy than the economic theory of
other post-Keynesian economists. That is, the financial
instability hypothesis leads to an investment theory of the
business cycle and a financial theory of investment.

INVESTMENT, CONSUMPTION AND THE THEORY OF EFFECTIVE DEMAND[5]

The distinction between investment and consumption demand,
and the differences in the variables, markets and considerations
that affect these demands are crucial to an understanding of:

1 Why a theory of effective demand is necessary.
2 The concept of equilibrium that is relevant for the understanding of an investing capitalist economy and how the relevant concept differs from the concept as used in standard economic theory (i.e. the difference between Keynesian and Walrasian ideas of equilibrium).
3 The behaviour of a capitalist economy that uses expensive capital assets in production and which has complex, sophisticated and evolving financial institutions and practices.

In recent years a considerable literature on the interpretation and true meaning of Keynes has been produced.[6] Part of this literature consists of interpreting 'Keynesian economics' as a 'disequilibrium state' within the framework provided by static Walrasian general equilibrium theory. In these interpretations assumptions about market behaviour, in the form of sticky prices, are introduced so that 'short side' sales or 'rationing' characterises the equilibrium. The 'short side outcome' or 'rationing' of jobs yields unemployment as an equilibrium of a constrained system. In these models wage, price and interest rate rigidities are constraints which lead to the unemployment result, which is taken to characterise Keynesian analysis.[7]

This disequilibrium approach completely misses the central problem that was identified by Keynes, which is that in a capitalist economy the variables and markets which determine investment demand are different from the variables and markets that determine the extent to which labour is applied to existing capital assets to produce 'current output'. Keynes worked with interdependent markets, but the interdependence stretched back and forth through time and the variables and markets that are relevant to one set of time-dependent decisions are not the same as those that affect other sets. In these interdependent markets the signals from current utilisation rates to investment demand can be apt, non-existent, weak or perverse depending upon relations and institutions that reflect the history of the economy.

The main issue in the controversy about what Keynes really meant is not the discovery of the true meaning of the 'Master's' text. Rather, it is how to construct a theory that enables us to understand the behaviour of a capitalist economy. Hopefully, understanding how a capitalist economy behaves will give us knowledge that will enable us to control and change it so that its most perverse characteristics are either eliminated or attenuated. In this quest Keynes provides us with the 'shoulders of a giant' on which we can stand as we do our little bit. Therefore an attempt to understand Keynes is a valid scientific endeavour.

To understand Keynes it is necessary to recognise that his analysis was not solely given to explaining unemployment. True the massive and continuing unemployment of the 1930s was a 'critical experiment' thrown up by history which forced a reconsideration of the validity of the inherited economic theory. However Keynes, while allowing for and explaining the time-to-time appearance of deep and persistent unemployment, did not hold that deep depressions are the usual, normal or everlasting state of a capitalist economy. The collapse of the world's financial order over 1929–33 was another 'critical experiment' that forced a reconsideration of inherited economic theory. Keynes' special theory argued that in a particular conjunction, where a financial crisis and a debt-deflation process had just occurred, endogenous market processes were both inefficient and quite likely perverse, in that they would tend to make matters worse with regard to eliminating unemployment. This state would not last for ever, but would last long enough to be politically and socially relevant.

Keynes' *General Theory* viewed the progress of the economy as a cyclical process; his theory allowed for transitory states of moderate unemployment and minor inflations as well as serious inflations and deep depressions. Although cyclical behaviour is the rule for capitalist economies, Keynes clearly differentiated between normal and traumatic cycles. In a footnote Keynes (1936) noted that 'it is in the transition that we actually have our being' (p.343). This remark succinctly catches the inherently dynamic characteristics of the economy being studied.

Disequilibrium theorists such as Malinvaud persist in

forcing the analysis of inherently dynamic problems into their static general equilibrium framework. In this framework constraints and rigidities are introduced to determine the characteristics of the 'equilibrium'. In doing so, Malinvaud hides the interesting and relevant economics in the market and social processes that determine the constraints. The dis-equilibrium theorists may construct logically sound models that enable them to demonstrate some degree of a theoretical virtuosity, but at the price of making their economics trivial.

Keynes' novelty and relatively quick acceptance as a guide to policy were not due to his advocacy of debt-financed public expenditures and easy money as apt policies to reverse the downward movement and speed recovery during a depression. Such programmes were strongly advocated by various econo-mists throughout the world. Part of his exasperation with his colleagues and contemporaries was that the policies they advocated did not follow from their theory. In the United States economists such as Professor Paul Douglas, Henry Simon and even Jacob Viner, all of whom were at the University of Chicago, advocated what would now be called expansionary fiscal policies well before *The General Theory* appeared. Before Herbert Hoover became President of the United States, he was Secretary of Commerce. As such he sponsored Commissions and Reports which advocated a budget that was balanced over the business cycle rather than annually (i.e. under his auspices contra-cyclical fiscal policies were advocated). However, these economists and politicians did not have and hold a theory of the behaviour of capitalist economies which gave credence to their policies: their policy advice was divorced from their theory. Keynes' contribution can be interpreted as providing a theory that made activist expansionary policy a 'logical inference from a tightly knit theory' (Blaug, 1976, p.164).

The concept of 'effective' or aggregate demand and the market processes that determine each transitory equilibrium of effective demand and supply are central to Keynes' theory and central to an understanding of the dynamic processes that determine the behaviour of the economy. Significant and serious market failures occur because market processes do not assure that effective demand will be sufficient to achieve full employment. Furthermore, when effective demand is sufficient, so that full employment is first achieved and then sustained, market processes will take place which lead to a 'speculative' investment and financial boom that cannot be sustained.

Effective or aggregate demand is the sum of two demands: consumption and investment (Government and the rest of the world are ignored for now). Businesses offer employment and thus produce output on the basis of the profits they expect to earn by using labour and the existing capital assets to produce and distribute consumption and investment output. In production and distribution demand for labour to use with existing capital assets depends upon what Keynes identified as 'short-run expectations'. In determining the price at which shoes will be offered to American and German distributors for the next season, Italian producers need to estimate their labour and material costs over this relatively short horizon. The American and German wholesale and retail firms have to estimate next summer's market for shoes in their country — which mainly depends upon their expectations of income, employment and price developments. Similar short-run considerations centring on investment projects under way, authorisations to spend on investment approved by business, and financing arrangements being made affect the employment and output decisions of the producers of goods used in investment. Employment offered in the construction industry, where projects are undertaken on the basis of 'orders in hand', also relate to short-run expectations. Thus, it is short-run expectations that lead to the production of consumer and investment goods. Standard gross national product statistics measure the result over a period of time of a set of short-run expectations.

In addition to deciding how to use existing capacity, business has to decide whether and how to expand capacity. Whereas the utilisation of existing capacity is determined by price, cost and therefore profit expectations over a relatively short run (six months, one or two years) the decision to expand capacity is determined by profit expectations over a much longer time horizon: 10, 20 or even 40 years. Thus uncertainty, in the sense that there is a need to decide and act on the basis of conjectures about future economic and political situations which in no way can be encompassed by probability calculations, enters in an essential way into the determination of that part of today's effective demand that is derived from investment behaviour.

Investment demand is financed in a different manner from consumption demand. It is true that in a world with consumer credit, banks and financial relations affect consumption demand, but consumer demand mainly depends upon income plus the demand for capital assets while investment truly depends upon the conditions under which short- and long-term external finance are available. Thus the demand for investment output is affected by the long-run expectations not only of businessmen but also of the financial community. Finance and financial markets enter in an essential way in generating the effective demand for investment output.

The distinction between the external financing of household demand — consumer financing and the financing of home ownership — and of investment demand and capital asset ownership by business centres around the time horizon of the credits and the expected source of the funds that will fulfil the debt obligations. Aside from the financing of housing, consumer debt is typically short-run. While the banking system does provide business with short-term financing, typically for activity based upon short-run expectations, the financing of investment and of capital asset ownership involves longer-term equity and debt instruments. The cash required to fulfil consumer debt and housing finance obligations normally is received as wages and other household incomes. The cash required to fulfil obligations on the instruments used to finance business debt will be generated by profits and the way in which longer-run profit expectations are transformed into asset prices. The role of debt financing and the considerations bankers need take into account are different for household and business debts.

Investment demand determines whether the short-run profit expectations of businessmen who make decisions to utilise the existing production capacity are validated or not. If investment demand is at the appropriate level then the various outputs produced with existing productive capacity will generate the profits that are expected. If such a result occurs, then business will be induced to offer the same employment to produce the same output, provided that the intervals between the first and subsequent production decisions are so small that the ongoing investments do not significantly affect production possibilities, and the liabilities issued to finance investment do not significantly affect cash payment commitments.

In as much as aggregate profits are generated by the way demand affects the utilisation of existing capacity, the validation of short-run profit expectations by realised profits depends upon the level of investment activity. It is financed investment demand that forces aggregate effective demand, by means of the multiplier, to the level at which savings equal investment. If investment is stabilised, then the aggregate flow of profits is determined and eventually, by a process of market adjustments, employment will settle at the level that is determined by correctly anticipating the volume of profits that follows from the hypothetically stabilised investment. Thus to each state of long-run expectations there corresponds a level of investment, and if short-run expectations adjust to the profits implicit in that investment level then there will be a level of employment at which the economy will settle. This level of employment which is consistent with the state of long-term expectations is the 'virtual' equilibrium of the system that Keynes considered: it is an implicit rather than an achieved equilibrium, for in truth the effects of investment and financing upon production capacity and payment commitments that are placed in the *ceteris paribus* bag will be taking place and these cumulated effects will change the implicit equilibrium of the system. Furthermore, if the short-run equilibrium implicit in the state of long-run expectations is attained and then sustained, a 'stable' or 'tranquil' behaviour of the economy will result. Such a stable or tranquil state, if sustained for a while, will feed back and affect long-term expectations about the performance of the economy. This will affect views of the uncertainties involved which, in turn, will affect asset values and permissible liability structures.

For the economy to sustain a virtual equilibrium of employment in which short-run profit expectations are consistent with financed investment, the profit flows must be sufficient to validate debts (i.e. business will be able to fulfil their cash payment commitments embodied in their liability structure). But such fulfilment of debt commitments will affect the willingness to finance debt by bankers and their customers: the value of the insurance embodied in money decreases as the economy functions in a tranquil way. Stability — or tranquillity — in a world with a cyclical past and capitalist financial institutions is destabilising.

If a transitory equilibrium defined by the existing short-run expectations differs from full employment the question arises as to whether labour, product or financial market reactions to the ruling situation will affect either short- or long-run expectations in such a way that a movement towards full employment takes place. Keynes' answer was that this depends upon how the market adjustments affect the state of long-run expectations that guide businessmen and their bankers as they hold and finance positions in capital assets, and as they plan and finance investment spending. In the years of the great contraction (1929–33) it seems clear that responses in labour, product and financial markets to unemployment, excess supply and difficulty in meeting financial commitments made things worse, not better. Falling wages and product prices, by increasing the burden of cash payment commitments due to existing debts relative to profit flows which depend upon current prices, outputs and wages, made the state of long-run expectations of businessmen and bankers less, not more, favourable to ordering investment output.

Thus there is a problem of effective demand failures in a capitalist economy that is not due to wages, price or interest rate rigidities. To recognise that such a problem exists it is necessary to specify that we are dealing with an investing capitalist economy that has sophisticated financial institutions. In such an economy employment is offered on the basis of short-run profit expectations, whereas investment demand, which depends upon long-run profit expectations, determines the profits that in fact are realised. Only if market reactions to unemployment change long-run expectations so that investment increases and if market reactions to excess aggregate demand change long-run expectations so that investment decreases can the system be considered as self-equilibrating, with its 'equilibrium' in the neighbourhood of full employment.

The financial instability hypothesis, by emphasising the way in which investment demand is generated by the combination of the valuation of the stock of assets, the financing available from internal funds and financial markets, and the supply price of investment output shows how a collapse of asset values, that occurs because of position-making problems of units engaged in speculative and Ponzi[8] finance, leads to a collapse of investment. Such a collapse will lead to a shortfall in the profit flows generated by capital assets, which in turn makes the fulfilment of business financial commitments more difficult, if not impossible. Financial structures and financial interrelations are the phenomena in a capitalist economy that make the development of those long-term expectations that lead to a collapse of investment an endogenous phenomenon in the particular circumstances that, in fact, arise in the aftermath of a sustained expansion.

A RESTATEMENT OF THE FINANCIAL INSTABILITY HYPOTHESIS

The financial instability hypothesis is rooted in the analysis of the two sets of prices that exist in capitalism: those of current output, which reflect short-run or current considerations, and those of capital assets which reflect long-run expectations (Minsky, 1974a). Thus it is a variant of Keynesian theory. However the financial instability hypothesis goes beyond what is explicit in *The General Theory* by integrating the liability structure and the cash payment commitments they imply into the analysis of the determination of capital asset prices and the financing of investment. The view of the economy is from Wall Street or the City. Economic activity is seen as generating business cash flows, and part of these is applied to validate debt. Anticipated cash flows from business operations determine the demand for and supply of 'debts' to be used to finance positions in capital assets and the production of new capital assets (investment output). Money is mainly created as banks finance business and acquire other assets, and money is destroyed as debts to banks are repaid or as banks sell assets.[9]

This Wall Street or City view looks upon the exchange of money today for money later as the key economic transaction. The money today part may involve a financial instrument, an existing capital asset or investment output. The money tomorrow part may be interest, dividends, repayment of principal *or* the gross profits after taxes from the use of capital assets in production. Acquiring capital assets in general and investment in particular are money today–money tomorrow transactions. Debt-financed positions in capital assets and investments involve two sets of money today–money tomorrow transactions: one set consists of the promises to pay on the debt instrument, the other consists of the returns that will be earned as the capital asset or completed investment good is used in production.

An economy with a Wall Street cannot be static. Yesterday's debts and capital asset acquisitions have to be validated by today's cash flows; today's cash flows are largely determined by today's investment; today's investment will or will not be validated depending upon the cash flows that are generated tomorrow. Therefore the economic theory that is relevant for an economy with a Wall Street cannot be static; it cannot abstract from time.

The cash flows that validate debt and the prices that were paid in the past for capital assets are profits. These profits are capital's share in gross national product, not the net profits of financial reports. The critical question for an economy with a Wall Street is 'what determines profits'. The answer that neoclassical theory gives is that the technical marginal productivity of capital generates profits. This obviously won't do in a world where output fluctuates and market power exists. Once the dynamic and cyclical character of the economy is accepted, the production function construct will not do as the basis for the theoretical analysis of either output or of relative factor renumerations.

The existing set of short-run cost curves, which reflect technical capabilities as embodied in capital assets, is the appropriate starting-point for the analysis of profit flows. These cost curves state the actual relation between out-of-pocket costs and output. When cost curves are combined with market conditions, variations in demand curves (that reflect variations in aggregate demand) translate into variations in gross profits. If gross profits are large enough, the debt structure and past investment decisions are validated.

If, with Kalecki,[10] we assume that workers spend all they earn on consumption and profit-receivers do not consume, we get

$$\pi = I \text{ (profits equal investment)}.$$

This is nothing more than a restatement of $S = I$ (savings equals investment). However, I is a function of (PK, PI(I), E π, Ext. Finance) where PK = price of capital assets, PI(I) = supply price of investment goods as functions of investment price, E π = expected profits and Ext. Finance = external financing conditions. Thus

$$I \rightarrow \pi. \text{ The causation runs from investment to profits.}$$

Investment calls the tune and finance affects investment. It can readily be shown that

$$\overset{*}{\pi} = I + DF,$$

when DF is the government deficit and $\overset{*}{\pi}$ is after-tax profits.

Furthermore,

$$\overset{*}{\pi} = I + DF - BPDF,$$

where BPDF is the deficit in the balance of payments. The

Kalecki model can also allow for consumption out of profits $C\overset{*}{\pi}$ and savings by workers SW which leads to:

$$\overset{*}{\pi} = I + DF - BPDF - SW + C\overset{*}{\pi}, \text{ so that}$$

$$\overset{*}{\pi} = 1 / 1 - C (I + DF - BPDF - SW).$$

Profits, rather than being determined by technology as in the neoclassical synthesis where production functions rule the roost, are determined by the economic, political, social and psychological relations that determine I, DF, BPDF, W, SW and $C\overset{*}{\pi}$ (Skouras, 1975).

This view of profits as the result of the way the economy in fact functions clearly identifies profits as cash flow. Viewing profits as cash flow quite naturally leads to an analysis of the different roles played by profits in a capitalist economy. Realised profits in a capitalist economy are: (i) the cash flows that may (or may not) validate debts and the prices paid for capital assets; (ii) the mark-up on labour costs that assure that what is produced by part of the labour force is allocated to all of the labour force. (This allocating of what is produced by a part to the whole is a device for generating a surplus); and (iii) the signals whether accumulation should continue and where the surplus should be used.

Profits — especially profits relative to the cash payment commitments on debts — affect the long-run expectations of business and bankers. Profits are the critical link to time in a capitalist economy: they are determined by the existing size and structure of aggregate demand, they determine whether the past debts and prices paid for capital assets are validated, and they affect the long-run expectations of businessmen and bankers that enter into investment and financing decisions. We are dealing with a capitalist economy with a past, a present and a future. In such an economy the extent to which present profits validate decisions taken in the past affects long-run expectations and thus present investment and financing decisions; present investment and financing decisions in turn determine the parameters within which future decisions will be made. By focusing on profits a theory based upon Kalecki's insights on how profit is generated clearly recognises that we need build our theory to be relevant for an economy that exists in history.

A capitalist economy only works well as an investing economy for investment generates profits. Profit expectations make debt financing possible and help determine the demand for investment output. Investment takes place because it is expected that capital assets will yield profits in the future, but these future profits will be forthcoming only if future investment takes place. Profits are the carrot and stick that make capitalism work.

Profits result from an excess of prices over unit labour and purchased input costs. The price system for current output allocates profits to particular outputs and thus to particular in existence capital assets. In the simple model where government and foreign trade are not taken into account, prices and outputs adjust so that profits equal financed investment. Relative price formation, production and employment take place within aggregate economic conditions that are determined by the need for profits to equal investment.

The identification of profits as a flow determined by the income generating process is but one ingredient in the financial instability view. This ingredient leads to the proposition that current investment determines whether or not the financial commitments on business debts can be fulfilled. At a sufficiently low level of investment, income, employment, and thus profits, a significant proportion of the contractual commitments on business debts cannot be fulfilled from the normal sources. Attempts by debtors to raise funds needed to meet commitments by recourse to extraordinary sources, such as the sale of assets, are part of the mechanism by which an initial financial tautness is transformed into a financial crisis. Fluctuations in investment determine whether or not debts can be validated; the question that now has to be addressed is: Why does investment fluctuate?

To answer this question, we turn to the financial system and the debt structure (Minsky, 1974, 1975a, 1975b). Any position (i.e. a set of owned assets) needs to be financed. The instruments used to finance positions set up cash flow commitments even as the assets 'in position' yield cash flows. We can distinguish three types of financial postures:

1. *Hedge finance.* The cash flows from assets in position are expected to exceed the cash flow commitments on liabilities for every period. As cash in exceeds cash out in every period the expected present value of a hedge finance unit is positive for every set of finite interest rates. The liability structure of a hedge unit consists mainly of long-term debts and equity, although short-term commercial credits to finance work in progress are consistent with hedge financing.

2. *Speculative finance.* The cash flows from assets in the near term fall short of the near-term contracted payments, but the income portion of the near-term cash flows, measured by accepted accounting conventions, exceeds the interest cost of the debt, and the expected cash receipts in the longer term are expected to exceed cash payments commitments that are outstanding. A unit engaged in speculative finance needs to roll over or refinance debt to meet its near-term financial commitments. The present value of the net cash flows of a speculative finance unit will be positive for one set of (low) interest rates and negative for other higher interest rates. Banks are speculative finance units.

3. *'Ponzi' finance.* The cash flows from assets in the near term fall short of cash payment commitments and the net income portion of the receipts falls short of the interest portion of the payments. A Ponzi finance unit must increase its outstanding debt in order to meet its financial obligations. Presumably, there is a 'bonanza' in the future which makes the present value positive for low enough interest rates. Although Ponzi finance is often tinged with fraud, every investment project with a long gestation period and somewhat uncertain returns has aspects of a Ponzi finance scheme. Many of the real estate investment trusts that came upon hard times in 1974–75 in the United States were, quite unknown to the household investors who bought their equities, involved in Ponzi schemes. Many of these trusts were financing construction projects that had to be

sold out quickly and at a favourable price if the debts to the trusts were to be paid. A tightening of mortgage credit brought on slowness of sales of finished construction, which led to a 'present value reversal' (see below) for these projects.

The mix of hedge, speculative and Ponzi finance in existence at any time reflect the history of the economy and the effect of historical developments upon the state of long-term expectations. In particular, during a period of tranquillity in which the economy functions at a reasonably close approximation to full employment, there will be decline in the value of the insurance that the holding of money bestows. This will lead to both a rise in the price of capital assets and a shift of portfolio preference so that a larger admixture of speculative — and even Ponzi — finance is essayed by business and accepted by bankers. In this way the financial system endogenously generates at least part of the finance needed by the increased investment demand that follows a rise in the price of capital assets.[11]

As the ratio of speculative and Ponzi finance units increases in the total financial structure of an economy, the economy becomes increasingly sensitive to interest rate variations. In both speculative and Ponzi finance units the expected cash flows that make the financial structure viable come later in time than the payment commitments on outstanding debt. At high enough short-term interest rates speculative units become Ponzi units and for Ponzi units the accumulated carrying charges at high interest rates on their outstanding short-term debts can lead to cash flow requirements that exceed the cash flow expectations that made the initial position viable (i.e. the initial short-run cash flow deficit is transformed into a permanent cash flow deficit by high interest rates).

External finance and interest rates enter the investment process at two quite different stages. The production of investment takes time and the early-on costs are compounded at the short-term interest rate in determining the costs of investment output. This is beautifully illustrated in the way construction is financed in the United States. The financing of a construction project leads to the drawing-down of funds made available by a bank; obviously, the interest charges on such funds have to be recovered in the 'delivered price' of the investment good (the delivered price of an investment good is a positive function of the (short term) interest rate).

An investment good, once delivered and 'at work' in a production process, is a capital asset. As a capital asset, its value is the present value of the anticipated gross profits after taxes (quasi-rents) that are imputed to its participation in economic activity. The present value of a capital asset is an inverse function of the (long-term) interest rate.

A rising investment demand leads to an increase in investment in process. As investment in process increases, an inelastic component of the demand curve for financing rises. If the supply curve of finance is infinitely elastic, then finance costs do not rise as investment increases. As more investment leads to greater profits, the prices of capital assets, at constant interest rates, increase. Such an increase is an incentive for more investment: the run-up of prices and profits that characterises a boom will result. However the internal workings of the banking mechanism or Central Bank action to constrain inflation will result in the supply of finance becoming less than infinitely elastic — perhaps even approach zero elasticity. A rising inelastic demand curve for finance due to the investment in process combined with an inelastic supply curve of finance leads to a rapid increase in short-term interest rates.

Sharp increases in short-term interest rates increase the supply price of investment output, and also lead to a rise in long-term interest rates. This leads to a fall in the present value of gross profits after taxes (quasi-rents) that capital assets are expected to earn. Rising interest rates shift the supply curve of investment upwards even as they shift the demand curve for investment, which is derived from the price of capital assets, downward. These shifts in the conditions of investment supply and demand lead to a fall in investment, which lowers current and near-term expected profits. Lower profit expectations lower the price of capital assets, and thus the price that business is willing to pay for investment output.

The fall in profits means that the ability of business to fulfil financial commitments embodied in debts deteriorates. In particular, when profits fall, some hedge units become speculative units and some speculative units become Ponzi units. The rise in long-term interest rates and the decline in expected profits play particular havoc with Ponzi units, for the present value of the hoped-for future bonanza falls sharply. The prior Ponzi units find they must sell out positions in assets to meet payment commitments, only to discover that their assets cannot be sold at a price that even comes near to covering debts. Once the selling-out of positions rather than refinancing becomes prevalent, asset prices can and do fall below their cost of production as an investment good.

What has been sketched is the route to a financial crisis. Whether a fully-fledged financial crisis takes place depends

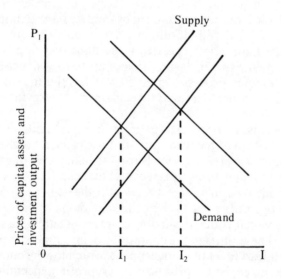

Figure 2.1

upon the efficacy of Central Bank lender of last resort behaviour, and whether gross profit flows are sustained by an increase in the government deficit or changes in the balance of payments. However, even if a fully-fledged financial crisis does not take place, the long-run expectations of business, bankers and the ultimate holders of financial assets will be affected by these developments. The risk premiums associated with investment projects will increase and businessmen and bankers will move towards balance-sheet structures that involve less speculative finance.

The recursive process between profits and the effective discount rate for business assets can continue even on to a 'present value reversal' (i.e. the supply curve of investment output can rise above the demand curve for investment output so that investment, and, with investment, profits collapse). Once profits collapse, the cash flows to validate even initially hedge financing arrangements will not be forthcoming (these relations are illustrated in Figures 2.1 and 2.2 — see Minsky, 1977).

In Figure 2.1, the 'normal' situation is illustrated. The demand and supply conditions for investment, taking financial conditions into account, might shift back and forth between I_1 and I_2 as profits, risk premiums and costs of production of investment output vary. In Figure 2.2 the situation in which the repercussions of a 'debt-deflation' have affected both profits and effective financing terms is sketched. In this case the fall of profits has lowered the demand price for capital assets even as the rise in 'lenders' risk' has raised the supply price of investment output for any given level of money wages. What is sketched is the extreme case in which the supply curve 'everywhere' lies above the demand curve.

In Figure 2.1, the shifts in the supply and demand curves for investment reflect changes in the variables that enter as proximate determinants of aggregate demand and supply even as the variables that enter into the determination of long-run expectations are unaffected. This in particular means that even though there have been variations in earned profits and in the terms upon financing contracts, the current expectations of longer-term profits, interest rates and acceptable financial

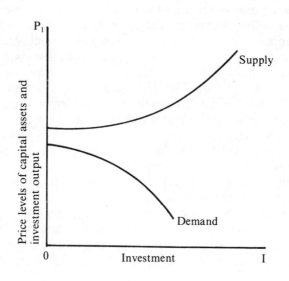

Figure 2.2

structures have not been changed. In Figure 2.1 a shift to the
left of the supply and demand curves can be offset by minor
changes in money market conditions, the government fiscal
posture and money wage rates.

In Figure 2.2, the position of the supply and demand curves
for investment output reflect changes in the long-run expectation about profits and desirable financing structure. The
shift from the situation illustrated in Figure 2.1 to that of
Figure 2.2 reflects the type of unfavourable experience with
inherited liability structures that we sketched in the discussion
of hedge, speculative and Ponzi finance. In the situation in
Figure 2.2, short-term changes in proximate profits, market
interest rates, money wages and the government fiscal posture

might sustain income and employment, but will not have a quick effect upon the supply and demand for investment output. In particular, in a regime of small government, such as existed when Keynes wrote *The General Theory*, neither wage deflation nor money market ease could quickly transform what is sketched in Figure 2.2 into that of Figure 2.1. In fact, because a key element in the emergence and continuation of the situation sketched in Figure 2.2 is the shortfall of profits relative to the financial obligations on inherited debt, a decline in money wages which leads to an expected decline in the dollar value of profits will make things worse. That is, whereas variation in market variables that are determined by supply and demand conditions in product, labour and money markets are effective governors of the rate of investment when long-run expectations are conducive to investment, variations in these same variables are not effective governors of investment once the shift in long-run expectations that occurs with and after a financial crisis has taken place.

Once a situation resembling that sketched in Figure 2.2 exists, the economy is well on its way to — or already in — a deep depression. However, whether such a situation develops fully and if it does, how long it lasts, depends upon the government's involvement in the economy; how promptly the government intervenes and how effective the intervention. In 1929–33 government intervention was minute and late. In particular in the United States the Federal Reserve virtually abdicated its responsibilities as a lender of last resort, which is to assure that those speculative and Ponzi financial positions which would be validated by longer-term cash flows at the current (pre-crisis) price level, at a reasonable approximation to full employment income, and at interest rates short of the rates that rule at the peak of the investment boom receive prompt refinancing.

In 1974–75 the emerging threats of a financial débâcle were met by extensive lender of last resort interventions by the Federal Reserve system and a virtual explosion of the Federal government deficit — which sustained aggregate business profits. The US economy — and with it the world economy — exhibited more resilience in 1974–75 than in 1929–33 because the government's involvement in the economy was much greater and more effective.

The essence of the financial instability hypothesis is that financial traumas, even onto debt-deflation interactions, occur as a normal functioning result in a capitalist economy. This does not mean that a capitalist economy is always tottering on the brink of disaster. There are situations where the short-term debt financing of business and households is modest, this leads to robust financial markets which are not susceptible to debt-deflation processes. There are also fragile financial structures which include a great deal of speculative and Ponzi finance of business and households. The normal functioning of an economy with a robust financial situation is both tranquil and, on the whole, successful. Tranquillity and success are not self-sustaining states, they induce increases in capital asset prices relative to current output prices and a rise in acceptable debts for any prospective income flow, investment and profits. These concurrent increases lead to a transformation over time of an initially robust financial structure into a fragile structure. Once a financial structure includes a sufficiently large weight of speculative and 'quasi-Ponzi' finance (of the interim financing of long gestation period investments) a run-up of short-term interest rates, as the demand for short-term financing increases rapidly, can occur. This will lead to 'present value reversals', especially if it is accompanied by a rise in the value of liquidity as some units fail to meet financial obligations. As the cost of investment output becomes greater than the value of capital assets being produced, take-out financing will not be forthcoming. This leads to a collapse of asset values even further below the supply price of investment output, which further decreases investment. But decreases in investment, by decreasing profits, makes things worse. The immediate market reactions to a decline in income in the context of a financial structure that is heavily weighted by Ponzi and speculative finance makes things worse; the set of interrelated markets is unstable.

POLICY IMPLICATIONS

The financial instability hypothesis has serious implications for policy. First of all, it points out that there are inherent and inescapable flaws in capitalism. That capitalism is flawed does not necessarily mean that one rejects it. The financial instability hypothesis emphasises the importance of institutions and the ability of institutions to modify the behaviour of the economy; thus, there are varieties of capitalism. The question may very well be which variety is better, not necessarily for all time, but for now.

In a capitalist economy with a small government, $\pi = I$, so that a collapse in asset values, which lowers I, not only decreases income and employment but it also lowers profits. This not only means that the value of capital assets falls, but also that outstanding debt payment commitments, especially by units that are 'into' speculative and Ponzi finance, cannot be fulfilled.

On the other hand, in a capitalist economy with a big government, $\overset{*}{\pi} = I + DF$, after tax profits equals investment plus the deficit. If a decrease in I is offset by a rise in the deficit, then profit flows need not fall; in fact, if the increase in the deficit is large enough, profits will rise. This is what happened in 1975 in the United States. The enormous government deficit in the first two quarters of that year helped abort a serious debt-deflation process by sustaining gross profits after taxes even as investment fell.

An implication of the proposition that prices must be such as to generate profits equal to investment is that any increase in the ratio of the total wage bill in the production of investment output to the total wage bill in the production of consumption goods is inflationary. Furthermore, any increase in spending on consumption goods financed by transfer payments or profit income is inflationary. As wages that are paid for overhead labour and ancillary business services such as advertising are best considered as allocations of profit, a rise in spending on advertising, executive suites, product research and development is inflationary. Thus, the emphasis upon growth through investment, the bias towards bigness in business, business styles that emphasise advertising and overheads, and the explosion of transfer payments are the main causes of our current inflation.

From the perspective of the financial instability hypothesis, inflation is one way to ease payment commitments due to debt. In the 1970s a big depression has been avoided by floating off untenable debt structures through inflation. Stagflation is a substitute for a big depression. However, the floating-off of debt through inflation is a game that can be played only a number of times; the propensity to expand into a boom will be atrophied as bankers become wary of Ponzi schemes. Alternatively, government intervention to sustain investment can become so overpowering that the 'sharp pencils' needed to assure that investment yields real rather than nominal, social rather than private, benefits become blunted.

Every businessman and banker knows that for every investment project worth undertaking there are literally an infinite number that are losers. Once the doctrine of salvation through investment becomes deeply ingrained into our political and economic system, the constraints on foolish investments are relaxed. This is especially so if the government stands ready to guarantee particular investors or investment projects against losses. A capitalism with a big government that is dedicated to full employment through ostensibly private investment can approach the inefficiencies of a Stalinist economy that refuses to use present value calculations.

In the aggregate, the foolishness of bankers, businessmen and government guarantors are floated off by massive government deficits that lead to profits which validate aggregate past investment and overall business liabilities, albeit at a price in inflation and increasingly inefficient business techniques. The inefficiency of the chosen techniques is reflected by the unemployment that accompanies inflation: stagflation is a symptom of an underlying inept set of capital assets.

Given that instability and inflation are due to the emphasis upon investment, transfer payments, and the need to bail out the threatened financial structure, the financial instability hypothesis indicates that an economy that is oriented towards the production of consumption goods by techniques that are less capital-intensive than those now being induced by policy will be less susceptible to financial instability and inflation. This suggests that the policy emphasis should shift from the encouragement of growth through investment to the achievement of full employment through consumption production. The financial instability hypothesis suggests that a simplification of financial structures is a way of achieving greater stability, although being rooted in an analysis of the historical dynamics of the financial structure, it also recognises that the enforcement of simplicity in financial arrangements will be difficult.

The financial instability hypothesis also suggests that while there are better ways of running our economy than the way it has been run in the recent past, there is no economic organisation or magic formula which, once achieved and set in motion, solves the problem of economic policy for all time. Economies evolve, and with the internal evolution of the economic mechanism the apt structure of legislated institutions and policy operations change: there is no way one generation of economists can render their successors obsolete. I am afraid economists can never become mere technicians applying an agreed upon theory that is fit for all seasons within an institutional structure that does not and need not change.

NOTES

* Earlier versions of this chapter were read at the Western Social Science Association meeting in Denver in April 1978, and in Southampton and London in July 1978. I wish to thank Thomas Buzzelton, Wallace Petersen, Victoria Chick and Maurice Townsend for comments, as well as the participants in these seminars.

1   Of the mathematical economists, perhaps F. H. Hahn has been most open about the limitations of mathematical theory (see Hahn, 1969, 1971, 1973. Also Arrow and Hahn, 1971, especially Chapter 14, pp. 347-69). In introducing their discussion, they note that in their earlier proof that a temporary equilibrium always exists they 'supposed that at the moment an equilibrium was shown to exist, economic

agents had no commitments left from the past' (i.e. there are no debts and no capital assets as we know capital assets). It is interesting to note that Arrow and Hahn head Chapter 14 with a quotation from W.B. Yeats, *The Second Coming*: 'Things fall apart, the centre does not hold.'

2   Perhaps the best references are Hicks (1937), Hansen (1949), Modigliani (1944) and Patinkin (1965).

3   Among the key works in the emerging post-Keynesian synthesis are Robinson (1971), Davidson (1978), Kregel (1973), Minsky (1975a), Weintraub (1966) and Chick (1973).

4   This is the outcome of the two Cambridge debates on capital theory, although the standard discussion and summary of the debate does not make this clear (see Harcourt, 1972).

5   This section reflects discussions with Jan Kregel and Ignazio Muzo and my reading of some of their work in progress.

6   Clower (1965) and Leijonhufvud (1968) are non-post-Keynesians who had a part in triggering the discussion of what Keynes truly meant.

7   Malinvaud (1977) is a sophisticated statement of this approach.

8   The label 'Ponzi' refers to a Boston event soon after the first world war in which a pyramid financing scheme swept through the working class and even affected 'respectable' folk.

9   Malinvaud (1977) introduces money as follows: 'Let us consider an economy with r commodities (h = 1, 2, . . . , r), the last one being money' (p. 18). Arrow and Hahn (1971, Chapter 14) write of the Keynesian model: 'Let the subscript "n" stand for money that we now regard as the non-interest-paying debt of some agency outside our formal system, say the government' (p. 349). It is clear that 'money' in Malinvaud and Arrow and Hahn has no relevant resemblance to the 'money' of those economies whose behaviour we are trying to understand when we do economic theory. Arrow and Hahn recognise that they are violating reality in their definition and offer apologies for the 'primitive monetary ideas' they explore. Malinvaud does not articulate any recognition of the 'heroic' nature of his abstractions, even as he offers his work as being 'relevant' to the analysis of policy.

10   Kalecki (1971, Chapter 7, pp 78-92). The financial instability hypothesis identifies profits, determined, as Kalecki shows, as a cash flow that does or does not validate past financial commitments: it integrates Kalecki's vision of the dynamic determination of profits with the capitalist institutional fact of a liability structure inherited from the past that commits current and future profits (the paper by Kalecki first appeared in 1942).

11   The shift towards speculative and even Ponzi finance is evident in the financial statistics of the United States as collected in the Flow of

Funds accounts. The movement to 'bought money' by large multinational banks throughout the world is evidence that there are degrees of speculative finance: all banks engage in speculative finance but some banks are more speculative than others. Only a thorough cash flow analysis of an economy can indicate the extent to which finance is speculative and where the critical point at which the ability to meet contractual commitments can break down is located. See Minsky (1975b) and Board of Governors of the Federal Reserve System (1976).

3. The Rise of Monetarism as a Social Doctrine

A. Bhaduri and J. Steindl

INTRODUCTION

It is hardly worthwhile to discuss the contents of monetarism. The really interesting question is how this ideology steadily gained ground to become the creed of the ruling circles in some countries and at least of very influential circles in others.

It should be noted at the outset that monetarism — in present-day practice, if not necessarily in theory — is associated with *restrictive* monetary and fiscal policy.[1] Our basic observation is that such restrictive policies have always been supported by banks and financiers (the City, Wall Street) more than by any other group in the economy. It is they who have consistently clamoured for high interest rates and for restrictive budgetary measures. The specific monetarist theory has found a home in those circles more than anywhere else.

CUI BONO?

The question immediately arises as to why this should be so. What interest is served by following restrictive monetary and fiscal policies? The answer comes most naturally on ideological grounds. Monetarism attributes to the control of money supply and to the banking system the central regulatory role, a strategic position almost comparable to the central planning office in a socialist state. This cannot fail to flatter the bankers' vanity. But more than being merely flattering to high finance, monetarism articulates an idological attack against Keynesian doctrine. Monetarism intends to displace Keynesian policies which threaten the social power of the banking system by relegating it to one of the instruments of government policy in maintaining full employment. It is by no means necessary to recall the 'euthanasia of the *rentier*' which bodes ill for the banks also, but it is quite sufficient to state that Keynesian policies entail an enormous strengthening of the national government's hand in the conduct of banking policy. This cannot find favour with the banks, unless they feel confident that the economic policies of the national government would be run more or less exclusively in the interest of high finance.

Faced with the historical experience of the inter-war years, J.M. Keynes, although in principle a liberal, was driven to support national economic policies designed to defend the level of home employment against depressive influences coming from the outside world. Such defensive national policies might involve devaluation, protectionism, exchange control, etc. These essentially entailed severe restrictions on the international role which the City had enjoyed under a Gold Exchange Standard with the pound sterling as a reserve currency.[2]

Let one of us (J.S.) indulge here in an historical reminiscence. Kalecki used to interpret the events in Britain around 1931–32 in terms of a shift of power from the City to industry. The interest of the City was overruled by abandoning the Gold Standard, adopting a floating exchange rate and establishing the Exchange Equalisation Account. Industry got protection again and free trade was rejected in a major turnabout of British economic policy. This change was connected with a decline in the international status of the City as the financial centre of the world. Kindleberger (1973) maintains that the City was neither able nor willing to plug the holes that had appeared in the network of international finance and thus prevent the snowballing effect which led to the breakdown of the entire structure in 1931. With this tarnishing of the international image of the City, the centre of gravity of British economic policy shifted to the home front in favour of domestic industries. This provided the necessary sociopolitical base for the acceptance of Keynesian policies.[3]

In order to answer the question 'Whose advantage?', it is worth stressing that a high interest rate policy is generally beneficial to banks under normal circumstances (i.e. as long as they do not become the victims of a financial crisis).

It is true that those financial institutions which have a lot of long-term investment committed at low interest and are forced to borrow short at very high interest tend to lose money on that account. In more extreme cases, they may even face financial ruin, as is apparent from the threat of bankruptcy which hangs over the head of many US thrift institutions at present. But, by and large, commercial banks neither in the US nor in the UK, although some in West Germany, have been locked in such a situation of borrowing short at a high rate and lending long at a low rate. Long-term government bonds are not a large part of the financial portfolio of the commercial banks either in the US or in the UK nowadays (of the order of one tenth perhaps), so that this consideration is not of overriding practical importance to them. In addition, new credit instruments have emerged which facilitate long- or medium-term lending at variable interest rates determined by a spread over the inter-bank lending rate (for example, LIBOR, i.e. the rate which the London banks charge each other for short-term money). The share of outstanding debt of developing countries carrying such floating interest rates is estimated to have increased from about 28 per cent in 1973 to nearly 60 per cent in 1980.[4] Increasingly, longer-term loans are being committed only on the basis of floating interest and the practice today extends in large measure even to newly-issued industrial bonds. Such new credit arrangements have helped to insulate the banks against the only disadvantage which an increasing level of interest rates may have for them.[5] Otherwise, high interest means increased earnings on loans advanced by banks, while small saving deposits usually do not get a proportionate rise in interest payments and demand deposits get none.

These general arguments find some empirical support in the fact that the British banks have done particularly well at a time

Table 3.1

UK banking Sector's Assets
(total lending £m)

	Public sector total		Private sector total		Overseas sector total		Total assets		GDP		Bank assets as per cent of GDP
	Index	total	Index	total	Index	total	Index	total	Index	GDP	
1970	100	7.474	100	10.786	100	15.471	100	33.727	100	43.530	78
proportion		22		32		46		100			
1979	232	17.305	497	53.602	832	128.678	592	199.585	592	163.647	122
proportion		9		27		64		100			

Source: CSO, *Annual Abstract 1981*

when industry has withered away under high interest rates (as can be seen in Table 3.1).

THE SHIFT OF POWER

The rise of monetarism from a local sect to worldwide emi-nence had been preceded by a shift of power from industry to the banks. Perhaps this shift was nowhere as clearly marked as in Britain. All existing evidence regarding the scope of opera-tion of traditional financial centres like the City or Wall Street tends to suggest that such a shift in relative power has indeed steadily been taking place over the last two decades or so.

Table 3.1 gives an indication of the extent to which the City has managed to extend its scope of operations during the 1970s. It shows that overseas lending has increased more than eightfold, lending to private domestic customers has increased fivefold and lending to the public sector has increased only twofold. The total assets of the UK banking sector were 78 per cent of the GDP in 1970 and 122 per cent in 1979. This illustrates the tremendous increase in the relative power and control wielded by the City. At the same time, the much faster growth of overseas operations allowed the banks to enjoy a certain degree of independence both from the national govern-ment and from the domestic public sector.

Table 3.2 shows the ratio of undistributed income of finan-cial companies to that of industrial and commercial com-panies. This ratio is seen to rise steadily in 1960–78 and then to jump to extraordinary proportions in 1979 and 1980, the years of consumption of monetarism when the banks continued to prosper while industry decayed. As Table 3.2 shows, the undistributed profits of the British banking sector as a per-centage of those of the industrial–commercial sector rose spectacularly from 7 per cent in the early 1960s to 28 per cent in 1980. In the absence of access to similar data from many other OECD countries, it is hard to judge how 'special' the British case is. Nevertheless, since the British banks' fortunes were connected with the rise of the Euromarket and the transfer of

Table 3.2

UK Profits: Industrial and commercial as compared to financial companies
(£m, annual averages)

	1960-64	1965-72	1973-78	1979	1980	1981
Undistributed income[1]						
1. Industrial and commercial companies	2468	3523	12251	19795	15238	16266
2. Financial companies	169	391	1664	3687	4290	3327
3. Financial in pc of industrial-commercial	7	11	14	19	28	20
Undistributed income plus dividends[2]						
4. Industrial and commercial companies	3584	5021	14108	24099	19306	20333
5. Financial companies	337	642	1998	4175	4882	3999
6. Financial in pc of industrial-commercial	9	13	14	17	25	20

1 Before providing for depreciation, stock appreciation and additions to reserve; net of taxes.

2 Dividends are net of tax after 1973; the data before and after 1973 are therefore not comparable.

Source: CSO, *Economic Trends, Annual Supplement* (1982 edn. and July 1982).

oil money, and since other countries' banks shared this experience, we may guess that a similar shift in the distribution of profits has taken place in other industrialised countries, although it has probably gone nowhere as far as in Britain.

It has to be pointed out here that a traditional divergence of interest exists between banks and industry in Britain owing to a general reluctance on the part of industry to indebt itself and borrow from banks (Samuels, Groves and Goddard, 1975). It is arguable that to a large extent this peculiar alienation has also been caused by the long-standing international position of the London-based banks, who often find their foreign business more profitable than lending to domestic industries.

The relative independence of finance from domestic industry in Britain owes a lot to the old tradition of the City as an international financial centre. Indeed, in the two historical reserve currency countries — the UK and later the US — the City and Wall Street could play their international financial role without necessarily being constrained by the growth of domestic industries.[6] In contrast, the transnational banks in countries like Germany and Japan, where industries have been reconstructed in the post-war period largely so as to poise them favourably in terms of international competitiveness, have had their operations grow more in line with the interests of their transnational corporate business.[7]

THE SOURCES OF THE BANKS' PROSPERITY

In attempting to understand the reason behind the shift in power from industry to the banking system which has taken place, it is essential to consider both the national and the international dimension of the problem. Undoubtedly, these two aspects have tended to reinforce one another in facilitating the process of shift of power in favour of the banking system, but for the sake of clarity in exposition we wish to separate them here.

On the *national level*, the long post-war prosperity of capitalism saw a renewed growth of *rentier* interests. It resulted in significant accumulation of personal savings held in the form of financial assets in most OECD countries (Steindl, 1982). Alongside grew the public debt which, in large measure, only reflected the growing *rentier* interest. As inflation tended to erode the real value of accumulated savings and the real interest rate, the *rentiers'* interest in trying to find compensation in the high interest rate of a 'dear money' policy became more pronounced. In so far as such a policy is normally also favoured by the banks, as we have seen above, the *rentier* becomes a natural political ally of the banks in his insistence that inflation is a more serious problem than unemployment.

In its *international aspect*, it hardly needs to be stressed that finance is a surface phenomenon reflecting the underlying relations of economic power between nations. The unchallenged 'reserve currency' status of the dollar under the Bretton Woods System merely reflected the new hegemonic role of the US in the international capitalist system. Both as an international unit of account and as a store of value, the dollar played the role of international money for more than a quarter of a century. And it was the store of value or reserve currency status of the dollar which also allowed the US to buy freely worldwide with her paper liabilities, which the foreigners willingly held as assets and considered 'as good as gold'. Thus, under the reserve currency status of the dollar, the US was able to finance not only some of her military expenditure, but also a large flow of private foreign investment into Europe. US multinationals were able to take over European firms, while the Europeans had to be satisfied with an equivalent dollar holding in exchange.[8] It needs to be stressed that these financing operations were increasingly routed, not through official transactions among Central Banks (as visualised under the Bretton Woods System), but through transactions conducted by large international commercial banks whose dollar claims became the basis for loans denominated in dollars. The result was the birth and growth of a massive *Eurodollar market*, where expatriate dollars, detached from their national monetary base, were held in commercial banks located outside the United States. It is hardly necessary to add that the motive for the expatriation of banking business from the US (as well as

Table 3.3

Role of private credit in current account financing of non-oil developing countries (1973-82) (in billions of US dollars)

	1973	1974	1975	1976	1977	1978	1979	1980	1981	1982	Cumulative total 1973-81
0. Total to be financed[1]	21	39	44	46	41	55	71	91	100	101	508
1. Borrowing from international markets (banks and bonds)[2]	11	16	16	23	18	34	44	50	52	N.A.	264
2. Credit from commercial banks[3]	N.A.	N.A.	N.A.	18	18	23	37	34	37	N.A.	N.A.
3. Publicised Eurocurrency lending to non-OPEC developing countries[4]	N.A.	N.A.	N.A.	N.A.	N.A.	14	27	24	33	N.A.	N.A.
4. Total publicised Eurocurrency lending[5]	N.A.	N.A.	N.A.	N.A.	42	70	83	77	133	N.A.	N.A.

Table 3.3 continued

| 5. Per cent share on non-OPEC developing countries in publicised Eurolending | N.A. | N.A. | N.A. | N.A. | N.A. | 20 | 33 | 31 | 25 | N.A. |

Notes

1 Row (0) is the algebraic sum of current account deficit and reserve accumulation giving ex-post financial requirement. Current account deficit is the net total of balances on goods, services and private transfers, as defined in IMF, *Balance of Payments Yearbook (Source:* World Bank (1982), Appendix B, Table 25).

2 Row (1) estimates finance raised through bank loans and bond issues. The latter item of bond issues is only around 10 per cent of the total for developing countries (1979-80). See *Economist* (1982a, p. 83) on the relative composition of bonds and bank loans, estimated from three different sources, namely OECD, the World Bank and Morgan Guaranty Co. Row (2) is compiled from IMF and BIS sources.

3 *Source: First Chicago World Report* (1981), in R. W. Lombardi, 'Multinational banking and the Third World', *International Herald Tribune* (1981b, p. 85).

4 *Source:* Morgan Guaranty Co, *World Financial Markets,* various issues. Morgan Guaranty estimates are somewhat lower than estimates by OECD and the World Bank (see *Economist,* 1982d for comparison); also *International Currency Review* (1980), No. 6, p. 9 using Morgan Guaranty estimates (for 1978-80).

5 *Source* as note (4) above.

from other countries where the same happened) was strengthened by the desire to escape from national monetary controls and national taxation.

In time, the Eurodollar market developed into an international commercial money market, comprising not only dollars but all other major convertible currencies, all of which were also detached from their national monetary base. The total value of such expatriate currencies held in the commercial banking system was estimated in November 1981 at 1.35 trillion US dollars — a 3353 per cent increase from the 39 billion US dollars recorded in 1965, the earliest measure of the Euromarket's size.[9] And, even as early as 1973, just before the quadrupling of the oil price, the volume of the commercial banks' transactions in such expatriate foreign currency exceeded the total value of foreign exchange transactions by all Central Banks and monetary authorities taken together (Engellau and Nygen, 1979).

Such a phenomenal growth of the Eurocurrency market dramatically altered the balance of power — at least temporarily — between the international commercial banking system and the national monetary authorities and their Central Banks. Like multinational corporations in their field, international commercial banks emerged as a main focus of financial power, largely independent of the control of national monetary authorities.[10] The Keynesian view of the economic autonomy of the national government in the conduct of economic policy and maintenance of full employment at home became almost anachronistic in this context. As economic power continued to shift steadily in favour of large commercial banks, a new economic ideology, as an antidote to Keynes, was called for.

Superimposed on this trend of growing independent financial power of international commercial banking has been, since the quadrupling of the oil price in 1973, the emergence of a class of international *rentiers* from the OPEC countries.[11] Not only did it vastly augment the deposit base of the large commercial banks, where most of the petromoney was held in short-maturing deposits, but is also made the entire international payments system crucially dependent on the commercial banks. The non-oil developing countries' current account deficits were increasingly met through commercial borrowing and the commercial banks' usual ability to create credit was applauded as an international virtue in the name of 'recycling' on a global scale (see Table 3.3).

A remarkable feature of Table 3.3 is the heavy reliance of non-oil developing countries on borrowing from international capital markets which financed approximately half of their financial requirements. Most of the credit came directly from commercial banks, which accounted for over 70 per cent of total borrowing during 1976–81 (Table 3.3, row 2 ÷ row 1). Well over half of such credit from commercial banks during 1978–81 was publicised Eurocurrency lending (Table 3.3, row 2 ÷ 3) which typically requires syndication of credit. Nevertheless, Table 3.4 also shows the somewhat self-contained nature of Eurocurrency lending in spite of all the attention paid to the global recycling phenomenon. It will be noted (from Table 3.4 row 1) that non-oil developing countries together account for about one-third of total Eurocurrency bank credit, while industrialised countries still have the major share (50–60 per cent).[12]

In light of this evidence on international bank credit, it would be rash to maintain that the present system of international banking is crucially dependent on the market for non-oil developing countries in general. Instead, the broad picture that emerges is the *crucial dependence of a few borrowers among non-oil developing countries* on the international banking system (see Table 3.4, row 2 and 3). It is on these selected few countries — less than a dozen in number, all belonging to the middle to high-income group among developing countries and most of them trying to industrialise typically through what are called 'open trade and investment policies' — that international banks' loans have been showered on an unprecedented scale during the last decade or so. At the same time, poorer non-oil developing countries have not had any significant access to large commercial loans. In the pattern that has increasingly emerged in recent years, the domestic savings of OECD countries and the liquid surplus of OPEC has merged to result in a powerful *rentier* interest tied to the smooth

Table 3.4

Eurocurrency bank credit concentration.

Shares of certain groups of recipients in total Eurocurrency bank credit in per cent

	1973	1974	1975	1976	1977	1978	1979	1980	1981	Average 1973-81
1. Share of non-oil developing countries[1]	19	21	39	38	32	38	43	31	26	32
2. Concentration according to region: share of Central and Latin America[2]	N.A.	N.A.	58	59	55	55	55	56	N.A.	N.A.
3. Concentration according to countries: share of 8 major borrowing countries[3]	N.A.	N.A.	53	54	52	53	56	55	N.A.	N.A.
4. Concentration according to income: share of 9 newly-industrialising countries[4]	N.A.	N.A.	69	67	63	65	71	74	N.A.	N.A.

Table 3.4 continued

Sources and Notes:

1 1981 figure relates to January to November. *Source:* Morgan Guaranty Co. Morgan Guaranty data relate to the non-OPEC developing countries, which corresponds fairly closely to non-oil developing countries data in this context.

2 Source: BIS, IMF and Morgan Guaranty Co.

3 Sources as in note (2) above. Includes 4 countries in the Americas (Brazil, Mexico, Argentina and Chile), and South Korea, the Philippines, Thailand and Malaysia in Asia. The 4 Asian countries account for about 10-12 per cent of total Eurocurrency bank credit, while the 4 countries in the Americas account for 43-45 per cent on an average.

4 *Sources:* BIS, IMF and OECD. These 9 countries are: Brazil, Mexico, Argentina, South Korea (as in note (3) above) as well as Greece, Spain, Portugal, Yugoslavia and Taiwan; they are on a comparable *per capita* income level.

operation of international commercial lending. On the receiving side of commercial loans were some OECD countries with serious balance of payments problems, a few socialist countries, as well as a handful of selected developing countries belonging to the middle-income group.

Commercial banks' dependence on their clients either as lenders or as borrowers has not been one sided, which has ensured them a position of relative autonomy. In particular, the relative importance of OPEC deposits in the total deposits of commercial banks has not shown any clear tendency to increase over time. The OPEC's share in total deposits has remained relatively stable at around 10–12 per cent throughout the period 1975–80.[13] As a consequence, commercial banks have not increased their dependence on OPEC depositors; instead, they have increasingly relied on international relending of domestic savings of OECD countries.[14] The fact that only a few selected developing countries in the middle-income range (led by Brazil and Mexico) have been the main borrowers implies that commercial banks' dependence on their borrowing clients in the developing countries has been highly specific. It would be wrong, then, to presume either a *general* dependence of developing countries on commercial banks or of the banks on developing countries' capital markets. More exactly, a few selected middle-income developing countries depend heavily on commercial borrowing,[15] while *rentiers* both from OECD and OPEC depend on profitable deployment of their financial savings through 'recycling' carried out by commercial banks.

ESCAPE FROM NATIONAL CONTROL

Given the concentration of international commercial banking in the traditional financial centres, large banks have increasingly shown a tendency to become more independent of their home governments and domestic industries. The development of Euromarkets, in allowing commercial banks to operate extensively in *foreign* currency, has also meant that the traditional business of international liquidity creation has largely become detached from the control of national monetary authorities. In a fundamental sense, therefore, restrictive national monetary policies no longer affect so severely the international commercial banking system; the banks can reap the benefits of a high interest policy without having to surrender to the control of central banks. The special attraction of monetarism for commercial banking lies precisely in this paradoxical fact that a restrictive national monetary policy is largely ineffective in curbing their international operations. And evidence seems to suggest that a 'dear money' policy hits domestic industries, while international commercial banks do not seem to suffer particularly from it (see Tables 3.1 and 3.2).

In the ultimate analysis, the social position of industry rests on its being a provider of jobs. It is evident that this function is inadequately fulfilled today by industry in spite of abundant support from the state. In most industrialised countries, basic and traditional industries mainly play the role of petitioners *vis à vis* the government, in some countries one might even say, of old age pensioners in constant need of support. The state subsidises industry even in the case of multinationals who sell their location by auction among the countries who desire their presence. In contrast, as representatives of the mythology of self-reliant private capitalism, the banks had been presenting a better image until recently. Their social influence rests on their nearly unilateral power to grant or withhold credit, to shift funds from country to country, and to influence the rate of exchange in a manner which is largely independent of particular national governments' policies. Even the US government and the Federal Reserve find themselves largely ineffective in regulating such international banking operations. The recent attempts by the Federal Reserve to gain some control of the Eurodollar market by imposing minimum reserve currency requirements (initiated in April 1980) have been almost scornfully rejected by the Central Banks in other countries in an attempt to protect the interest of international commercial banking located in their respective countries.[16] Banking seems to have become internationalised and independent both of domestic industries and of national governments to an extent where even the most powerful of national governments can exert little control over international banking operations. Nevertheless, there is a reverse side to this picture that is now becoming increasingly apparent. The international lending structure, particularly the Euromarket, is exposed to considerable risks which need not to be dwelt upon here. In the event of large-scale defaults the banks would have nobody to turn to but the monetary authority and the government of their home country. This implies serious qualifications to the statement about the freedom of international banks. Their independence has a limit in the consideration they have to show to their home government and Central Bank, in order to facilitate intervention on their behalf in case of need. The bond to the home base can never be broken completely.

These considerations touch on the inner contradictions in the position of the banks. There seems to be a good deal of double-talk in their embrace of monetarism. They praise the restrictionist policy at home in so far as it gives them high interest and high margins, but they escape the restrictions on volume by seeking expansion abroad. The dramatic expansion in the volume of international credit has largely resulted from fierce competition among banks. But the paradoxical outcome of the ensuing recycling process carried out by international banks during the last ten years or so is only now becoming apparent. Most of the handful of developing (and some socialist) countries to which the banks lent heavily (see Table 3.4) are now in a sort of *borrower's debt-trap*, where they cannot avoid increasing recourse to borrowing, if only to serve their outstanding debt. The mirror image of this is the situation in which the banks now find themselves. The fear of technical default by a few of these heavily indebted borrowers can set in motion a chain reaction of defaults, the risk of which has been further aggravated by the 'cross-default' clause of the usual syndicated lending. A dear money policy encouraged by monetarism and recent devices such as floating interest loans which shifted the burden of debt-servicing to these borrowers have only contributed further to the fear of widespread default which the international banking system must try to avoid in its own interest (*Economist*, 1982b, pp. 21–4). As a result, banks now find themselves in an uncomfortable *lender's trap*, where they have to keep on lending, rescheduling and rolling over their debts to already heavily indebted borrowers who probably can never pay back. And such debt-rolling must continue to keep the present fragile structure of international finance from crumbling.

It is in this context that we must judge the recent deviations from more orthodox monetarism. The tight money policy is now being relaxed by the Federal Reserve and the West German Bundesbank, followed by several other Central Banks; and, interest rates have also begun to decline.[17] While these developments may be connected in an obvious way with the compulsions of electoral processes in these countries, it appears to be more than a merely temporary manoeuvre. Restrictive monetarism has begun to become irreconcilable with the uncomfortable position in which the banks have landed themselves. The insolvency of many of their debtors makes it necessary for Central Banks to intervene as lenders of last resort and the Bank of International Settlements has already felt compelled to create at least some modest facility to bail out banks in difficulty. Neither the necessity to inject money into the system to unfreeze bad loans nor the strain of high interest on debt-servicing can be overlooked by the bankers any more, while such demands also cannot easily be reconciled with the tight money policy.

It may be concluded that tight money policy cannot continue unless the Central Banks refuse to intervene effectively, as they did in 1931, which would inevitably have the same consequences it had then (Minsky, 1982). This is not to say that trouble could not arise even if the Central Banks are prepared to advance credit: in so far as a financial crisis may be an international currency problem as well, it would require a coordinated international action of monetary authorities to deal adequately with it.

The precarious position of the banks is only the logical consequence of their policy and that of the US government allied to the Federal Reserve. The harm done to both the developing countries and to industry in advanced countries by the high interest policy and the long-lasting refusal of the US government, upheld at Toronto, to expand lending facilities of the IMF would certainly have come back with a vengeance to the banks if the US had maintained its position.[18] But then, as Keynes (1972, p. 156) once said: 'Banks and bankers are by nature blind.' It might be added that some governments, with their monetarist spectacles, have been hardly better off.

SUMMARY AND CONCLUSION

The ascent of monetarism to worldwide influence can be explained as a social and political phenomenon. Without going into its broader political aspects, this chapter has been concerned with the question of how monetarism has been able to gain so much power despite the evident damage it is doing to industrial capitalism. Monetarism, seen as the ideology of the banks and of the *rentiers* whose interests are defended by the banks, serves as an antidote to Keynesian ideology which assigns to the banks the role of instruments of the government's full employment policy and therefore deprives them of their autonomous power and influence on policy. Moreover, the high interest rates which usually result from monetarist policies are, in most cases, directly beneficial to the banks as long as there is no danger of a financial crisis. The rise of monetarism since the early 1960s can be explained by the increase in the banks' influence and power which resulted from the expansion of their business, chiefly through operations in the Euromarket. By 1981 the volume of the Euromarket had expanded to 40 times its size in 1965. The lending was not confined to less-developed countries; 50–60 per cent was lent to industrial countries. The sources of the banks' funds were both the financial surplus of the OPEC countries and the savings of the industrial world. The Euromarket thus constitutes a network of financial relations extending over all parts of the world.

A major attraction of the Euromarket is the escape-route it provides from national monetary controls. The large transnational banks, in their support of monetarism, play an ambiguous role: they favour tight money policy which keeps interest high; but at the same time, through their participation in the Euromarket, they escape the tight credit policy imposed by the monetary authorities. Historically, the basis for such a successful policy of expansion of banking business was provided first by the expansion of trade and investment, and subsequently by the recycling of petromoney. Since both these favourable conditions have vanished, the reverse side of the monetarist medal has become visible. Owing to the protracted recession, to which tight credit policy has largely contributed, the safety of the banks' customers is threatened, both in industrial and in less-developed countries. At the same time, the complicated network of international lending increases the dangers implicit in the instability of the banking system. As a result, the position and the point of view of the banks has undergone a fundamental change: their interest is now in easier money because they want more liquidity, so that their customers, threatened with insolvency and forced to borrow, can at least service their debt. This explains the turnabout of the Federal Reserve policy since August 1982 when interest rates were permitted to decline in the US, followed by those in Europe.

The conclusion is that monetary policy has been of singular short-sightedness, because it has disregarded the interests of the banks' customers in both industrial and less-developed countries until their economic plight reacted back on the banks. With a recession lasting longer than expected, and the fear of growing insolvencies, a return to a high interest policy is not likely.

NOTES

1 Historically this was not always the case. In 1929 the proto-monetarists Foster and Catchings were inveighing against the Federal Reserves' policy of stopping the stock market boom by tight credit policy (Tavlas and Aschheim, 1981). This stance of bygone times is still reflected in Milton Friedman's monetary history (Friedman and Schwartz, 1963).

2 A recent issue of the *Economist* (1981) recaptures this change of mood:

'In the particular circumstances of 1931, it is easy to accept the macro-economic argument that devaluation was a better short-term remedy than yet another attempt to drive down wages and salaries. There was then a downward spiral of expectations of lower prices and costs'. The *Economist* then argues that a depreciating sterling is no alternative (to wage cut) today. Indeed, a stable and highly valued sterling serves the interest of the City, and that is our point.

3   Or, in particular, that aspect of Keynesian policy which argued for the economic autonomy of the state in managing demand through public works to provide a sufficient market for domestic industries so as to maintain full employment. The attitude of Keynes was already evident in his opposition to the return to the Gold Standard (1925), a policy which meant putting the interests of the City above the interests of industry.

4   Its consequence has been not only to increase the general debt-service ratio (i.e. interest and amortisation payments as a percentage of exports of goods and services) for the borrower developing countries, but to increase the particular component of interest payment ratio dispropor-tionately. Thus the group of middle-income net oil-importing develop-ing countries which account for most of the commercial debt had an almost fourfold increase in their interest payments ratio between 1973 and 1982 while their overall debt-service ratio during the same period doubled. See World Bank (1982), Table 33 in particular.

5   The corresponding reduction in bond prices is likely to affect far more adversely thrift institutions with long-maturing portfolios.

6   In the case of US banks, during the 1960s their expansion into Europe was linked to takeovers and opening of subsidiaries by US multi-national corporations. But we suspect that, once the Eurocurrency market assumed its vast size, even US banks could begin to operate relatively independently of their corporations. In the case of Britain, this is a more clearly established pattern.

7   This impression distinctly emerges from an as yet unpublished survey of 84 transnational banks (with 3941 foreign entities) conducted by the UN Commission on Transnational Corporations: *Transnational Banks: Operations strategies and their effects in developing countries*. With regard to Germany, however, it must be added that the Bundesbank has an exceedingly strong position of power and that since 1967 it has pursued time and again restrictive policies to the detriment of employ-ment and of domestic industry, contributing very largely to the weak-ness of private investment in all that time. This happened although Germany, unlike Italy for example, has not been under the compulsion of a chronic and serious balance of payments problem.

8   United States' balance of payments figures for the period 1960–67 suggest that USA ran an average annual export surplus of goods and

services of the order of 6 billion dollars. But US grant and aid plus net transfer on official exchange account (annual average 5 billion dollars) and foreign private investment (annual average 3 billion dollars) resulted in an overall payments deficit.

9 This figure was reported in *International Herald Tribune* (1981a) — see Carl Gecoirtz, 'Euromarkets: a gawky adolescent begins to settle down', p. 15.

10 The main reason for this is the Euromarket of expatriate dollars, Deutschmarks, Swiss francs, sterling, guilders, French francs, yen, Belgian francs and various smaller convertible currencies, as well as composite units such as Units of Account, European Currency Units and Special Drawing Rights, which form a varied currency base of commercial banking operations, detached from national monetary bases.

11 Mainly 'low-absorber' OPEC countries (i.e. Saudi Arabia, UAE, Kuwait, Qatar) who accounted for 33.6 billion out of a total OPEC surplus of 34.1 billion dollars in 1977 (see *World Financial Markets*, September 1976 and June 1977). On an average till the end of 1980, OPEC invested around 40 per cent of their financial surplus in Euromarkets according to US Treasury and Bank of England data.

12 A more exact percentage breakdown based upon Morgan Guaranty data is the following:

	1970-73	1974-76	1977-79	1980-81
Industrialised countries	66.2	48.0	38.5	57.8
Non-OPEC developing countries	19.4	30.9	37.8	28.3
Others	14.4	21.1	23.7	13.9

13 The data relate to banks reporting to the Bank of International Settlements (BIS).

	1975	1976	1977	1978	1979	1980
Ratio of OPEC's deposit in total bank deposit	0.11	0.12	0.12	0.10	0.11	0.12

Source: BIS

14 See *International Herald Tribune* (1981a).

15 For example, 3 Latin American countries (Brazil, Mexico and Argentina) accounted for 78 per cent of gross commercial lending to Latin America at the end of 1979, which amounts to 51 per cent of the total lending to non-oil developing countries. Similarly, almost the entire commercial lending to Asia is concentrated in a few countries (South Korea, Indonesia, Malaysia, the Phillipines and Thailand).

16 See *International Currency Review* (1980), where the letters written by several Central Banks to the Federal Reserve are quoted in part. Thus, the Bank of England wrote: 'These proposals appear to us to carry with them an implication that the US authorities consider it necessary to extend their regulatory jurisdiction into the affairs of non-American banks. We would find this a troublesome principle and one which, if generalised, could materially damage effective international cooperation in this field. We feel sure that these concerns could also be shared by a number of other major countries to whose banks these proposed regulations would apply' (p. 16) — letter dated 11 January 1980. Soon the same point was repeated by Deutsche Bundesbank as well as the Bank of Japan in their letters.

17 This was written soon after the Federal Reserve changed their stance in August 1982.

18 The administration has in the meantime consented to an increase of the quotas by about 50 per cent. The effect of this on the lending capacity of the IMF will not be felt immediately because of procedural delays.

4. Keynesians, Monetarists and Keynes: The End of the Debate — or a Beginning?

V. Chick

INTRODUCTION*

In *The Theory of Monetary Policy* (Chick, 1977) a major chapter (Ch. 3) was devoted to arguing out Keynesian and monetarist propositions concerning the mechanism and efficacy of monetary policy on the ground-rules at that time accepted by major participants in the debate. These ground-rules included the use of the comparative static method supplemented by dynamics of adjustment according to the correspondence principle. Additionally, both sides at that time assumed that the mode of introduction of new money was a matter of indifference. These ground-rules are not satisfactory.[1]

In 1972, Friedman paved the way for considering different modes of monetary change, in a backhanded sort of way. He argued that the mode of financing fiscal policy was important, fiscal policies being more effective if accompanied by monetary changes than by changes in interest-bearing debt or tax changes. Here at least is recognition that monetary changes always entail a change in some other economic variable as a counterpart. Friedman's well-known, because colourful, assumption that money rains down on the economy from a helicopter has one supreme methodological attraction: it permits us to hold to the established method of analysing a change in only one variable at a time, *ceteris paribus*. Recognising that all monetary change involves some other change as well forces us to relinquish that method.

Realism also suggests that the comparative–static method is suspect: in the real world the effects of monetary change (or any other sort of change) work their way through time and the final equilibrium result obtained by comparative–static analysis is never reached. This is not just due to the length of calendar time required: that would not be a serious problem if we could be sure that the approach to equilibrium was always monotonic, for we at least could reach conclusions about the direction of change. But there have been too many studies of monetary questions in which overshooting of the final position figures prominently[2] for us to rest our case on that. More fundamentally, however, the path to equilibrium is likely to alter the structure of the economy, so that comparative–static results do not apply.

This chapter represents a change of ground-rules: The effects of monetary changes of different types are examined by a process analysis. Because of the complexity inherent in the use of process analysis (Faxen, 1957), the effects of monetary change cannot be traced through very many periods. Nevertheless, the results using this method are quite powerful. As a result of the analysis,

(1) a new interpretation of Keynes' position on the relative efficacy of fiscal and monetary policy is offered;

(2) the difference between Keynes' analysis in *The General Theory* and the subsequent Keynesian position is clarified; and

(3) the fundamental unity of the monetarist and Keynesian positions is made more apparent — thus continuing the process begun in Chick (1977).

Where unity is demonstrated, debate should cease. But the approach presented here is intended also to point analysis of monetary policy in a new direction.

MODES OF MONETARY CHANGE

A change in the money stock of a closed economy can come about in several different ways. There are, for a start, two suppliers of money: the monetary authorities and the banking system, supplying high-powered and deposit money, respectively. When the monetary authorities allow the supply of high-powered money to increase an interest rate policy is being pursued, whether implicitly or explicitly. If, for example, the government, for contra-cyclical reasons, is running a deficit and — also for contra-cyclical reasons — it is undesirable to allow the interest rate to rise, then where the deficit is financed by issuing government debt to the public, the Central Bank simultaneously provides the money wherewith to purchase it; that is, the form of financing by borrowing is preserved, but the usual need to raise interest rates in order to sell the securities is obviated and the net result is a rise in the money supply. As a shorthand, this process will be designated fiscal policy financed by new money.

Open market operations can, of course, occur even in the absence of the need to provide new government finance; these constitute the second main source of monetary change. The third main influence of the authorities over the money supply is exercised through the various means of affecting bank lending: calls or releases of special deposits, limits on the expansion of advances, etc. Finally, the banks themselves can initiate monetary change, either because they have reserves in excess of those demanded by the authorities, acquired in a period of pessimism and uncertainty, or because they have some (though in the UK quite limited) power to encourage a flow of funds to them by raising rates of interest on their liabilities or indeed, by creating new, more attractive, forms of liability such as negotiable certificates of deposit.

Keynes did not stress these differences. In a passage which, read superficially, provides the source of the Keynesian contention that money (M) affects income (Y) chiefly through the interest rate (r), Keynes (1936) treats the monetary financing of government deficit and bank expansion as equivalent:

The relation of changes in M to Y and r depends, in the first instance, on the way in which changes in M come about. ... [If] changes in M are due to the Government printing money wherewith to meet its current expenditure ... [the] new money accrues as someone's income. The new level of income, however, will not continue sufficiently high for the requirements of M_1 [transactions and precautionary balances] to absorb the whole of the increase in M; and some portion of the money will seek an outlet in buying securities or other assets until r has fallen so as to bring about an increase in the magnitude of M_2 [speculative balances] and at the same time to stimulate a rise in Y to such an extent that the new money is absorbed either in M_2 or in the M_1 which corresponds to the rise in Y caused by the fall in r. Thus at one remove this case comes to the same thing as the alternative case, where the new money can only be issued in the instance by a relaxation of the conditions of credit by the banking system, so as to induce someone to sell the banks a debt or a bond in exchange for the new cash. It will, therefore, be safe for us to take the latter case as typical. (p.200)

It is not safe. Keynes, while beginning the passage by emphasising the importance of the transaction which is the counterpart of the monetary increase, ends by saying it makes no difference. We shall establish that it does.

DEFICITS FINANCED BY NEW MONEY

Monetary finance of government deficits is not unusual in the UK: monetary policy in the 1960s was directed toward the interest rate, often mitigating its fluctuations. To the extent that the rate was stabilised, fluctuations in the government deficit were reflected in changes in the money supply.

The important feature of the direct financing case is that autonomous expenditure and the supply of high-powered money increase together as one and the same transaction. The government's expenditure plan is made effective by the creation of new cash. There should be no dispute, therefore, about the first-round consequences of this policy action. The monetary increase, which the monetarists regard as the active element of the policy, is simply the counterpart of the income generated by government expenditure, the aspect focused on by Keynesians. In the first round, the government purchases goods and services in exchange for money, providing income paid in the form of money to the suppliers of those goods and services.

Both Keynesians and monetarists should be able to agree that there is now an excess supply of money. Their disagreement concerns the reaction to that excess supply. Keynesians assume that the public react solely by buying bonds; this is the foundation of their assertion that the effect of a monetary increase on income takes place through interest rate changes. Monetarists, on the other hand, would argue that the new money will raise the demand for goods. It is widely believed that this difference of view stems from contrasting assumptions about the substitutability of money for commodities and financial assets. At the extreme, Keynesians are said to believe that the only relevant margin of choice is between money and bonds, while an equally extreme classical view acknowledges only the transactions motive for holding money, thus predicting that an excess demand for money falls entirely on the market for goods. Tobin (1961, 1969) and Friedman (1956) have proposed less extreme versions which, respectively, still preserve the Keynesian emphasis on the money–bond choice, and support the monetarist prediction that a change in the money supply is manifest mainly in changes in output and/or price rather than changes in the interest rate.

The question of relative substitutability is a reflection of the ground-rule of employing a static method, and is quite beside the point. In the context of process analysis, which was undoubtedly the method of Keynes' analysis in the passage just quoted, our modern antagonists are referring to different stages in the sequence of events following the monetary change. Let us return to Keynes' description. In the period in which the deficit occurs, M and Y increase by the same amount, the amount of the deficit. The need for transactions balances rises with increased income but not to an equal extent: the Cambridge k is less than one and there are economies of scale in precautionary holdings also.[3] The money not absorbed by transactions and precautionary balances will find its way into the speculative sphere. Initially, there is no demand for speculative money holdings (the interest rate is unaltered). Purchases of bonds then lower the interest rate until the speculative demand rises sufficiently to take up all the new money not absorbed by income-related demands. That occurs in the period subsequent to the introduction of new money. The lower interest rate stimulates investment and raises income (and transactions and precautionary demand) still further, somewhat reversing the initial fall in interest rates. It is only to this second reaction in the process, the disposal of money not absorbed by M_1 balances, that the 'Keynesian bond–money margin' pertains.

Let us explore the transactions demand further, for it is here that the money–goods margin is important. Unlike precautionary demand, which is also used for the purchase of goods but only occasionally, transactions balances circulate continuously in exchange for goods. They are not really 'held', except on average. Some might suppose that people, or firms, would hold additional transactions balances as a luxury (Friedman, 1959), using some of their increased income to lengthen the period between trips to the market or to the bank (Clower, 1969, 1970). For simplicity, however, it is helpful to assume that changes in the money supply leave the pattern of payments unaffected. Then the increased transactions balances unambiguously would be used in the purchase of commodities, if the new money accrued to households, or raw materials and labour if it accrued to firms.

RESPONSE OF CONSUMERS

When household incomes rise, it is typically assumed that both consumption and saving rise. Some of the new money finances the incremental consumption; the rest — saving — may (depending on expectations of interest rate changes) be used to purchase bonds. In other words, that part of the new money which is added to transactions balances as it circulates in exchange for goods finances what Keynesians call the multiplier, creating income changes in addition to the initial change arising from the deficit.

From the monetarist point of view, the stimulating effects of government expenditure arise from the propensity of those who acquire additional money balances to spend those balances on commodities. But what is the difference? To Keynesians, increased income is an incentive to spend, and financing is rather ignored, it being assumed that income is paid in the form of money. To monetarists, money burns a hole in peoples' pockets, no matter how it gets there. Whether it represents additional income, as in the case being considered, or as an increment to wealth, income remaining unchanged as in the helicopter case the new money raises the budget restraint. A spending decision needs money to finance it, and a rise in the budget restraint (extra money) does typically result in an increment of spending. Keynesians and monetarists should agree on this point. It is awkward for both if they do not, for if Keynesians wish to deny the monetarists' 'direct effect' they must repudiate the multiplier; and if monetarists are to sustain the importance of the direct effect, they must accept its consequence, the multiplier.[4]

Conflict may still arise, however, both about the fundamental issue of causation and about the extent of expenditure in all rounds after the initial change. First, causation. The monetarist position is that monetary changes cause changes in income, so the initial fiscal action, in which money and income increase simultaneously rather than in causal sequence, does not relate to their theory: it is the subsequent rounds of income change which are relevant. Their theory would describe events as follows: each person in the multiplier chain receives an increment of income in the form of money, which is more than sufficient to cover the old level of transactions. The excess supply of money is spent on goods, which generates income. Thus the monetary increase plays a causal role in the rise of income. From a Keynesian point of view, the desire to increase expenditure comes from the realisation of a higher level of income. The increased volume of money balances (larger pay packets) merely enables that desire to become effective in the market place: its role is not causal.

Second, the extent of induced expenditure. Keynesians would insist that the amount was given by the marginal propensity to consume in each round. The monetarist position is less clear, for they approach the problem as one of adjusting to an excess stock of money. There is, on the face of it, no simple relationship between the existence of this excess stock and the rate at which consumers attempt to get rid of it by spending. This is a question of adjustment speed, for which we need to make some assumption such as equality of marginal and average income velocity (the timing of payments remains unchanged; the extra expenditure is spread evenly over the expenditure period).[5] If, by such an assumption, the two approaches were made comparable, it is likely that monetarists would assert a larger impact on the goods market than would Keynesians. This can be inferred from the monetarists' tendency to play down, or even deny, an interest-rate effect of monetary change. For there to be no interest-rate effect it would appear that one of three assumptions must be adopted: either (i) the marginal propensity to save is zero (with its attendant problems for stability); or (ii) the rate of increase of private[6] financial assets keeps pace with the desire of savers to place money at interest; or (iii) savers hold all the unspent portion of their new incomes as idle money. It is difficult to imagine modern monetarists owning up to any of these propositions,[7] particularly the last which, ironically, is the liquidity trap.

Monetarists have avoided having to adopt one of these alternatives by changing the definitions of consumption and saving. Keynes, pursuing the effects of money flows, defined consumption as consumers' expenditure on commodities. Saving, therefore, could take the form only of acquisitions of financial assets or of idle money-holdings. Monetarists have adopted the Fisherian schema, in which consumption is the stream of utility from commodities; saving, therefore, may take the form of purchases of claims to future utility streams through the acquisition of durable goods. This change of concept permits monetarists to save face when confronted with the choices given above, but does not, of course, contribute to the settlement of differences with Keynesians.[8]

RESPONSE OF FIRMS

We now turn to the response of firms whose sales have risen as a result of government purchases. If the increase in sales is thought to be more than transitory, a revision of output and pricing plans is called for. Assuming an upward-sloping marginal cost curve in the short run, the likely outcome is an increase of both price and output. The increased cash flow from sales will finance the rise in outlays for raw materials and labour to prepare for an expansion of output. Again, these expenditures will have multiplier effects and again, if the incremental cash flow exceeds the increased outlays, the remainder will probably be placed in short-term securities pending an investment decision. The extent to which the multiplier consists of real output changes rather than price changes is decided here. Once again, both income and the interest rate are affected in ways which both Keynesians and monetarists should be willing to accept.

FURTHER CONSIDERATIONS

Overshooting of the interest rate is virtually inevitable, due to the fact that changes in income through the multiplier take time. Keynes shortcircuits this process, leaping straight from the interest-rate effect to the final equilibrium with his phrase 'at the same time to stimulate a rise in Y to such an extent that the new money is absorbed'. It will not happen 'at the same time', of course. Assuming (unrealistically) that the initial monetary increase is not repeated during expansion, money which goes into bonds as a temporary abode of purchasing power will return to active circulation as income grows over time (perhaps quite a long time) and the initial fall in interest will be reversed at least to some extent and perhaps completely. It is even possible that the final equilibrium rate will be higher than the rate obtaining before the deficit is undertaken (the reason for this ambiguous outcome can be glimpsed in what follows).

To assume no further monetary increase is unrealistic for two reasons. First, the initial fall in interest is likely to stimulate investment, an activity typically financed by borrowing, and often financed initially by *bank* borrowing (which increases the money supply) and funded later. Second, the deficit was financed by high-powered money, the bulk of which would not normally remain in the hands of the public but would find its way to the banking system, where it would constitute an increase in reserves and a base for new lending, just at the time when the demand for bank loans is increasing on account of the favourable prospects for investment. By now it is obvious that to trace out the full effects would be a formidable task. And it would only divert us from our main purpose, which is to explore the difference between new money which finances a government deficit and new money arising from bank lending.

MONEY CREATED BY BANK LENDING

We now turn to examine the policy of money creation achieved by stimulating an increase in bank lending. Suppose, beginning in bank portfolio equilibrium, that the Central Bank releases special deposits. Banks have been provided with excess reserves, other things being equal. So the banks should now be willing to expand their earning assets at every given rate of return: their supply of loans function has shifted to the right. Assuming no previous rationing of credit and given a downward-sloping demand curve for loans, a fall in the loan rate is required if the *actual* volume of loans is to increase (a stable demand curve for loans implies no change in borrowers' expectations. This is to some extent unrealistic in the circumstances postulated. We shall return to this point later). The

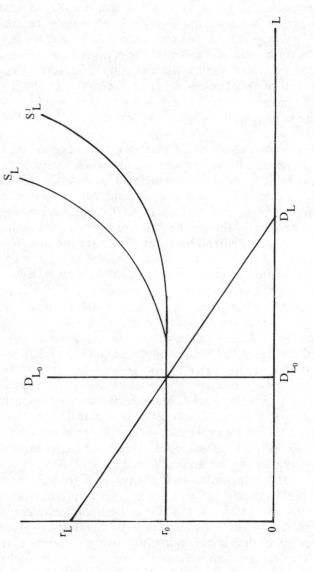

Figure 4.1

money supply (deposits) will not rise until loans *have* increased. Thus a fall in the interest rate (now the bank loan rate; in the previous section it was the rate on securities) must occur *prior to* and as a precondition of a money supply increase. While the interest rate in the deficit/new money case played a role in the transmission of policy in the periods *after* the initial increase in the money supply, the role of the interest rate in the transmission of this present form of monetary policy is to convert an increase in bank reserves — which *are not* money — into a rise in deposit holdings of the private sector, which *are* money.

This is the point at which Keynesians evoke the image of the horse that will not drink. The argument that in a depression an increase in bank reserves will not increase loans, while seeming plausible in a verbal presentation, is harder to sustain in the face of some simple geometry. In Figures 4.1 and 4.2 let D_{L_0} be the demand to maintain the stock of already outstanding loans, D_L to total demand for loans (hence at r_0 no new loans are sought; at higher rates borrowers wish to repay), and S_L the banks' willingness to issue and maintain a given level of loans. S_L shifts to S^1_L as a result of the provision of reserves. For loans not to expand, either banks are in their own 'liquidity-trap' (Figure 4.1) or the demand for loans is totally inelastic (Figure 4.2). A case has been made for the former in recession, though it has been strongly challenged:[9] it has been supposed that banks react to the greater uncertainty and higher probability of bad debts by holding excess reserves rather than expanding loans. And clearly the less responsive borrowers are to interest costs the less the expansion provoked by a given fall in interest rates — though some increase in lending will still take place, even given unchanged expectations, as long as D_L has some elasticity.

The monetary authorities have always relied to some extent on an expectation effect of a monetary policy shift. In relaxing a constraint on the banks, the authorities indicate an expansionary stance, which firms should see as favourable to profits and investment, thus encouraging borrowing. In terms of the figures, the D_L function shifts to the right, and bank lending may increase without any fall in the loan rate. Thus when

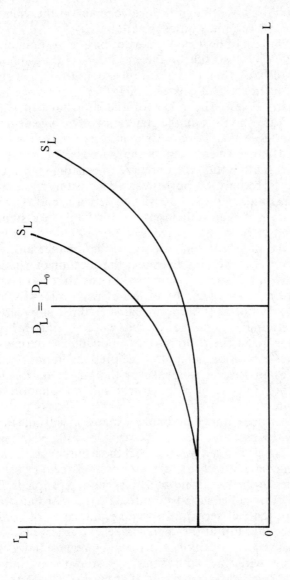

Figure 4.2

expectations are allowed to change, a change in the interest rate is not *essential* to the transmission of this form of monetary policy. Its significance depends on the 'announcement effect' of policy on expectations.

The amount of new money created by a relaxation of special deposits, then, depends on the elasticities of the demand and supply of bank finance and on the extent (if any) of shifts in these functions. But for simplicity we have bypassed an important point. The effect of the monetary increase on expenditure and thus on the generation of *income* depends on the extent to which the banks' expansion takes the form of new loans (whether overdrafts or the purchase of newly-issued securities) rather than the purchase of existing securities, and on the intentions of borrowers. Expansion of new loans provides funds to those who wish to deficit-spend. Those who issue liabilities against themselves can reliably be assumed not to intend to hold the proceeds of borrowing as idle money, except for the short time for which the 'finance motive'[10] is relevant.[11] However, there remains the question of whether the proceeds will be spent on commodities or on securities. In the case of firms borrowing by means of new issues of securities (which will not bulk large in bank credit in any case) it is extremely unlikely that the proceeds will go to finance holdings of other securities, though for individuals purchases of securities cannot be ruled out. The preponderance of existing securities in the market ensures that most of the money channelled into securities markets will not support deficit expenditure.

Furthermore, not all the banks' expansion will take the form of new loans: they too may make purchases of existing securities.[12] It is often asserted that these purchases could have an immediate effect on expenditure, as people sell their securities to the banks in order to spend the proceeds. This is quite a reasonable supposition for a particular individual — people often sell securities to make purchases of consumer durables, say. But at the *aggregate* level it is less plausible. It supposes that security-holders in aggregate have, simultaneously with the authorities' decision to expand bank reserves, decided to spend out of accumulated wealth — that is, to dis-save. Clearly such behaviour in aggregate presumes a shift in preferences. Analysis is usually conducted against the background of stable preferences; we wish to adhere to this convention. It implies that at most, sellers of securities in aggregate spend their capital gains (more of this below).

To fix ideas, define a_1, a_2, a_3 as the banks' marginal propensities to increase deposits by expansion, of overdrafts and purchases of new securities and outstanding securities, respectively. The a's sum to unity. Then define b_1, b_2, b_3 as borrowers' marginal propensities to use overdrafts to purchase goods, buy securities, or hold the proceeds idle; c_1, c_2, c_3 as the marginal propensity to allocate the proceeds of new issues to the three uses, respectively; and d_1, d_2, d_3 as the same three uses to which are put sales of securities out of one's portfolio. Each set of marginal propensities sums to unity. It is being asserted that $a_1 > a_3 > a_2$; a_2 is small; $b_1 > b_2$; $b_3 = 0$; $c_1 = 1$; $c_2 = c_3 = 0$; $d_2 < d_3$ and d_1 is small.

To the extent that deposit expansion results from new loans, expenditure on goods may reliably be assumed to increase. If b_2 were zero, initial expenditure rises by the same amount as the rise in the money supply. This is perhaps the sense in which bank lending is similar to public works financed by new money, as Keynes suggested. The earlier remarks on the Keynesian and monetarist positions apply.

To the extent that the banks' expansion takes the form of purchases of existing securities, those purchases will lower the rate of interest on securities to the extent required by the interest elasticity of money demand. Idle balances willingly held thus have increased, not *in response to* an excess supply of money, as in the previous case, but as *a counterpart to* bank expansion. It is obvious that this portion of the rise in the money supply works through the interest rate. It does not affect expenditure and income directly, except for capital gains. Here, the Keynesian transmission mechanism holds, and monetarists would be hard pressed to deny it — unless, of course, they accept absolute liquidity preference on the part of the public!

In summary, monetary policy operating through a relaxation of credit conditions will increase initial transactions balances and expenditure by the amount $a_1b_1 + a_2c_1 + a_3d_1$. The largest component is a_1b_1, representing new bank borrowing encouraged by a fall in the loan rate and/or a rise in expectations. Idle balances will increase to the extent a_3d_3, which arises from banks' purchases of existing securities from the public. The *immediate* expenditure increase will be less than the increase in the money supply to the extent $a_1b_2 + a_3d_3$.

Subsequent effects occur as before. The new expenditure will have a multiplier effect, and further borrowing (on securities markets rather than from banks) may follow from the fall in security yields caused by the banks' demand for securities. But for any given increase in the quantity of money, these income effects will begin from a smaller first-round income change, compared with the fiscal deficit case. So if the *rate* at which the multiplier proceeds, and the *rate* at which investment responds to lower interest rates, and the *rate* at which savings are placed in securities markets are assumed to be given, then at any point in time the position of the economy will be different according to the manner in which money is increased. Differences may diminish over time, as the decisions of many periods outweigh differences in initial conditions, but the independence of long-run equilibrium from the path taken to reach it is an article of classical faith, not a demonstrated proposition. And in any case policy-makers are interested in the short run.

OPEN MARKET OPERATIONS

And so to the third method of increasing the money supply, which we can deal with fairly quickly. The interesting feature of an open market operations is that it is concerned entirely with the composition of the public's financial wealth. An open market purchase increases the supply of money and decreases the volume of bonds outstanding. Typically the rate of interest falls, to persuade bond-holders to sell to the government broker; the extent of its fall is given by the interest-elasticity of liquidity preference. There are some capital gains for those who sell — there is no initial change in income proper. Surely, this is the case in which the Keynesian transmission mechanism is most obviously appropriate and relevant.

The monetarist direct effect could play a major role if it were reasonable to assume that the intervention of the government broker determined only the timing of the sales of securities on the part of households which were intending to spend but were waiting for a favourable moment to sell their assets. But, as pointed out above, this amounts in aggregate to a desire to dis-save — an extreme assumption which monetarists have never explicitly endorsed. The monetarist direct effect may have a role to play, but it is more properly limited to that portion of capital gains which are spent on commodities.[13]

For the Keynesian transmission mechanism to be the exclusive means of transmission, all capital gains must be ploughed back into the speculative sphere as idle money-holdings. This is not as implausible as it sounds. The reasoning is as follows. Bond-holders have sold to capture a capital gain. If they expect the policy to work in the traditional manner, the fall in the interest rate will encourage investment; this will increase the demand for funds on the securities market and raise the interest rate once again. Those who sold securities may be waiting for that rise, after which securities become cheap again; they are holding money idle meanwhile. If this behaviour is typical, the interest rate is the *sole* transmitter of this form of monetary policy. In any event, one can say with confidence that because capital gains are small relative to the monetary change effected by open market operations, the monetarist direct effect is far smaller in this case than in the other two modes of monetary increase which we have analysed.

RESOLUTION: A BEGINNING?

Is it not possible to come to some agreement? It would seem plausible to suggest that when Keynes talked of monetary policy he had in mind the type most prevalent in his time (and still): open market operations. With a minor qualification, this is the type of policy for which it is most obviously true that money has its chief effect through the interest rate. This fact has nothing to do with the absence of a money–goods margin of choice; it arises *because of the way money enters the system.* In an open market operation, the government broker *poses* a money–bonds choice. What happens subsequently depends on how people spend out of accumulated wealth and capital gains, questions on which, unlike expenditure out of income, there is no widely accepted presumption of behaviour. They may not plan to spend any of it, but if they do, the amount is most unlikely to be significant.

Contrast the cases explored above with the helicopter policy. The new money is clearly a windfall. No effort has been expended to earn it, so it is perceived as an increase in wealth, not income. It comes all at once, not gradually as payment for goods or services. With this increase in wealth, the incentive to save is far less than it would be if the money accrued gradually as income, where even though wealth has increased it is less obvious to the receiver. The very prudent might place some of this new helicopter money at interest, but it is not implausible that most of the money will be spent on commodities. It does not matter whether the commodities are durables, which in the Fisherian income scheme counts as saving: the point is that there is expenditure on goods rather than on financial assets. The monetarist direct effect naturally dominates — would not Keynesians agree?

For the other cases explored in this chapter, it has been shown that it is important for Keynesians and monetarists to see that there is a unity in the idea that income determines the plan to spend and money makes it possible, for otherwise each is placed in an absurd position: for Keynesians to refute the direct effect they may have to disown the multiplier, and monetarists may have to embrace the liquidity-trap to prevent interest rate changes from absorbing some of the adjustment to monetary change. But the most important message is the futility of talking about the transmission mechanism divorced from the type of monetary change being considered. A debate which is not at cross-purposes is more likely to take place if the specific properties of different policy options are taken into account and their effects examined by an analysis based on time sequence, for actual policy has its impact in a temporal world.

NOTES

*The author wishes to thank Charles Goodhart and Thanos Skouras for their comments, without implicating them.

1 Almost as this chapter was being written (1978), the monetarist–Keynesian debate was shifting ground, away from issues of monetary policy proper to the macroeconomic system as a whole, particularly the operation of the labour market. Simultaneously, many commentators emphasised the political and social–philosophical nature of the conflict of views. The analytical issues discussed in this chapter are no longer at the forefront of the discussion, but they have slipped from attention without ever having been resolved. It is still important to resolve them, especially in these gloomy days of restriction.

2 Tucker (1966), Laidler (1968) and Tanner (1969) are some good examples.

3 See Patinkin (1965, pp. 82–8) and Appendix by A. Dvoretsky.

4 Cf. Friedman and Meiselman (1963), in which the direct influence of money on income is sharply contrasted to the multiplier.

5 Since the new money also represents an increase in the wealth of the private sector, the above argument should be equally acceptable to those using a consumption–wealth relation in preference to or in addition to the consumption–income relation.

6 An increase of government bonds has been ruled out by assumption.

7 Even the classical writers didn't; although at times they skated close to accepting the first proposition, it is difficult to pin them down to anything so bold, particularly in the short run, which is our concern here.

8 Friedman (1959) has argued, additionally, that the interest-rate effect will be slight because there are so many financial markets over which the demand to place excess money balances may be spread. One could equally well argue that the 'direct effect' is vitiated by the existence of a multiplicity of goods. It is not convincing.

9 Morrison (1966, Chapter III), reviews this hypothesis. See also Brunner and Meltzer (1968), who apparently worked independently of Morrison,

as they do not refer to his study. Both studies are quite critical of the hypothesis for a variety of logical reasons, and adduce evidence against it.

10 Keynes (1937c). His definition differs from the better-known one of Davidson (1965).

11 I have seen, not infrequently, references in the literature to borrowing in order to increase one's money-holdings. Outside the (rather trivial) finance motive, this strikes me as patently absurd. Indeed, in an overdraft system, overdrafts and the money supply do not expand until those granted an overdraft actually make use of it.

12 While overdrafts bear a higher rate of return, bank expansion usually includes some securities to maintain liquidity. In general, banks may be supposed to be indifferent between new and old securities. In the UK they typically buy 'seasoned' securities, leaving it to the discount houses to buy at tender.

13 Friedman (1957) suggests that windfalls are spent on durables. But are capital gains which are actively sought by those 'playing the securities market' regarded as windfalls?

5. Is There Any Crowding-out of Private Expenditure by Fiscal Actions?

P. Arestis

INTRODUCTION*

It is the contention of the simple Keynesian multiplier analysis that an increase in government expenditure or a decrease in the rate of taxation induces repeated rounds of spending. Similarly, a multiple reduction of total spending is said to result from fiscal changes opposite to those just mentioned. It is true to say, though, that this analysis pays little attention to the way deficits or surpluses are financed. Thus, an expansionary impact on the economy, for example, can be achieved by a rise in government spending matched by either an increase in tax receipts, or an increase in the money supply, or, indeed, by borrowing from the public through bond issues.

This contention, however, has been severely challenged by a number of economists who argue that government spending financed by taxes or by borrowing from general public savings may reduce other spending to such an extent that there will be little, if any, net increase in total spending. In other words, increases in government expenditure, which are not accompanied by money creation, induce temporary increases in nominal income with no net effect over a longer period of time. This is frequently referred to as the crowding-out of private expenditure by fiscal actions, known to Keynes as diversion (1929) or 'congestion' (1937c). It is thus asserted that government spending financed by either taxation or borrowing from the public is mainly a resource transfer from the private sector to the government, with little net effect on total spending. It can have a strong stimulative influence on the economy if, and only if, the increased government expenditure is financed by monetary expansion.

When increases in government spending crowd out an equivalent amount of private expenditure, so that the impact on total spending is zero, then we have the notion of *complete* crowding-out. On the other hand, crowding-out is *partial* if the increased government expenditure is accompanied by a reduction in private expenditure smaller than the increase in government expenditure. In addition, *overcrowding-out* occurs when the decrease in private expenditure is greater than the increase in government expenditure. Finally, if the increase in total expenditure is the same or greater than the increase in government expenditure, then there is *no crowding-out* (these definitions could be couched in both real or nominal terms, in which case we may have the distinction between *real* and *nominal* crowding-out).

The current debate on crowding-out focuses on the impact of the method of financing government spending and, in turn, has led to increased analysis of the so-called government budget constraint (Christ, 1968, 1978; for a comprehensive review of the literature, see Currie, 1978). This constraint specifies that the total flow of government expenditure must equal the total flow of financing from all sources. The total flow of financing includes taxes, net government borrowing from the public, and the net amount of new money issued. Budget deficits or surpluses alter the size of public debt, and the method of financing such deficits or disposing of such surpluses affects the composition of private wealth. Hence, any discussion of the effects of fiscal policy actions should distinguish the different monetary repercussions that result from such alternative modes of financing budget deficits or disposing of budget surpluses.[1] The inclusion of this constraint, which provides the necessary link between the fiscal sector and the rest of the economy in most recent models, has shed new light on the impact of alternative modes of financing budget deficits or disposing of budget surpluses. Neglect of this constraint results in introducing a bias in the policy effects; that is, in the magnitude of both the short-term and the long-term multipliers.[2]

The discussion so far has concentrated on the financing of government expenditure and the possible subsequent crowding-out of private expenditure; this is termed in the literature as *financial* crowding-out. When, however, attention is directed to the size and share of public expenditure, then a different type of crowding-out may occur. This refers to the contention that public expenditure can only expand at the expense of private expenditure, which must contract to provide the necessary room; this is the so-called *resource* crowding-out, and it is of the kind discussed by Bacon and Eltis (1976) (for a critique of the validity of the conceptual framework of the Bacon-Eltis thesis, see Ietto Gillies, 1978 and Hadjimatheou and Skouras, 1979). Clearly, in a situation of full employment with real constraints (because of capital, raw material or labour shortages) one could see how this may come about: resources would have to be diverted from the private sector to the public sector.[3] But in less than full employment situations, the extra resources required to meet the increased public demand could be mobilised from unemployed factors of production. The following comment by the Bank of England is quite interesting in this context; it has been argued that resource crowding-out is actually 'neither interesting analytically nor relevant in the present conjuncture' (Treasury and Civil Service Committee, 1980, p. 22) of excess capacity in the UK (see also Bacon and Eltis, 1979). At full employment, though, arguments can be constructed to show that expansion of the public sector need not be contractionary of the private sector. In the short run fiscal policy may be expansionary — without creating inflation — by raising the level of capacity and labour utilisation. In the longer run an expanded public sector could enhance profitability and investment in the private sector, thus creating the climate for the economy to shift onto a higher growth path (Currie, 1981, p. 13).

This chapter attempts to review the theoretical foundations of the crowding-out debate, and to summarise the major empirical results that have been published in the literature. The main conclusion is that although it makes a lot of difference how changes in government expenditure are financed, crowding-out is never complete, at least in the short run.

THEORETICAL FOUNDATIONS OF CROWDING-OUT

The crowding-out debate is not new. Adam Smith, as early as 1776, argued that some types of labour were unproductive, and condemned the transfer of resources from the private sector to the government whether through taxation or borrowing. For Smith 'saving is spending', because one man's saving becomes another man's investment; thus borrowing funds from the public to finance government spending was asserted to involve the 'destruction of some capital which had before existed in the country; by the perversion of some portion of the annual produce which had before been destined for the maintenance of productive labour, towards that of unproductive labour' (Smith, 1937, p878). Later classical economists, such as James Mill, and J.B. Say, argued along similar lines: government spending was considered unnecessary as a stabilisation tool because private investment was sufficient to utilise the funds provided by private saving.

The neoclassical economists argued that government expenditure financed by borrowing from the banks bid resources away from other sectors, thus increasing the purchasing power of the government, which would drive up the price level even under full employment conditions. The higher price level would serve as a deterrent to 'real' consumer or private investment spending which would otherwise have taken place. A good example of this view is found in the testimony of R.G. Hawtrey before the Macmillan Committee in 1930. Hawtrey argued that increases in government expenditure financed out of taxes or loans from savings to bring England out of stagnation would merely replace private expenditure, with no net impact on total expenditure. He also rejected the idea of increases in government expenditure financed out of new bank credit because the result of such a policy would be inflationary, forcing up the bank rate of interest and causing credit contraction.[4] These views were shared by the Treasury at the time (the so-called 'Treasury view'):

The large loans involved, if they are not to involve inflation, must draw on existing capital resources. These resources are on the whole utilised at present in varying degrees of active employment, and the great bulk is utilised for home industrial and commercial purposes. The extent to which any additional employment could be given by altering the direction of investment is therefore at the best strictly limited. (White Paper, 1929, Cmd. 3331, p. 53)

The Bacon–Eltis (1976) thesis also belongs to the neo-classical tradition. They argue that in Britain the increased taxation necessary to finance the expanding public sector has been entirely borne by profits, with workers being able to shift any rise in taxation onto capital. Private investment and exports have been crowded out as a result. At the same time, the successful resistance of workers to bear part of the increase in taxation has led to rising inflation, which has also contributed to the crowding-out of private expenditure in this country.

There is a Marxist counterpart to the neoclassical thesis on crowding-out: increases in public spending lead directly through taxation to an equivalent fall in surplus value, and to the extent that the extra employment in the public sector is not productive, then a *complete* crowding-out of private accumulation occurs (Bullock and Yaffe, 1975); indeed, *overcrowding-out* could easily occur according to this analysis, if public spending also crowds out an amount of personal consumption expenditure.[5]

Perhaps the best argument for the existence of the crowding-out effect can be found in Keynes own words:

If, for example, a Government employs 100,000 additional men on public works, and if the multiplier ... is 4, it is not safe to assume that aggregate employment will increase by 400,000. For the new policy may have adverse reactions on investment in other directions .... The method of financing the policy and the increased working cash, required by the increased employment and the associated rise of prices, may have the effect of increasing the rate of interest and so retarding investment in other directions, unless the monetary authority takes steps to the contrary; whilst, at the same time, the increased cost of capital goods will reduce their marginal efficiency to the private investor, and this will require an actual fall in the rate of interest to offset it. (Keynes, 1936, pp. 119-20)

It is very important to note that Keynes recognised that crowding-out constituted one of the most fundamental elements of his monetary analysis. An increase in government expenditure will create 'congestion'; in particular 'The investment market can become congested through a shortage of cash. It can never become congested through a shortage of saving. This is the most fundamental of my conclusions within the field' (Keynes, 1937c, p. 669).

We may summarise these statements within the so-called IS–LM framework (Figure 5.1). The increase in government spending, is, of course, represented by a shift in the IS curve to IS_1 (from IS_0) and, with LM being LM_0, a sharp rise in the rate of interest ensues (from r_0 to r_1) and little or no change in income (Y_0 to Y_1). This kind of crowding-out has been referred to in the literature as the *Hicksian* crowding-out (Meyer, 1980) or *transactions* crowding-out (Friedman, 1978); it must be recognised, though, that this crowding-out could very well be ascribed to the restrictive monetary policy than to the expansionary fiscal policy (Buiter 1977a). For allowing the LM curve to shift to the right (to LM_1 from LM_0), through monetary expansion, a significant rise in income occurs (from Y_0 to Y_2), thus allowing the full expansionary effects of fiscal policy to materialise.

Keynes recognised a second way, based on business psychology, through which government spending could crowd out private spending: 'With the confused psychology which often prevails, the Government programme may, through its effect on "confidence" increase liquidity-preference or diminish the marginal efficiency of capital, which again, may retard other investment unless measures are taken to offset it' (Keynes, 1936, p. 120). In other words, the increase in

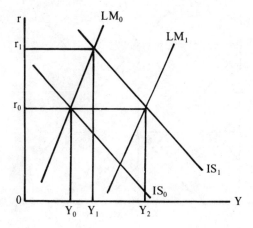

Figure 5.1

government spending, shown by the shift of IS to IS_1 in Figure 5.2, may have adverse effect on liquidity-preference, the LM curve which shifts to the left (to LM_1), and income increases only slightly, from Y_0 to Y_1. If the marginal efficiency of capital is adversely influenced, then the IS shifts from IS_1 back to IS_2 and with the LM being unchanged at LM_0 the result is again a small increase in income as before, i.e. from Y_0 to Y_1. We may note that when both, the IS and the LM, shift due to a simultaneous increase in liquidity-preference and lower marginal efficiency of capital, income may in fact turn out to decrease not increase.

More recently the discussion on the existence of crowding-out has concentrated on the slope of the LM curve. In order for crowding-out to occur, the proponents of it must assume that the demand for money is nearly perfectly interest-inelastic,

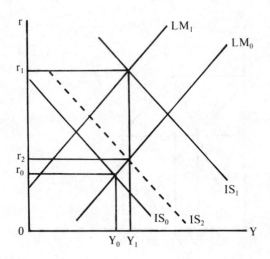

Figure 5.2

that is to say, the LM curve must be essentially vertical. Critics have argued that the majority of empirical studies produce estimates that do not support a zero interest elasticity of money demand. Friedman (1972)[6] has argued, though, that the slope of the LM curve is largely irrelevant to the crowding-out debate. In particular, Friedman has pointed out the necessity of distinguishing between initial and subsequent effects of fiscal actions. According to Friedman an 'expansionary' fiscal action might first be reflected in a rise in output, but the financing of the deficit would set in motion contractionary forces which would eventually offset the initial stimulative effect.[7]

We illustrate this point by referring to Figure 5.2. In the short run the IS curve tends to shift to IS_1, following an increase in government expenditure, but in the long run the IS curve would revert back to its original position (IS_0); the reason is that there is a 'reduction in the physical volume of assets created because of lowered private productive investments' (Friedman, 1972, p.917). In other words, Friedman is implicitly assuming that increases in government expenditure are at the expense of private investment expenditure, and that government expenditure does not create capacity but merely 'absorbs' resources. (For a critique of this view, see Gillies, 1978). For Friedman, therefore, potential output in the future will be lowered relative to what it otherwise would have been with the transfer of resources from private investment, which generates the future capital stock, to government spending, which absorbs the capital stock. These subsequent effects will continue as long as a deficit exists. Eventually, the stock of private wealth will be reduced relative to what it otherwise would have been because of reduced investment, thereby reinforcing the leftward movement of the IS curve. The total volume of wealth would fall because of the rise in the rate of interest which reduces the market value of the existing stock of government bonds. Friedman (1972, p.916), in fact, believes that wealth effects are about equal in magnitude and opposite in direction to the initial expansionary effect of an increase in government spending.[8]

More recently Floyd and Hynes (1978) (see also Butkiewicz, 1979) have demonstrated that when the wealth effects of deficit financing are properly included in the demand for money, then even the initial, or first-round, positive effects of deficit financing are associated with first-round crowding-out (irrespective of whether the deficit is financed by borrowing or printing money); however, 'whether or not crowding-out is complete, incomplete, or more than complete, depends on the magnitudes of the relevant parameters; the issue cannot be settled on theoretical grounds, regardless of the degree of homogeneity of the various wealth effects on the demand for money' (Floyd and Hynes, 1978, p.104).[9]

An additional possible source of crowding-out could arise from price effects, when the price level is not assumed to be given; in situations like these, changes in prices not only alter the real volume of wealth[10] — in which case the usual wealth effects become operative — but they may affect real expenditure through price-expectations (see, for example, Arestis and Hadjimatheou, 1982). This kind of crowding-out may be contained, though, if price expectations cause the real rate of interest to fall; the extent of this type of impact would naturally depend on whether interest-sensitive expenditures are affected by real, rather than nominal interest rates (Currie 1981, discusses this point in more detail). Additionally, changes in prices may crowd out investment expenditure via their impact on profitability (Redhead, 1978). To the extent that prices lag behind costs, inflationary pressures following increases in government expenditure could so affect profits that investment expenditure may be significantly curtailed. One should also mention the possibility of crowding-out arising from the so-called 'ultrarationality hypothesis'. According to the latter (see, for example, David and Scalding, 1974) government expenditure is a close substitute for private expenditure. This hypothesis rests on the assumption — which has yet to be empirically supported — that the combined savings ratio of the private and public sectors is more stable than that of either of the two alone. It, therefore, follows that an increase in government expenditure would reduce private expenditure by an equivalent amount, without necessitating any changes in interest rates, prices or wealth. In other words, the private sector behaves as if government is an extension of itself, so that government expenditures are considered as substitutes for private expenditures. Thus, crowding-out may take the form of direct substitution independently of any adjustment in the interest rate, inflation or the exchange rate. Barro (1974) also reaches the same conclusion on grounds of 'ultrarationality'. Increases in government expenditure not financed by money-creation will leave total expenditure unchanged since the private sector perceives debt-finance as simply deferred tax liabilities.

A number of studies have been critical of the crowding-out thesis. Davidson (1978) has attacked Friedman (1972) by pointing out that his results depend critically on 'the marginal propensity to purchase securities out of each period's savings' (p. 404); the argument here is that it is only when the marginal propensity to purchase securities is equal to zero that the Friedman scenario holds true. In view of Keynes' belief that the marginal propensity to purchase securities is greater than zero but less than one, the Keynesian argument will then be that crowding-out could only be partial.

Tobin (1978) argues that the David–Scalding (1974) ultra-rationality hypothesis is not, in fact, supported by their empirical study of private savings behaviour. In the same paper, and in a critique of Barro (1974), Tobin demonstrates that crowding-out need not occur even at full employment. For the increased government expenditure at full employment and the inflationary pressures that ensue will make money a less attractive asset, and encourage economic units to save in other forms of assets, including real capital. Thus, increased government expenditure enhances rather than reduces the economy's capital stock (contrary to Friedman's, 1972, claim). Similarly, Mitchell (1981), employing a post-Keynesian framework, concludes that budget deficits do not produce destabilising results, for they provide the means through which the nominal growth in the economy can be accommodated.

The study by Friedman (1978) is interesting in that it accounts for crowding-out phenomena within the context of a model that includes money, bonds and capital (see also Meyer, 1980). Friedman demonstrates that crowding-out crucially depends on 'the ratio of the substitution coefficient between bonds and money to the substitution coefficient between bonds and capital' in relation to 'the ratio of the respective wealth coefficients on the demand for money and capital' (Friedman, 1978, p. 629). The importance of this study is that it relates to an issue which is completely ignored by the studies that emphasise the wealth effect in the demand for money, as in Floyd and Hynes (1976), for example. Since it is implicitly assumed in these studies that government bonds are closer substitutes for capital than money, it is taken for granted that the sign of the wealth effect in the demand for money is positive. This, however, need not be the case; as Friedman (1978), Tobin (1971) and Tobin and Buiter (1976) argue, the substitutability between bonds and money may be stronger than between bonds and capital. Clearly, if this were the case, then crowding-out of the Floyd and Hynes-type could not be sustained: the increase in wealth that would follow from bond-financed increases in government expenditure would decrease the demand for money, and with no higher interest rates it becomes very difficult to see how crowding-out could ever occur. In fact, the available evidence on this substitutability condition would support, according to Friedman (1978, p. 639), the non-existence of crowding-out effects.

Blinder and Solow (1973, 1974, 1976a; see also Buiter, 1977a) have directed a rigorous theoretical attack on the crowding-out thesis. They employ an IS–LM model extended to incorporate wealth effects in both the consumption and demand for money functions, as well as a government budget constraint providing for government debt interest payments. Their conclusion is that if government expenditure, financed by bond issues, is more expansive than government spending financed by money-creation their model is stable, otherwise the model is unstable. In other words, if government expenditure, financed by bond issues, is contractionary, as monetarists claim, or expansionary but less expansive than government expenditure financed by money-creation, then the model is unstable. Fiscal policy, therefore, is effective. The Blinder–Solow conclusion derives from the inclusion of interest payments in the government budget constraint. For the model to be stable, the budget must balance in the long run to ensure unchanging stocks of money and bonds. In order for the budget gap to close following the initial increase in government expenditure, income must rise by a larger amount in the case where the increased government expenditure is financed by bond issuance than by money creation. The inclusion of interest payments in the government budget constraint would always ensure that higher tax receipts must be induced to offset the increased interest payments on the government debt and higher tax receipts could only come about through higher income; thus government expenditure is more expansionary in the bond-financed case.

The Blinder–Solow contribution, though, suffers from a number of problems. First, their analysis completely neglects price effects. Secondly, their model's consistency depends critically upon the existence of a wealth effect in the consumption function. Thirdly, they completely fail to account for the fact that wealth includes not only public debt but also the stock of capital. Fourthly, there is the unsatisfactory implication that at the steady-state capital accumulation ceases which, within the type of analysis employed by Blinder and Solow, must require reducing aggregate income to the extent that a zero savings rate is reached (for an elaboration on this and other problems [11] see Turnovsky, 1977, pp. 130-3). Fifthly, it has been demonstrated by Tobin and Buiter (1976) that if coupon payments are treated as government transfers — Blinder and Solow define government expenditure net of coupon payments — then the long-run government expenditure multiplier does not depend on the mode of financing; it is, in fact, equal to the inverse of the marginal tax rate as in Christ (1968). Currie (1978) argues that even in this case the possibility of instability remains (p. 70) — Scarth (1976) uses empirical estimates to demonstrate this possibility — while Buiter (1977b) shows that when the effects of complicated lag structures are accounted for, the stability problem becomes a more complex issue.

The interest payments in the Blinder–Solow (1973–74) analysis refer to the service costs of added debt; if in addition, interest payments on existing debt is accounted for, then we have the type of coupon effect discussed by Artis (1978). This can arise when increases in government expenditure are financed through borrowing which leads to an increase in interest payments not only for the new debt but also because any refunding of existing debt will have to be made at higher interest rates; the implication here is that the additional interest cost would have to be met by borrowing. Needless to say, of course, the increased debt-service payments in this case are expected to increase consumption and income more than in the Blinder–Solow case. Artis (1978), though, concedes 'that there is something a little bizarre about the dominance of this effect' (p. 175) (see also Wilson, 1979).

Another attack on the crowding-out thesis is the study by Hendershott (1976) who argues that not only may crowding-out not occur but, indeed, we may have the phenomenon of 'pulling in'. This can happen when investment depends on the level of income as well as on the rate of interest. Fiscal expansion may, in this case, increase investment although the fiscal operation raises the interest rate.

Finally, the monetarist claim that failure to account properly for the role of wealth in the demand for money leads to erroneous conclusions as far as crowding-out is concerned, has also been challenged. Modigliani and Ando (1976) argue that even if a wealth effect is included in the demand for money it could never produce significant crowding-out; this is so because wealth could not rise unless savings increased, which would require income to increase. Thus an increase in income should be accompanied by a rise in wealth. However, the gradual accumulation of wealth would affect the rate of interest via the demand for money and, therefore, some crowding-out of the interest rate-sensitive-type of private expenditures would ensue. Modigliani and Ando, though, went on to say that there is no reason for this process to be so fast as to cause complete crowding-out. But they had a stronger argument to support the view of a very low wealth elasticity in the demand for money: 'with well-functioning markets, and in the presence of a short-term asset involving no risk of principal, the demand for money must depend only on the short-term rate and the volume of transactions (as well as on transaction costs), but must be independent of either wealth or $\dot{P}$' (Modigliani and Ando, 1976, p. 28); they also reported that no significant wealth effects could be found in the demand for money of the empirical model they used for the purposes of their study — the MIT–PEN–SSRC (MPS) model for the US economy. Goodhart (1975) seems to share the Modigliani–Ando view when he argues that 'the wealth elasticity of demand for money, when narrowly defined, should be very low' (p. 48). Currie (1981), however, has demonstrated that the wealth elasticity of demand for money is likely to be higher the wider the definition of the money supply adopted.

The analysis so far has been concerned with a closed economy. In the open economy case, where the existing literature is not as rich as for the closed economy, the above analysis would still be valid but, in addition, one would have to distinguish sharply between a regime of fixed exchange rates, and a regime of flexible exchange rates (Currie, 1981). When fixed exchange rates prevail a fiscal stimulus would inevitably result in a deficit in the balance of payments, with higher imports in response to increased home demand. This, of course, would limit the size of the multiplier, but could hardly be considered as crowding-out — this is essentially Thirlwall's (1978) 'balance of payments constraint'; see also Ward (1981). It was the case, none the less, especially in the UK during the post-war fixed exchange rate era, that in situations of severe balance of payments difficulties, the authorities would increase the bank rate along with a battery of credit squeeze measures such as hire purchase controls, requests to the banking sector to restrict lending, calls for special deposits, etc. Two kinds of crowding-out could take place in this environment: first, there is the crowding-out that could come about from higher interest rates, following the increase in bank rate. Second, the worsened balance of payments may be accompanied by higher prices of imports which may work through to higher costs and wages thus raising significantly the general price level; in this case the domestic inflationary pressures could conceivably crowd out some private expenditures as explained above. A further impact arising from the balance of payments deficit, is the subsequent decline in private sector wealth; in the absence of sterilisation, this drain on wealth will take the form of a decline in the money stock. There is, though, an opposite impact on wealth arising from the capital account of the balance of payments. The higher interest rates resulting from the fiscal stimulus may induce capital inflows which, again in the absence of sterilisation, will mitigate the drain on wealth due to the deficit in the trade account of the balance of payments. Needless to say, the capital account effect would depend crucially on the degree of capital mobility.

In a regime of flexible exchange rates, the possibility of crowding-out could arise in a more direct manner. A fiscal stimulus would, as above, worsen the balance of payments situation, which now would tend to depreciate the exchange rate, raising import prices, and the resulting inflationary pressures could crowd out some expenditure. This tendency of crowding-out through inflation would be restrained, though, to some considerable extent by the improvement in competitiveness which, if it persists, could very well outweigh the tendency for crowding-out, via increased exports (but see Thirlwall, 1978). This process will also be influenced by any potential capital movements induced by the higher interest rates — themselves caused by the fiscal stimulus. Any inflow of capital would, of course, tend to mitigate the fall in the exchange rate. One should also account for any wealth effects arising from the balance of payments, as in the case of fixed exchange rates.

The analysis so far of both the fixed exchange rate and the flexible exchange rate regimes may be more appropriate in the case where expansionary fiscal policies are financed through taxation. When the financing is done through borrowing or money creation, the following comments are in order. In the money-financed case, fiscal expansion will be at least as powerful with floating exchange rates as with fixed ones. Since, though, long-run stock equilibrium in the flexible exchange rate regime will require income to increase to a level sufficient to balance the budget, whereas in the fixed exchange rate long-run stock equilibrium could occur at a lower level of income (because the budget deficit could be matched by an equal balance of payments deficit), it follows that fiscal policy in the flexible exchange rate case could be more powerful and the degree of crowding-out smaller than in the fixed exchange rate regime. Bond-finance, by contrast, is likely to be unstable. Stability in this case is only ensured when the wealth effects on expenditures are greater than the wealth effects on the demand for money; it therefore follows that stability is less likely to occur in the bond-financed case regardless of the foreign exchange rate regime prevailing (for more details on these conditions and, indeed, for more details on the effects of fiscal policy and crowding-out in the case of an open economy, see Currie, 1981).

EMPIRICAL EVIDENCE ON CROWDING-OUT

The origins of recent empirical work on the crowding-out question can be traced primarily to the results published by Andersen and Jordan (1968) and supporting studies by Keran (1969, 1970). These results have indicated that crowding-out occurs; that is, a change in government spending financed by either borrowing or taxes has only a negligible effect on gross national product over a period of about a year. It is, in fact, suggested that expansionary fiscal actions have an initial positive effect which is followed in later quarters by an approximately off-setting negative effect. Crowding-out, therefore, occurs within a very short time period.

The response to these empirical results has been substantial. Corrigan (1970) has argued that the results reached by Andersen and Jordan are questionable in that the indicator of fiscal policy used by the authors, the 'full employment surplus', which is an estimate of the overall national income account budget at some arbitrarily defined full employment level of economy activity, suffers from a serious defect. This defect refers to the upward trend in full employment growth in nominal incomes; thus, increases in full employment receipts would come about even in periods when tax policies and expenditure were unchanged. It is argued that a superior indicator of the direction and magnitude of short-run changes in discretionary fiscal policy is the so-called 'initial stimulus' which is supposed to be more independent of the level of economic activity than the equivalent variable utilised by Andersen and Jordan. The 'initial stimulus' is the algebraic sum of the initial effects of changes in government expenditure and the initial effects of changes in government tax policies on an accounting basis. It, therefore, seeks to identify and quantify those elements in the government budget that actually represent changes in discretionary fiscal policy. In this way it is, therefore, more independent of the level of income than the full employment surplus indicator of fiscal policy.[12]

At an empirical level Corrigan provides results which indicate that the association between changes in gross national product and changes in fiscal policy as measured by the initial stimulus is stronger than is the case with full employment surplus. In addition, when the initial stimulus is used as the indicator of fiscal policy its impact on total spending is significant; the Andersen and Jordan study, therefore, appears to have overstated the case against fiscal policy, particularly with regard to the impact of tax changes on gross national product (see also DeLeeuw and Kalchbrenner, 1969). Similar tests have been carried out by Artis and Nobay (1969) confirming this last result. In general, they found a stronger fiscal multiplier, but a very weak monetary multiplier. More recently Friedman (1977) has provided evidence to show that, using updated series which include the 1969–76 period, even the Andersen–Jordan reduced form now 'believes in' fiscal policy. Carlson (1978), however, has defended the Andersen–Jordan thesis by arguing that Friedman's results were defective in that they were characterised by a 'non-constant error variance'. This study showed that once this statistical problem was tackled, the Andersen–Jordan equation still did not 'believe in' fiscal policy (Carlson, 1978, p. 19). This particular result has prompted Vrooman (1979) to suggest that 'Carlson may be right, and that Friedman may have been wrong, but also that Carlson may have been wrong, and Friedman right' (p. 111). His argument is that Carlson correctly observed the statistical problem in the Friedman study, but the method Carlson utilised to cure for the statistical weakness was not satisfactory; in fact, 'Carlson was wrong in his method and his conclusion' (p. 113). Vrooman finally concludes that Friedman was right in as much as there had been a significant increase in the impact of fiscal policy.

Davies (1969) argues that the surprisingly high association between money and gross national product is a reflection of common trends in gross national product and the monetary aggregates, particularly during the 1960s. He also adds that another weakness of the Andersen–Jordan study is the absence of a detailed transmission mechanism: what are the channels through which instruments of policy are supposed to influence ultimate targets? For, according to Davies (1969) 'We need to see precisely how money is supposed to produce the results it appears to produce in the Andersen–Jordan equation' (p. 131).

Gramlich (1971) demonstrates that the reduced form approach of Andersen and Jordan is not satisfactory at all in one very important respect. This can be shown by considering the impact coefficient of government expenditure on gross national product which in the Andersen–Jordan study is less than unity. Since the government spending component of gross national product automatically rises by the amount of the expenditure, the impact coefficient of less than unity for government spending indicates that some endogenous component of total spending falls by a large amount as expenditures rise, and that the marginal propensity to consume must be very low. If, then, one could determine exactly what was falling and why, and if one knew what the implied consumption function looked like, one would have some guidance on the Andersen–Jordan findings, and presumably one would find them easier to accept. Reduced forms, however, provide no internally consistent description of the various relationships involved, 'Thus the reduced form technique, while it may be indicative, does not seem to be very conclusive' (Gramlich, 1969, p. 530). What is needed is for

the monetarists to spell out in detail precisely how they think the transmission process works. Moreover, this description must be translated into an econometric model with a reasonable degree of structural detail ... only after such a project is carried out, and carried out successfully, will most economists really be prepared to believe that money matters as much and as fast as it seems to in St Louis. (Davies, 1969, p. 131)

Reduced forms have also been attacked as being biased because of the presence of association between the policy variables included in the reduced form and other exogenous variables (Modigliani, 1971; but see also Modigliani and Ando, 1976). Additionally, reduced forms would be biased if, over the period of estimation, the policy variables included in them were actively used for stabilisation purposes (Goldfeld and Blinder, 1972). In this case the reduced form coefficients will underestimate the true response to the variable used for stabilisation purposes, and overestimate the response to other policy variables included in the reduced form.

The methodology of single-equation estimates has been severely critised by Modigliani (1977) who argues that reduced forms are a very poor representation of what actually takes place in an economic system; while Modigliani and Ando (1976) provide empirical evidence for this claim. Their evidence is based on an exercise designed to test whether the Andersen–Jordan reduced form could reproduce the output generated by a fairly complex 'black box' which purports to have characteristics similar to the US economy's. Simulation exercises have shown that this is the case. The black box chosen for this exercise is a multi-equation model of the US economy. Modigliani and Ando (1976) conclude that the reduced form provides results which were very different from the true ones. They were thus able to suggest that the reduced form was 'both a severely biased and quite unreliable method of estimating the response of a complex economy to fiscal and monetary action' (p.42), and that the evidence produced by large macro-economic models is expected to be much more reliable and dependable than that of reduced forms. Inevitably, then, 'there are no viable alternatives to the painstaking task of looking inside the black box. When this is done, one cannot fail to conclude that the effects of macro fiscal actions are certain to be long-lasting and likely to be substantial' (Modigliani and Ando, 1976, p.42. Schwartz (1976) has attacked the Modigliani-Ando (1976) study, arguing that since the multi-equation model used to represent the black box suffers from some severe short-comings [13] it actually proved nothing (see also Darby, 1976). This criticism, though, is completely irrelevant, for Schwartz misses the whole point of their paper when she criticises the specification of the model they use. The point here is that the Modigliani-Ando study does not make any claims about the correct specification of their model (Gordon, 1976, p. 59).

The studies that have been concerned with large models, however, reveal that crowding-out can occur over time. The way that crowding-out is studied in these empirical works is usually through simulation results which show the implied government expenditure and tax multipliers. The model simulations, then, have not always produced evidence which would support the standard Keynesian presumption of positive government spending multipliers; and as Fromm and Klein (1973) point out:

Conventional textbook expositions generally depict real expenditure multipliers approaching positive asymptotes. In fact, most of the models here show such multipliers reaching a peak in two or three years and then declining thereafter in fluctuating paths. At the end of five to ten years, some of the models show that continued sustained fiscal stimulus has ever-increasing perverse impacts. (p. 393)

These results should not be interpreted to suggest that government spending does not matter: it would seem that it does matter over a certain period. Moreover, if government spending were to accelerate rapidly than be held to a once-for-all increase, the impact on gross national product would be considerable over the period of acceleration and also over some periods beyond. It would, therefore, appear that these estimates of the fiscal multiplier are not as damaging to the Keynesian position as they initially appear (Klein, 1973, pp. 9–12). After all, it takes a considerable length of time in some of the models for the government spending multiplier to approach zero or turn negative, and policy-makers historically have shown little concern for the long run. Nevertheless, before such a conclusion is finally reached a much more detailed analysis is required to establish whether demand management can still be effectively implemented even with crowding-out occuring within a period of 2–3 years. This particular question has been dealt with by Arestis and Karakitsos (1980), who clearly show that fiscal policy can be relied upon to achieve the ultimate targets for inflation and unemployment under different modes of finance. The framework used in this study is that of 'optimal control' within the National Institute of Economic and Social Research model of the UK economy.

The above studies refer mainly to US experience; in the case of the UK similar results have been reported. Bisham (1975) derives a GDP multiplier of 0.98 after 11 quarters for the

National Institute of Economic and Social Research model with respect to an increase in government expenditure; Ball, Burns and Miller (1975) for the London Business School model, report a real multiplier of 1.11 after 24 quarters, while in the study by Evans and Riley (1975), where the Treasury model is employed, the multiplier is 1.33 after 16 quarters. In the study of Laury, Lewis and Ormerod (1978), the multipliers are 0.68, 1.06 and 1.09 for the above models, respectively. What is interesting about these multipliers is that they 'indicate rather less disagreement than one might have been led to expect from similar US studies', and with respect to the pattern of fiscal policy impact, 'the British models are telling much the same story' (Laury, Lewis and Ormerod, 1978, p. 64). The same results are reached in the studies by Taylor (1979) and Lewis and Ormerod (1979), and National Institute of Economic and Social Research (1981). In the study by Fetherston and Godley (1981) the dynamic multiplier is 3.27 after five years for the Cambridge Economic Policy Group model, while in the study by Ball, Burns and Warburton (1979) the multiplier is 0.65 in the case of the London Business School model.[14] The latter study is interesting in as much as the increase in government expenditure is financed through money-creation; as such it shows little, if any, crowding-out. Nevertheless, by the end of the experiment (32 quarters) the increase in real government spending is roughly equal to the fall in real consumer spending; it is only because other components of aggregate expenditure are not crowded out that the overall impact on aggregate output is positive.

In a more recent study Arestis and Karakitsos (1982) employ the 'optimal control' technique, which they show to be superior to the standard simulation technique used by the other studies, to conclude that within the National Institute of Economic and Social Research model crowding-out is never complete; and although the dynamic multipliers derived in this study do differ from the ones of the other studies of the UK economy mentioned above, due to the superior technique utilised in the Arestis-Karakitsos study, the pattern of results, in terms of crowding-out, are, in fact, similar. All these studies employ the three models mentioned above. In the study by

Arestis (1979) a small dynamic model is used, which again provides similar results. Studies with small models, but, utilising US and Canadian data, include Cebula's (1978) and the Zahn's (1978) papers. They show that although the level of private investment spending is crowded out by government budget deficits (financed through borrowing), crowding-out is not complete in as short a period as the studies by Andersen–Jordan and Keran suggest. A further result of the Cebula (1978) study is that the partial crowding-out which is evident in his paper has an important inflationary impact on the economies of Canada and US. This result is important in that the inflationary potential of fiscal policies is derived from supply considerations and not from the traditional demand considerations. The Zahn (1978) study (using US data) clearly indicates that the crowding-out that occurs is never large enough to outweigh the expansionary influence of government spending — except perhaps in the very long run. This last comment suggests a progression of the debate on crowding-out from 'Does it exist?' to 'What is the time period required for it to set in?' The answer to the latter question must be that in the short run at least, no complete crowding-out is evident (Meyer, 1980).

Finally, a word on *resource* crowding-out of the Bacon–Eltis (1976)-type. It has been demonstrated quite convincingly, by Hadjimatheou and Skouras (1979) that the available empirical evidence does not support the conclusions reached by Bacon and Eltis. They have shown that the data used by Bacon and Eltis are misleading, and that proper and detailed examination of the statistical evidence provided by Bacon and Eltis does not substantiate their arguments. When Hadjimatheou and Skouras attempt to correct for these deficiencies their own evidence seems to contradict that of Bacon and Eltis. Furthermore, Ietto Gillies (1978) has argued that not enough evidence exists to support the Bacon–Eltis contention that industry has been squeezed out of resources by the expansion of the public sector. Also Thirlwall (1978) argues that the growth of the public sector has not been an autonomous development in the economy but a response to the economy's inability to grow at a rate compatible with full employment because of a serious balance of payments constraint.

CONCLUSIONS

Whether crowding-out exists or not is, of course, a very important issue in contemporary economic analysis and policy. Indeed, the acceptance or rejection of crowding-out phenomena constitutes a fundamental difference between monetarists and non-monetarists (Blinder and Solow, 1973; Stein, 1976a; Tobin and Buiter, 1976).

The theoretical review and the summary of the empirical results on the existence of crowding out provided in this chapter, clearly indicate that:

(i)   in none of the non-reduced form studies does complete crowding-out occur, at least in the short run.

(ii) In the long run we may have complete crowding-out, but there is, of course, the inevitable problem of what constitutes the long run; and in any case 'in the long run we are all dead'. Furthermore, there is the argument that when crowding-out occurs, this can only be so because of an inappropriate mix of the policy instruments employed by the policy-makers (Currie, 1981).

(iii) Not enough evidence exists to show that resource crowding-out has occurred, at least in the UK.

We may, therefore, conclude by saying that theoretical considerations and the available empirical evidence clearly indicate that complete crowding-out does not occur. Thus fiscal policy matters — indeed it matters a great deal — for even if crowding-out were complete, or even over-complete, fiscal policy would still be important in the sense discussed by Buiter (1977a), Arestis and Karakitsos (1980), and Currie (1981).

NOTES

*   I am extremely grateful to D. Currie, G. Koolman, G. Hadjimatheou, E. Karakitsos and D. Jones for their valuable comments and suggestions. Any remaining errors and omissions are, of course, my responsibility.

1   See Arestis (1979), Cebula and Curran (1978) and Choudhry (1976) for typical examples.

2   See Choudhry (1976, p.408) who reaches the same conclusion after a 'synoptic' discussion of the literature. See also Christ's (1968, 1978) contributions on this point, as well as the papers by Carlson and Spencer (1975) and Spencer and Yohe (1970).

3   Peston (1981) demonstrates that 'at full employment a reduction in public sector employment *allows* an increase in private sector employment, but it does not guarantee it' (p.26).

4   For a more detailed discussion on this view, see Klein (1968), pp.45–6.

5   Those Marxists who accept the underconsumption hypothesis argue, however, that government intervention is necessary in order to create additional effective demand by absorbing part of the continually mounting volume of surplus which could not be absorbed through private channels (Baran and Sweezy, 1966).

6   See also the papers by Brunner and Meltzer (1972, 1976), but see McGrath (1977) as well as Silber (1970) and Rasche (1973).

7   Meyer (1975) provides a numerical example clearly showing the expansionary initial effects as well as the subsequent contractionary effects of fiscal action in an IS–LM framework.

8   There is the question here of what constitutes wealth: for although there is little disagreement that high-powered money and capital stock ought to be included in the definition of wealth, the same cannot be said for government bonds and bank demand deposits. The controversy surrounding the treatment of these two items as wealth has been summarised by Currie (1981).

9   It has been pointed out to me by Currie that the argument of Floyd and Hynes (1978) is flawed in that it is likely to be actual, not 'permanent', wealth holdings that are relevant for considerations of portfolio balance.

10 It should be clear by now that changes in wealth may come about through three avenues: from changes in the quantity of outstanding assets included in wealth; from changes in interest rates which cause the value of the existing stock of fixed interest bonds and equities to alter; and from changes in the aggregate price level which induces the real value of wealth to change. For an elaboration on all these changes, see Currie (1981).

11 For a further critical analysis of the Blinder–Solow reasoning, see Infante and Stein (1976) to which Blinder and Solow (1976b) responded, defending their 1973–74 contributions.

12 For more details on the notion of the indicator 'full employment

surplus', see *Council of Economic Advisers* (1974) and Artis (1978). On the meaning of the 'initial stimulus' indicator, see *Federal Reserve Bank of New York* (1965).

13 The shortcomings Schwartz refers to are points which non-monetarists, like Modigliani and Ando, would reject in any case on purely theoretical grounds. For example, one such shortcoming Schwartz suggests is the inclusion of real money balances in the consumption function. Presumably Modigliani and Ando would not accept this proposition as being theoretically valid.

14 It must be stressed that the dynamic multipliers of these large-scale models may change as the specification of the structural relationships of these models are up-dated.

6.   Post-Keynesianism: Quite Wrong and/or Nothing New

G. C. Harcourt

Those who are strongly wedded to ... 'the classical theory', will fluctuate ... between a belief that I am quite wrong and a belief that I am saying nothing new.

(J. M. Keynes, *The General Theory*, p.v)

INTRODUCTION*

My aim in this chapter is to attempt to give an overview of, and to sieve out some of the more grandiose claims made for, the body of thought which comes under the general heading of post-Keynesianism. I start by saying that I certainly do not think that the approaches that come under this heading, though they provide important and substantial insights, have yet reached a coherent steady-state. Indeed, the people who come under this umbrella are a heterogeneous lot, sometimes only combined by a dislike of orthodox or neoclassical economics — all brands, or at least their conception of it/them. A characteristic of some post-Keynesian writers — no names, no pack drill — is that their positive contributions are superior to their presentation and knowledge of the work of the people which they are attacking and which they are attempting to supersede. Nevertheless, there are enough common strands running through their writings to make it worthwhile to try and pick them out (see, for example, Eichner and Kregel, 1975).

POST-KEYNESIAN PERSONALITIES

First, let me list the main contributors. I start in the USA, not because this is where the movement necessarily originated but because its members are now numerically the strongest, grouped around the *Journal of Post Keynesian Economics* (*JPKE*) which is enthusiastically and aggressively edited by Paul Davidson and Sidney Weintraub. The US group has its roots firmly planted in Keynesian soil, especially the Keynes of the *Treatise* (1971, V, VI) and the *General Theory* (1971, VII) and also the papers that grew out of *The General Theory* — 'The General Theory of Employment' (1971, XIV), 'Alternative Theories of the Rate of Interest' (1971, XIV), 'The Theory of the Rate of Interest' (1971, XIV), and *How to Pay for the War* (1971, XXII). Together with Keynes' influence is Marshall's, especially his theoretical methods (supply and demand analysis, his way of handling time) which influenced Keynes as well.

Davidson and Weintraub are two important names: Davidson especially for his monetary theory (Davidson, 1978, for example); Weintraub for his provision of a theory of activity and distribution and his thoroughly Keynesian stress on the central importance of the money wage, its level and rate of change, for the functioning of the entire system (Weintraub, 1977). Davidson's pupil, Jan Kregel (1973, for example), is also very important, not only for his contributions which are amongst the most substantial and useful, but also because he has strong links with the UK–Italian subset, and because he tries to build a bridge between these two often unsympathetic groups — unsympathetic because, on the one hand, most of the Americans do not want to know about the classical–Marxist roots which come to the other strands through Piero Sraffa, Pierangelo Garegnani and Krishna Bharadwaj and also through Michael Kalecki and Joan Robinson. On the other hand, the Italian members in particular do not wish to be associated with some of the more (to them) neoclassical vestiges of Keynes' thought, especially in Chapter 17 of *The General Theory*, which is crucial to the structure of the US post-Keynesians (in Chapter 17, Keynes attempted to show

how the essential and peculiar properties of money, together with his monetary theory of the rate of interest, were capable of producing an underemployment equilibrium). Again, in the United States, we must mention Hyman Minsky (1975a, 1978) for his challenging interpretation of *The General Theory* as an endogenous cyclical process, the outcome of interrelationships between real and monetary factors, and also for his greater tolerance, because of his early Marxist sympathies, towards a classical–Marxist input into the construction of alternative approaches to orthodoxy. We should also mention the contributions of Donald Harris because he, perhaps more than anyone else, has been able to combine the classicals and Marx with Keynes, Kalecki, Robinson, Kaldor and Harrod into a comprehensive framework (see my review — Harcourt, 1980 — of his 1978 book, Harris, 1978).

Now we move to Europe, specifically to Cambridge, England and to Italy. We discuss two strands which are intertwined, though not altogether comfortably. First, there is Sraffa, whose life's work has been devoted to a rehabilitation of the classical method and approach, in particular to what Garegnani (among others) has called the surplus approach to value and distribution. Around this core there can be placed theories of output and employment as a whole and also theories of growth (the most comprehensive account of modern classicism, with which is combined a description of its historical roots and a comparison with neoclassical general equilibrium theory, is Walsh and Gram's *Classical and Neoclassical Theories of General Equilibrium*, 1980). The method is one which is concerned with the characteristics of long period positions — those centres of gravity which in the classical schema are the chief explanators of the levels of market prices and their movements over time and which result from those elements at work in an economic system which can be regarded as dominant and persistent. To this group, Keynes' revolutionary contribution *must* be a theory of the *long period* levels of output and employment (around which actual levels would oscillate) to be placed alongside the theories of natural prices — prices of production in Marx's terms, long period normal prices in Marshall's. '[B]y long-period is meant not that which occurs in a long period of time but ... that which is determined by the dominant forces of the system within a period when those are constant or changing but slowly' (Eatwell, 1979, p.4). A good example of this point of view in *The General Theory* is Keynes' definition of 'the long period employment corresponding to a [given] state of expectation'. Keynes writes:

If we suppose a state of expectation to continue for a sufficient length of time for the effect on employment to have worked itself out so completely that there is ... no piece of employment going on which would not have taken place if the new state of expectation had always existed, the steady level of employment thus attained may be called the long period employment corresponding to that state of expectation. It follows that, although expectation may change so frequently that the actual level of employment has never had time to reach the long period employment corresponding to the existing state of expectation, nevertheless every state of expectation has its definite corresponding level of long-period employment. (1971, VII, p.48)

Keynes is applying here to the theory of employment a lesson learnt from his teacher, Marshall, concerning the theory of price: 'a normal price ... [is] the price which any one set of conditions tends to produce' (Marshall, 1920, 1961, p.371).[1]

It is interesting to note that Meltzer (1981) gives a similar interpretation of Keynes — that Keynes was providing a theory of a long period underemployment equilibrium level of employment and activity, though obviously Meltzer comes to the question from a different starting-point, and his ideological purposes and policy implications are very different from those of the group under discussion. A key quote for all these writers is from *The General Theory*.

[We] oscillate, avoiding the gravest extremes of fluctuation in employment and in prices in both directions round an intermediate position appreciably below full employment and appreciably above the minimum employment a decline below which would endanger life.
    But we must not conclude that the mean position thus determined by 'natural' tendencies, namely, by those tendencies which are likely

to persist, failing measures expressly designed to correct them, is, therefore, established by laws of necessity. (p.254)

Apart from Sraffa himself (for an evaluation of Sraffa's contributions, see Harcourt, 1982), the most important names here are Garegnani, Pasinetti, Krishna Bharadwaj and, in Cambridge itself, John Eatwell and Murray Milgate.[2]

Uncomfortable allies of this group are Joan Robinson and the Robinsonians, especially A. (Tom) Asimakopulos in Canada and her Australian fans, Keith Frearson, Peter Groenewegen, David Clark, Joseph Halevi, Bruce McFarlane, Peter Riach, Geoff Harcourt (see Peter Groenewegen's, 1979, paper on radical economics in Australia). Robinson's and Kahn's interpretation of Keynes' purposes and methods differ considerably from the interpretation of this other group, though through the influence of Kalecki, Robinson *does* wish to reach over 100 or so years interim of neoclassical economics in order to graft the modern developments by Keynes, Kalecki and Sraffa onto Marx and the classical economists, especially Ricardo (see her paper with Amit Bhaduri — Bhaduri and Robinson, 1980). Her slogan is 'history versus equilibrium' which she took to be the methodological revolution in Keynes' work and which made her very partial to Kalecki's view that it is the short period where the action is, and that the long period has no independent existence, being nothing but the growth out of a succession in short periods: 'the long-run trend is but a slowly changing component of a chain of short period situations ... no independent entity' (Kalecki, 1971, p. 165). Indeed, Robinson's definition of long period *equilibrium* goes even further:

The short period is here and now, with concrete stocks of the means of production in existence. Incompatibilities in the situation ... will determine what happens next. Long period equilibrium is not at some date in the future: it is an imaginary state of affairs in which there are no incompatabilities in the existing situation, here and now. (Robinson, 1965, p.101)

A prominent issue which is currently being debated between

these two groups is the operational significance of the concept of a centre of gravity in the analysis of movements over time of modern capitalist economies (see Harcourt, 1981a). The differing views on Keynes are to be found in issues of the *Cambridge Journal of Economics* and in the papers from the Conference at the Villa Manin in September 1981. There, Kregel and Garegnani clashed over the significance of Chapter 17 of *The General Theory* for the theory of effective demand in the long period, and whether we need a theory of effective demand for the long period[3] (see also Eatwell, 1979; Garegnani, 1981; Kregel, 1981).

I should also mention the post-war work of Nicholas Kaldor,[4] who is a group by himself, and the Cambridge Economic Policy Group led by Wynne Godley and Francis Cripps. I have not the space to say much about them in this chapter, but at the level of policy in particular, they are a very important influence and, of course, Kaldor's theoretical contributions are remarkable. Moreover, with his unique blend of theory and policy, including his involvement in policy, he probably more than anyone else carries on Keynes' role in Cambridge, certainly with the breadth and volume of his papers, not to mention his membership of the House of Lords. Just as in the United States the *Journal of Post Keynesian Economics* has been the outlet for the writings of the American post-Keynesians, so the *Cambridge Journal of Economics* is the outlet for those of the English/European group (of course, the pages of neither are confined to any particular nationality but the 'lines' of each are determined by these two groups in their respective countries).

POST-KEYNESIAN CHARACTERISTICS

So much for the background and personalities: now for some characteristics. At the deepest level of analysis, the following points stand out. First, there is a preoccupation with time and how it should be modelled. Now obviously this is common to all economics, but I mention it because the motivation of these groups — especially the Americans and Robinson — derives from it, particularly in relation to their dissatisfaction with what they conceive to be the orthodox way of handling time. The latter often seems to be to reduce it to the same dimensions as space (i.e. to smuggle back in the equivalent of an assumption of perfect foresight or to model 'as if' there were perfect foresight) the latest example of which is the approach of the 'rational expectations' school. One of the ironies of modern economics has been the declining star of John Hicks — as far as the profession in general assesses his later contributions — just when some of us have thought that he was getting better and better! (see the independently written but very similar reviews — style and elegance apart — of his 1977 collection of papers by Leijonhufvud, 1979, and myself, 1979a, in the *Journal of Economic Literature* and the *Economic Journal*, respectively). These reactions are in large part due to Hicks' changing views on how to model time, which have moved more and more towards those of Robinson in particular, as Hicks himself has acknowledged.

Robinson has attacked the neoclassical pendulum analogies of equilibrium in so far as they have been applied to an ongoing economy in which the past is gone and the present stands between it and a future which is uncertain and unknown and yet to come: witness her famous remark about time running at right-angles from a point on the blackboard. Here Keynes in his 1937 *Quarterly Journal of Economics* article is very influential: 'We simply do not know' (1971, XIV, p.114); and 'I accuse the classical economic theory of being itself one of these pretty, polite techniques which tries to deal with the present by abstracting from the fact that we know very little about the future' (1971, XIV, p.115). Nevertheless, decisions have to be made now and so rules-of-thumb, practical modes of behaviour, must be devised which, just because they have to be based on expectations which can come badly unstuck, may prove to be very unstable bases. In fact, post-Keynesians in recent years have become fond of distinguishing between neoclassical rational behaviour, which implicitly or explicitly includes perfect foresight, 'perfectly informed about the future as well as the past', as Chick (1978, p.1, n.2) puts it, and

Marshall's common-sense behaviour, 'reasonableness' in Clower's term; that is to say, acting sensibly with given information — 'one's [limited] knowledge' (Chick, 1978, p.1, n.2). G.L.S. Shackle has as much as anyone, and more than most, illuminated our understanding of this crucial aspect of Keynes' central message. To quote him directly:

[I]nvestment is a highly hazardous business, a gambling question, for the businessman at the time of his decision does not know whether he will make profits or not, especially in future years. In these circumstances, businessmen are swayed by the current state of the news and can lose their nerve, keep their money in the bank and so unemployment starts — it's as simple as that (see Harcourt, 1981b, p.141)

Allied with these views is a stress which goes back to the classicals but which was picked up again by Keynes, the sequence nature of production in a money-using economy whereby the bulk of production is in anticipation of future sales and so employment is offered *ahead* of the validation by sales of the production that results from the employment (I have a copy of a physics research student's notes of Keynes' 1933 lectures in which, in the second lecture, he quotes with approval Marx's sequence, $M - C - M'$). And in a recent issue of the *JPKE* (Summer, 1981) Roy Rotheim takes up this point in his discussion of Keynes' distinction, which did not survive to the final draft of *The General Theory*, between the cooperative economy, the neutral economy and the monetary or entrepreneur economy. In the last, a *general* state of unemployment could emerge, as it could not in the former two, because of fluctuations in effective demand which themselves are a monetary phenomenon (see Rotheim, 1981, pp. 574-83). Chick is very good on this in her 1978 paper where, whatever you may think of her critique of Clower, the positive contributions are illuminating: '*The General Theory* presents a model of a *production* economy, using *money* moving through *time*, subject to *uncertainty* and the possibility of *error*' (p.5).

It is from these factors that we get the Robinsonian version: the concentration on the importance of the short period and

the insistence that long period equilibrium is imaginary —
though long period and short period decisions come together
at this particular juncture in time. Asimakopulos perhaps
more than anyone else has made all this very clear. He is always
careful to list what is given: including the institutions and
social relationships of the economy to be modelled (see, for
example, his 1978 paper on Marshall and Wicksell); what
length of time he has in mind (see, for example, the opening
pages of his 1974 paper with John Burbidge on tax incidence in
the short period); and, of course, he utilises Keynes' central
analytical contribution of a balance between injections and
leakages, with the investment dog wagging a savings tail (see
James Meade, 1975, in the Milo Keynes collection) rather than
the other way around as used to be thought and supply-siders
still would have us think.

Associated also with this last point is a distinction, which
both Chick and Davidson make (see Davidson, 1980, p.153),
namely, that neoclassical equilibrium is concerned with
market-clearing prices, 'a point where supply equals demand',
whereas Keynes' concept concerns rest states, 'a point of rest:
forces leading to change are either absent or countervailing'
(Chick, 1978, p. 17). Markets, in particular labour markets,
may not clear in the neoclassical sense, but there is nothing
which can effectively be done about this by those most
intimately concerned, the wage-earners, because those who
make decisions about prices, employment and investment are
not able to get signals from the system which suggest to them
that they ought to change *their* behaviour.

If firms [get] all the labour they require and sell all their output at the
price they set, all their expectations have been met ... no reason to
change their plans. ... Households ... [may] *like* to sell more labour
... but they have no power to effect a change .... [T]he setting of
wages is up to the firms .... Households have no means of informing
firms that demand could be stronger if employment were higher.
(Chick, 1978, p.18)

The next main point, which follows from the above, is the
importance of social relationships and institutions in post-

Keynesian theory. The principal variable of post-Keynesian analysis is not the isolated economic agent so beloved of orthodoxy. This is true even of those orthodox economists who are apart from the mainstream — for example, Clower, Leijonhufvud — who, of course, have made important contributions to our reassessment of Keynes and to our assessment of *how* our economies work and could be made to function better. Post-Keynesians, following the classical tradition, look at the behaviour of groups (classes) and their functions in capitalist economies. Thus, running through Kalecki's version of the main propositions of *The General Theory* is a simple theory of distribution and employment in the short run, summed up in the phrase 'workers spend what they earn and capitalists earn what they spend'.

Robinson (1977, pp.7–17) has provided a neat exposition of this and I digress to present it here, using the simplest case of no consumption by *rentiers*, no saving by workers and no overseas or government sectors. Then the national accounts are:

$$C + I \equiv E$$
$$W + \Pi \equiv Y$$
$$E \equiv Y$$
$$C \equiv W$$
$$I \equiv \Pi$$

For Kalecki's reasons ('capitalists may decide to ... invest more in a given period than in a preceding one, but they cannot decide to earn more ... therefore, their investment ... decisions ... determine profits ... not vice versa' (Kalecki, 1971, pp.78–9), $I \rightarrow \Pi$.

Now consider Figure 6.1 in which costs and prices are measured on the vertical axis and total employment in the consumption and investment goods sectors on the horizontal axis. We assume that the marginal product of direct labour in the short run is constant up to capacity in the consumption goods trades (the reverse L-shaped marginal cost curve) and that investment *in real terms* is given for the period we are considering and requires AB of the available work force. The consumption spending of the investment trades workers

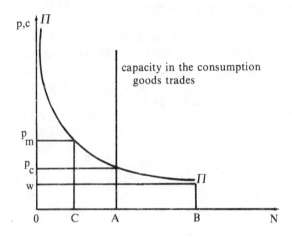

Figure 6.1

constitutes the total profits of the consumption goods trades. Whatever the employment in the latter, they get their costs (which are wage costs for the sector as a whole) back from the spending of the consumption good workers. $\Pi\Pi$ is a rectangular hyperbola which subtends the area $w \times AB$ where w is the money wage and AB is total employment in the investment goods trades. $w \times AB$ is, of course, the profits of the consumption goods trades. If there were competitive forces in price setting, a price of Op_c would tend to be set with accompanying full employment of the existing stock of capital goods in the consumption goods trades, OA employment of the workforce and profit per unit of employment of wp_c. However if, as Kalecki argues, there is administered pricing in the consumption goods trades — his degree of monopoly theory — and those with discretion do not set a price of Op_c but, say, a higher one of Op_m, there will be unemployment of CA, basically because the real wage of the workers is *lower* than in the first situation. The money wage is the same but the price is higher because of the higher amount of profit per unit of employment, wp_m.

The prices of the capital goods and the profits of the investment goods trades are not explicitly determined in this model. However, as investment expenditure in real terms is fixed in the model, whatever process determines the mark-up in the investment goods trades will ensure that the money expenditure on investment goods will cover the wage costs and the total profits implied by the size of the mark-up.[5]

The above analysis leads up to a consideration of the microeconomic foundations of post-Keynesian macroeconomics, a vital part of their contribution, especially with the recent emphasis in modern orthodox economics on the importance of microeconomic foundations, with the accusation added that neither the post-Keynesians nor the Keynesians have other than *ad hoc* foundations, if any at all. We should also note in passing that there are as well *macroeconomic* foundations of microeconomics. This is the meaning of Marx's schemes of reproduction and the modern versions of them by Kalecki, Robinson, Harrod (without knowing it) and others, for example, Pasinetti (1970). '[The theory] is macroeconomic because it could not be otherwise' (p.109). If decision-makers do not make decisions which are consistent with *overall* social and technical constraints we are liable to get a crisis situation. Harris has a fine paper on this — see Harris (1975) — and it is one of Robinson's major themes, which has often been misunderstood when her 'golden ages' have been taken to the descriptive rather than the mythical benchmarks which their very name implies.

Returning to our main theme, the seminal work is again Kalecki's — the notion that a model of a capitalist economy can be split into two sectors, one, the raw materials-producing sector where Marshallian-type supply and demand pricing rules, the other, the 'manufacturing' sector (it is obviously more than this) where because individual firms (or at least the price leaders(s)) have discretion, and because of oligopolistic interdependence mark-up pricing rules (this has been refined in one variant as the normal cost pricing hypothesis of Neild, 1963, and Godley and Nordhaus, 1972, among many others). Associated with these hypotheses are, as we have seen, the stylised facts of reverse L-shaped cost curves in the short run. In Kalecki, the mark-up is determined by the degree of monopoly in each industry and overall, though Kalecki never solved satisfactorily what he meant by an industry — neither has anyone else — nor the aggregation problem for the economy as a whole, that is to say, how to move from the degree of monopoly for each industry to the degree of monopoly for the economy as a whole.[6] In the more recent versions of this Kaleckian contribution, the mark-up has been taken either as constant (in the normal cost pricing hypothesis, perhaps in order to bring in a target rate of return, the size of which is determined by the macroeconomic characteristics of the system — here Marx is relevant) or, in another variant, as determined by the financial needs of the firms for investment expenditure. The most developed examples of the latter are Wood (1975) (Ball developed essentially the same argument in 1964), Eichner's work, which culminated in his 1976 book and — I like to think anyway — Harcourt and Kenyon (1976), where we introduce vintages into the analysis.[7]

The distinction between the two forms of pricing has been taken up by Kaldor and Hicks, the former for his model of growth and distribution in the world economy, the latter in his flex price/fix price dichotomy which he used, for example, in his Mills Memorial lecture (Hicks, 1976), to illuminate recent inflationary experiences in the capitalist world. As far as the fix price sector is concerned all variants have in common the rejection of profit-maximising, at least in its simplest forms, partly for reasons associated with oligopolistic inter-dependence. In so far as we are concerned with the distribution aspects of the theory, there are two major objections: 'the complementarity of inputs ... precludes the estimation of marginal products for individual inputs; and the inability to define ... a demand curve for individual firms means that marginal revenue product curves cannot be estimated' (Asima-kopulos, 1980–81, p.164).[8] Burbidge (1979), in writing about post-Keynesian approaches to international trade, also makes use of the distinction when classifying different countries according to the characteristics of their traded goods.

The Kaleckian underpinnings are also relevant for the recent debates in Australia about the real wage overhang (the alleged tendency for the real wage to increase at a faster rate than productivity), as Riach has pointed out. Riach took exception to the simple-minded view that higher real wages *caused* unemployment in Australia and are still doing so — the Pigouvian revival in the Treasury and at the ANU through Max Corden. Riach responded — first with Graham Richards in their 1979 paper on the lessons of the Cameron experiment — and now in his paper to the Political Economy Conference in Adelaide, 1981 — 'Labour-hiring in Post-Keynesian Economics' (Riach, 1981), in which he sketches in the supply-side response in post-Keynesian theory — 'An explicit account of the labour-hiring decision in a ... world where price and quantity may be positively related' (p. 4) (Kurt Rothschild as well as Kalecki and Robinson should take a bow here[9]).

The implication for labour of the product market behaviour which we sketched above is that

reduction in real wages is *not* necessary to seduce the entrepreneur into increasing employment. Once the real wage has been determined, along with the profit margin, the representative firm's input of labour is determined solely by aggregate demand in the product market ... Instead of price and quantity being the simultaneous outcome of the Marshallian scissors, the real wage and employment ... are determined by separate forces. ... It is not meaningful to talk of a 'labour market' in the traditional sense of an arena in which trading between buyer and seller establishes a market-clearing equilibrium price. There is no price which establishes a state of rest — output and employment are fluid in response to changes in demand, without any need for a real wage change. (Riach, 1981, pp.7–8)

Riach's approach reflects the 'horses for courses' approach of post-Keynesian theory — a number of outcomes are possible, depending upon concrete situations and circumstances, rather than the simple, slightly dogmatic, views which follow from the universalist nature of much modern neoclassical theory — the sort of theory which allows people to give advice as they step off the plane, as Eric Russell used to put it (see Russell, 1978, p.199). Thus, additional labour *can* be hired in a situation of higher real wages, but there is no functional relationship between the two variables, because wages and employment are controlled by independent forces. The move is not 'from one equilibrium to another ... rather [it is] a process taking place over historical time' (Riach, 1981, p.8).

I want, finally, to mention two more characteristics: first, the role of money in post-Keynesian analysis. Here I think (apart from Keynes, of course) the outstanding contributions are by Davidson and Minsky (see also Moore, 1979). Davidson has amalgamated the analysis of the *Treatise* and *The General Theory* in terms of Marshallian supply and demand analysis of spot and future markets to describe the determination of investment expenditure and the cost and availability of finance. The same contrast between spot and future markets (and their respective prices) is used by Davidson (and Kregel) to illuminate the analysis of Chapter 17 of *The General Theory* where, again, they argue that the real forces associated with the accumulation of capital goods and the monetary forces determining the rate of interest come together. The vital clues are the peculiar and essential properties of money or, rather, liquidity, which Keynes developed in embryonic form in his 1933 lectures (see Rotheim, 1981), whereby an underemployment equilibrium is possible because switching demand from goods to money does not necessarily create compensating employment opportunities. This is because liquid assets have two essential properties — negligible elasticities of production and substitution.[10]

Minsky takes the argument even further to produce an endogenous cycle theory as a result of the interaction between real and monetary factors. His views are summarised in the following three quotes from his works:

What we have is the bare bones of a model in which the path of income, in the sense of the aggregate budget constraint depends crucially upon two phenomena: the determination of total investment demand and the external financing of investment through monetary changes. Thus, it is the views of businessmen and bankers about the appropriate financial relations that call the tune for aggregate demand and employment. These views are volatile, responding to the past of the economy, and they change as the economy transits among the various types of behaviour (boom, crisis, debt-deflation, stagnation, and relatively steady expansion) which characterise the performance of capitalism. (Minsky, 1975, p.136)

A capitalist economy ... is characterised by two sets of relative prices, one of the current output and the other of capital assets. Prices of capital assets depend upon current views of future profit (quasi-rent) flows and the current subjective value placed upon the insurance against uncertainty embodied in money or quick cash: these current views depend upon the expectations that are held about the longer run development of the economy. The prices of current output are based upon current views of near term demand conditions and current knowledge of money wage rates. Thus, the price of current output — and the employment offered in producing output — depend upon shorter run expectations. (Minsky, 1978, pp.4–5)

Businesses offer employment and thus produce output on the basis of the profits they expect to earn by using labor and the existing capital assets to produce and distribute consumption and investment output. In production and distribution, demand for labor to use with existing capital assets depends upon what Keynes identified as 'short run expectations'. ... In addition to deciding how to use existing capacity, business has to decide whether and how to expand capacity. Whereas the utilisation of existing capacity is determined by price, cost and therefore by profit expectations over a relatively short run (six months, one or two years) the decision to expand capacity is determined by profit expectations over a much longer time horizon
. . . .
   Investment demand is financed in a different manner than consumption demand. It is true that in a world with consumer credit, banks and financial relations affect consumption demand, but consumer demand mainly depends upon [wage] income ... while investment ... depends upon the conditions under which short and long term external finance are available. Thus the demand for investment output is affected by the long run expectations not only of businessmen but also of the financial community. (Minsky, 1978, pp.8–9)

The different forces determining consumption goods' prices as compared to those determining capital goods' prices date back to the *Treatise* where Keynes distinguished between available and unavailable goods, and profits and incomes inflation, the latter distinction being related to the former. In a sense Minsky is spelling out what is implied in the methods of *The General Theory*, methods which have been so well documented by Kregel in his 1976 *Economic Journal* article, where he pointed out that Keynes has three models running through *The General Theory* and the papers that followed it. The purposes of these models were, first, to make the central point about effective demand unhampered by puzzles about how or if the economy could actually get to such a level, and then to bring in further complications in order to analyse the happenings in an economy over time. As early as 1923 Keynes was arguing that economists set themselves 'too easy ... a task' if they did not do this even though he was still, then, a quantity theorist (indeed, he still *thought* he was in the *Treatise* even though by then he had produced a theory of sectorial price levels which was inconsistent with the quantity theory). Let me quote what Keynes actually said since most of us are only familiar with one sentence:

But this *long run* is a misleading guide to current affairs. *In the long run* we are all dead. Economists set themselves too easy, too useless a task if in tempestuous seasons they can only tell us that when the storm is long past the ocean is flat again. (1971, IV, p.65)

CONCLUDING REMARKS

This quote brings us back to the last issue which I wish to emphasise: the methodological debates between Davidson, Weintraub and, on this issue, the Robinsonians, on the one hand, and the Sraffians, on the other, which concern this long run. The latter group, especially Garegnani, worry about the concentration on the short run because it gives over much emphasis to the importance of expectations so that definite results might not be possible (this, of course, might be a strength), and sustained and dominant forces are dismissed, or at least played down. In particular, the surplus approach to value and distribution will not get a role because supply and demand (or its variant in marginal utility theory) will explain value and distribution. Furthermore, they fear that if Chapter 17 is made the central part of post-Keynesian analysis, the investment theory, at least that coming from Keynes himself, is subject to the critique of the capital theory debates whereby well-behaved relationships between capital and the rate of profits, and investment and the rate of profits, are not able to be established (see Garegnani, 1978, 1979). So we have the recent vigorous debates between Garegnani and Kregel, and Garegnani and Robinson, over these issues.

As I have argued elsewhere (see Harcourt, 1981a), the issue turns partly on whether centres of gravity can be regarded as operational concepts in a model of a modern capitalist economy with oligopolistic market structures and in which rapid technical advances are occurring. Garegnani's point is that there is enough stability in the dominant forces — in particular, the dominant techniques — to make the concept operational and thus the surplus approach applicable, at least as a framework within which the other issues can be set. I think that Bhaduri and Robinson (1980) come close to accepting this when they graft Kalecki's analysis onto Sraffa's. Certainly Harris has made a good fist of doing this, at least as a first approximation, with his models of crises with Marx on the left and Robinson, Kaldor, Kalecki and Harrod on the right (see Harris, 1975).

On the left-hand side of Figure 6.2 we have the sphere of production. At any moment of time technology and social factors between them allow a particular combination of wages and rates of profits potentially to be established. Here, we suppose the current state of the class struggle dictates a wage of w^* which implies that the maximum rate of profits which may be received is r^*. On the right-hand side of the figure we have the sphere of distribution and exchange. We show, first, in terms of rates of growth of the stock of capital goods, the rate of profits that would be established from post-Keynesian expression, $r = g/s_c$ where s_c is the marginal propensity to save of the capitalists. We also show the accumulation function, $g^* = g^*(r^*)$ — the desired rate of accumulation is a function of

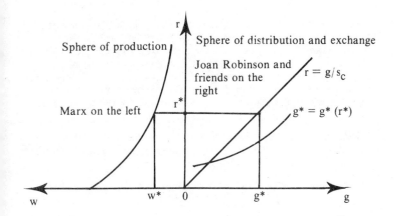

Figure 6.2

the expected rate of profits, for any given financial situation and state of long-term expectations. Provided the economy is within the area bounded by g^*, r^* and is below $r = g/s_c$, no contradictions arise; but once it is outside here, a variety of crisis situations are created and changes must occur in order to resolve the contradictions which gave rise to them in the first place.

I have neither the space nor the time to mention the importance of institutions (see Davidson, 1980, pp.162–4), nor Weintraub's stress (like Keynes') on the importance of the relative stickiness of the overall money wage for the stability of the system, nor the important contributions of Josef Steindl (on processes in mature capitalism) and Paolo Sylos-Labini (on pricing on oligopolistic industries). But that does not mean that I regard them as unimportant, only that time is a device to stop everything happening at once, just as space is a device to stop it all happening in Cambridge (see Dhamar Kumar in Harcourt, 1969, p.369, n.1).

NOTES

* This chapter is a revised version of a paper given at a seminar at the Reserve Bank of Australia in Sydney on 16 October 1981. I am indebted to Tom Asimakopulos, Vikas Chitre, Bob Dixon, Bruce McFarlane and the editors of the *Thames Papers* for their comments on a draft of the paper. Sadly, since it was written, Joan Robinson, Piero Sraffa and Sidney Weintraub have died. I refer to the writings of Keynes by giving first the date of publication and then the number of the volume of the *Collected Writings* in which they are to be found.

1 Vikas Chitre has reminded me that this concept of the long period should be distinguished from the concept associated with the secular stagnation thesis of Alvin Hansen and Roy Harrod.

2 For the link between Sraffa and Marx, see Steedman (1977) and my review of Steedman (1977), Harcourt (1979b).

3 Robinson might have been surprised to be reminded that she wrote in 1933 (in her report on the state of development of the embronic *General Theory*) that 'it was only with disequilibrium positions that Mr Keynes was consciously concerned when he wrote the *Treatise*. He failed to notice that he had incidentally evolved a new theory of the long period analysis of output' (Robinson, 1951, p.56).

4 In North America, John Cornwall at Dalhousie has made outstanding contributions by marrying Kaldor's analysis, together with his own substantial inputs, with empirical findings. See Cornwall (1972, 1978).

5 For a fuller account of this sort of model, see Harcourt (1972, Ch.5, especially pp.205–14, 232–40).

6 Peter Kriesler (1981) of Sydney University has written an excellent M Ec thesis, on all this.

7 See also, for a very recent, thoughtful contribution, Shapiro (1981).

8 Bob Dixon has pointed out to me that it would be argued that the firms do not need to know their MRs and so on, they just have to keep experimenting with changes in prices and quantities until they observe maximum profits. By implication, at these points, MRs = MCs, but it is by implication, not by conscious calculations of them directly. This argument runs smack-bang into Robinson's principal objection to the static method and its inability to handle time, as expressed in the Preface to the second edition of *The Economics of Imperfect Competition* (Robinson, 1969). She regards as a 'shameless fudge' the notion that businessmen can find the position and shape of their individual demand curves by a process of trial and error which in effect assumes that demand curves stay put 'long enough for ... firm[s] to discover [them],

and [that] the experiments of raising and lowering ... [prices] ... have ... negligible cost[s] and no reaction upon the behaviour of the [firms'] customers' (Robinson 1979b, p.112).

9 See also the fine paper on 'The Labor Market' by Appelbaum (1979).

10 Davidson also (with Hines) pioneered the reawakening of interest in Keynes' finance motive — that an important element of the demand for money is the need for finance to be arranged before extra non-routine expenditure can be undertaken. See Davidson (1965, 1967, 1972); Hines (1971) and Smith (1977).

7. Towards a Post-Kaleckian Macroeconomics

M. Sawyer

INTRODUCTION*

This chapter has two central purposes. The first is a comparison between the work of Kalecki and Keynes as an appropriate starting-point for the development of macro-economics which will serve as an alternative to the current Keynesian-monetarist orthodoxy.[1] The second is to outline some of the key features of an alternative macroeconomics stemming from Kalecki, and which I label post-Kaleckian.

The use of the term post-Kaleckian may seem unnecessarily pedantic especially in a volume on post-Keynesian economics. I wish to use the term post-Kaleckian for three reasons. First, it serves to stress the break with the post-war macroeconomic orthodoxies in a way which the term post-Keynesian does not: the latter term has often been used to signify little more than the standard Keynesian economics (e.g. Kurihara, 1955; Okun, 1981). Indeed, Davidson (1981, p.152) is reduced to distinguishing between post-Keynesians (with a hyphen) and post Keynesians (without a hyphen) with the former being the advocates of the neoclassical orthodoxy. There is an urgent need to break out of the stranglehold imposed by the Keynesian–monetarist debate. The importance given to that debate has served to shift the ground sharply in the monetarist direction, and virtually to force economists to declare for one side or the other. Yet the real challenge to monetarism does not come from Keynesian economics but, as I hope to show, from post-Kaleckian and post-Keynesian economics. In this context, it is interesting to note the categorisation used by Meade (1981) of positions taken on macroeconomics, where anyone taking a post-Keynesian or post-Kaleckian view would appear to be declared a non-person.

Second, on grounds of historical accuracy, the work of many post-Keynesians owes more to Kalecki than to Keynes (e.g. Eichner and Kregel, 1975, and their acknowledgement of the work of Kalecki).

Third, and to my mind most importantly, the term post-Keynesian is used by some post-Keynesians to cover a wide range of approaches to economics (see Davidson, 1981, pp.154–5, and the range of opinion encompassed by members of the editorial board of the *Journal of Post Keynesian Economics*). Indeed, in Davidson's usage, the term post-Keynesian covers virtually all non neoclassical economists. In her introduction to Eichner (1979), Robinson focuses on the importance of the uncertainty of expectations about the future, such that 'from this point post-Keynesian theory takes off. The recognition of uncertainty undermines the traditional concept of equilibrium' (p.xi). Whilst the distinction between economic theory based on certainty (whether about the outcome or the frequency distribution of outcomes) and theory based on uncertainty is important, I think that it is necessary to be clear about the nature of the economic environment within which uncertainty operates. A particularly important distinction so far as macroeconomics is concerned is that between environments which are essentially atomistically competitive and those which are essentially oligopolistic. Below, I argue that Keynes adopted the competitive view, whilst Kalecki adopted the oligopolistic one. Thus the use of the term post-Kaleckian can be used to signal a macroeconomics based on oligopolistic behaviour rather than competitive behaviour, within the range of post-Keynesian macroeconomics.

KALECKI OR KEYNES AS THE STARTING POINT?

I would like to begin by setting out what I see as the main differences between the macroeconomics of Michal Kalecki and the macroeconomics of John Maynard Keynes. Later I shall argue that the macroeconomics of Kalecki provides not only a more realistic starting-point for the development of an alternative macroeconomics (to the dominant monetarist–Keynesian orthodoxy), but fits in well with many widely-accepted features of developed capitalist economies, such as mark-up pricing, investment dependent on demand and profits. In focusing on the work of Kalecki, I do not wish to suggest that we dismiss the work of Keynes, nor in calling the approach post-Kaleckian wish to underrate the contribution of post-Keynesians. Indeed, I hope that many post-Keynesians (specifically in the terminology of Davidson, 1978, 1981, the neo-Keynesians and the socialist-radical groupings) would find much of what I say below acceptable. However, I diverge from the neo-Keynesian approach when it argues that at the firm level growth aims determine the price which is set to generate funds for the required investment, rather than the Kaleckian view that the firm aiming for the largest surplus of revenue over costs, with the investment decision influenced by profitability, growth prospects, etc. I also stress the importance of real wage targets held by workers rather than the money wage targets.

Kalecki and Keynes can both be credited with the discovery of the concept of effective demand, and there appears a strong case for believing that Kalecki was a couple of years ahead of Keynes in publishing the discovery.[2] However, there are differences even in the determinants of aggregate demand. In Keynes, aggregate demand is the sum of consumer expenditure (which depends on income) plus investment (related to the rate of interest and expectations). In Kalecki, consumer expenditure depends largely on wages and investment on an accelerator mechanism and profits.[3] Already, it can be seen that the distribution of income between wages and profits has a role to play in the Kalecki approach. However, there are many differences between Kalecki and Keynes. Before going into details, we can divide the differences into four broad groups. First — and in my view most importantly — Kalecki adopts an essentially oligopolistic view of a developed capitalist economy, whilst Keynes maintains an essentially atomistic competitive view of the world. Below it will be seen that this oligopolistic or competitive view of the world is pervasive in the analysis of Kalecki and Keynes, respectively. Second, the nature of financial assets and crucial financial and real flows are perceived rather differently. For example, for Kalecki private investment is financed by retained earnings and bank borrowing, whilst for Keynes it is largely financed by issue of bonds. Third, the view of Kalecki and Keynes on the uses of equilibrium analysis are rather different. Fourth, the relative importance to be given to political factors, institutions and ideas are assessed differently by the two men.

In both their approaches, there are three major markets which have to be examined, namely the markets for output, for labour and for finance. In each case, Kalecki adopted a basically oligopolistic view whilst Keynes adopted essentially an atomistic competitive view. In the output market, it is well known that Kalecki adopted an oligopolistic approach with price determined as a mark-up over average direct costs, where the mark-up was determined by the degree of monopoly, and the mark-up and average direct costs were taken, as a first approximation, as constant with respect to output. Kalecki's degree of monopoly theory of income distribution derived from this pricing policy, is surely one of the most misunderstood theories in economics.[4] For my purpose here, it is sufficient to say that the degree of monopoly theory is not a tautology. Kalecki was quite clear that the degree of monopoly determined the mark-up, and that the factors determining the degree of monopoly included 'the process of concentration in industry ... tacit agreements ... development of sales promotion, advertising, selling agents, etc.' (Kalecki, 1971, pp. 49-50)[5]. Formalisations of the degree of monopoly approach are given in Cowling (1981, 1982) and Sawyer (1982a, 1982b). Formalisation makes it quite clear that the factors isolated by

Kalecki are fully in line with modern oligopoly theory, and that the theory is not a tautology (though it may be difficult to test). Many investigations of structure–profitability relationships in industrial economics indicate that testing of that theory is possible, though most of those investigations have been more akin to data-mining than to serious hypothesis testing (Cowling, 1982, pp. 256; Sawyer, 1982c).

The assumption that average direct costs are approximately constant with respect to output is often adopted in the belief that it corresponds to a 'stylised fact'. The difficulties which such an assumption creates for neoclassical economics are well known. Here, I merely wish to point out that constant unit costs, reflecting excess capacity held by the firm, are likely to be a feature of oligopoly (in part using excess capacity as an entry barrier — Spence, 1977; Cowling, 1982). Thus an apparently innocuous assumption of constant unit costs reinforces the need for an oligopolistic view of the world.

In Keynes (1936), prices play a more limited role than wages, whilst for Kalecki the position is reversed. In discussing the output market, Keynes does not appear ever to state specifically that he is assuming atomistic competition. But, from sentences such as 'in a single industry its particular price level depends partly on the rate of remuneration of the factors of production which enter into its marginal costs, and partly on the scale of output' (p.294), it is difficult to put any interpretation other than the assumption of atomistic competition. It can be noted in this respect that, following publication of *The General Theory*, Ohlin wrote that 'in this respect [the assumption of perfect competition] as in other respects Keynes does not seem to me to have been sufficiently radical enough in freeing himself from the conventional assumptions. When reading his book one sometimes wonders whether he never discussed imperfect competition with Mrs Robinson' (Moggridge, 1973, p.196).[6] Further, as far as I am aware, all the work stemming from the reinterpretation of Keynes (Clower, 1965; Leijonhufvud, 1968) has assumed atomistic competition, and analysed the consequences of price rigidity or sought to explain price rigidity.

Kalecki played much less attention to the labour market

than to the product market. Indeed the most significant way in which the post-Kaleckian approach below diverges from Kalecki's writing is in respect of the labour market. However, it is clear that Kalecki did not view the labour market as atomistic competitive. In one of his last published papers, he wrote that 'high mark-ups [of price over costs] ... will encourage strong trade unions to bargain for higher wages since they know that firms can "afford" to pay them .... To sum up, trade union power restrains the mark-ups.' And later that

it follows from the above that the class struggle as reflected in trade-union bargaining may affect the distribution of national income but in a much more sophisticated fashion than expressed by the crude doctrine: when wages are raised, profits fall *pro tanto*. This doctrine proves to be entirely wrong. Such shifts that occur are: (a) connected with widespread imperfect competition and oligopoly in the capitalist system; and (b) they are contained in fairly narrow limits. However, the day-to-day bargaining process is an important co-determinant of the distribution of national income. (Kalecki, 1971, pp.161–4)

In his prescient article 'Political Aspects of Full Employment' (1943) (in Kalecki, 1971, ch.12) he stressed the impact of the maintenance of full employment on workers, where

'the sack' would cease to play its role as a disciplinary measure. The social position of the boss would be undermined and the self-assurance and class consciousness of the working class would grow. Strikes for wage increases and improvements in conditions of work would create political tension ... [The] class instinct [of business leaders] tells them that lasting full employment is unsound from their point of view and that unemployment is an integral part of the normal capitalist system. (pp.140–1)

Keynes appears to have given greater emphasis to the labour market, particularly to money wages with the device of measuring other variables in terms of wage units. Chapter 2 of *The General Theory* deals in detail with wages and wage adjustment, with one mention of trade unions (and that in connection with classical explanations of unemployment). Indeed, as Tobin (1972) argued in connection with the explanation of rigidity of money wage in the presence of unemployment, Keynes 'did not appeal to trade union monopolies or minimum wage laws. He was anxious, perhaps over-anxious to meet his putative classical opponents on their home field, the competitive economy' (p. 3).

There is much work which traces its origin to Keynes which emphasises the problems which arise when wages fail to adjust to excess demand or supply (notably Clower, 1965; Barro and Grossman, 1976), or which investigate why wages may be slow to change in ostensible competitive conditions, invoking implicit contracts, attachment of workers to particular job, hiring and firing costs, etc. (discussed and extended in Okun, 1981).[7]

The finance capital market postulated by Kalecki is imperfect in the technical sense since 'access of a firm to the capital market, or in other words the amount of *rentier* capital it may hope to obtain, is determined to a large extent by the amount of its entrepreneurial capital. It would be impossible for a firm to borrow capital above a certain level determined by the amount of its entrepreneurial capital' (Kalecki, 1971, p. 105). There is also the principle of increasing risk that 'the heavier the borrowing the greater will be the danger of such a contingency [of being driven out of business whn profits cannot cover interest payments]' (p. 106). The importance of these remarks is

that the expansion of the firm depends on its accumulation of capital out of current profits. This will enable the firm to undertake new investment without encountering the obstacles of the limited capital market or 'increasing risk'. Not only can savings out of current profits be directly invested in the business, but this increase in the firm's capital will make it possible to contract new loans ... the limitations of the size of the firm by the availability of entrepreneurial capital goes to the very heart of the capitalist system. Many economists assume, at least in their abstract theories, a state of business democracy where anybody endowed with entrepreneurial ability can obtain capital for starting a business venture. This picture of the activities of the 'pure' entrepreneur is, to put it mildly, unrealistic. The most important prerequisite for becoming an entrepreneur is the *ownership* of capital. (pp. 107, 109)

Finally, and of particular relevance for macroeconomics is that 'one of the important factors of investment decisions is the accumulation of firms' capital out of current profits' (p. 109).

There are difficulties in establishing clearly the assumsption made by Keynes about the nature of the finance capital market. But his discussion of investment and the marginal efficiency of capital would seem to imply that the rate of interest was constant so far as the investing firm was concerned, and independent of the source of finance (i.e. essentially a Modiglian-Miller, 1958, world). The only deviation from that type of world is the discussion of risk. At a number of places, Keynes (1936) talks of the pure rate of interest (e.g. p. 208) with a borrower required to pay a risk premium above that rate. The risk premium may vary between borrowers and with the level of interest rate. But it would appear that for each borrower the level of interest rate payable is invariant to the size of loan. It is a little strange that this view was maintained, given the apparent stress on risk and uncertainty. For the risk of bankruptcy leads to the principle of increasing risk, imperfect capital markets and the importance of internal finance.

There would seem to be one departure from the perfect capital market assumption in Keynes, in that the full force of the consumption function and the dependence of consumer expenditure on current income relies on the absence of borrowing and cumulated savings with which to maintain consumer expenditure in the face of declining income.

Once the oligopolistic view is substituted for the competitive view, then numerous changes follow in its wake. Profits share is strongly influenced by the degree of monopoly, rather than being linked with the marginal productivity of capital. Real wages are influenced by the degree of monopoly and union bargaining power, rather than the interplay of supply and demand of labour. Imperfections in the capital market lead to retained earnings as an important element in savings, and profits as a key factor in the determination of investment.

Keynesian macroeconomics has always required some element of price rigidity (whether of relative or absolute prices) to explain unemployment. Price inflexibility seems a thin reed on which to rest the explanation of unemployment, particularly during periods of inflation or during prolonged periods of unemployment.[8] In this respect I agree with Kaldor (1978) who wrote: 'it is difficult to conceive how production in general can be limited by demand with unutilised capacity at the disposal of the representative firm as well as unemployed labour — unless conditions of some kind of oligopoly prevails' (p.xxi, n.1).

I now come to the nature of the financial system as characterised by Kalecki and by Keynes. For Kalecki, savings are largely made directly or indirectly out of profits, with savings out of labour income often taken as zero. Finance for investment comes from retained earnings, borrowing from banks and new share issues. Savings made by households out of dividend payments, self-employment income, etc. return to firms via the banks or new share issues. Bonds are essentially government debt used to help finance any deficit. The money supply would appear to be largely credit money created by banks in response to the demand for loans. The interrelationship between planned increases in investment leading to changes in the money supply if the investment is to come to fruition is clear in Kalecki's description of the multiplier process (Kalecki, 1971, p.29). Little is said about the determination of the rate of interest on government bonds, whilst Kalecki (1954) argues that 'the short-term rate [of interest] is determined by the value of transactions and the supply of money by banks; and that the long-term rate [of interest] is determined by anticipation as of the short-term rate based on past experience and by estimates of the risk involved in the possible depreciation of long-term assets' (p.73). He uses the equation $MV(r) = T$, where M is the supply of money determined by the banking system, $V(r)$ the velocity of circulation function depending on r, the interest rate of short-term assets (labelled bills by Kalecki), and T the nominal volume of transactions. With M and T determined elsewhere in the system, this equation serves to determine the rate of interest r.

In Keynes, it would appear that, as a first approximation,

savings are determined by households (based on income), whilst investment decisions are made by firms.[9] The precise manner by which investment is financed is not clear in Keynes, with most attention paid to the cost of finance and its impact on investment. Profits do not appear to be mentioned. The characterisation of financial assets derived from Keynes and embedded in the IS–LM model is a two-asset world — money and bonds. Leijonhufvud (1968) argued that the aggregates used by Keynes and those used by Keynesians were somewhat different, and the main issue surrounded whether capital goods were amalgamated with consumer goods (as in Keynesian treatments) or with non-money financial assets (as, he argued, in Keynes) under the label of bonds.[10] This basic two-asset dichotomy still prevails in many macroeconomic models, including many essentially monetarist models (e.g. Stein, 1976b; McCallum, 1978). Since, as I shall argue below, money is treated as exogenously determined by Keynes, the only route by which savings flows back to firms to finance investment is through the issue of bonds, though in this context bonds means a spectrum of assets.

It is difficult to pin down the definition and nature of money assumed by Keynes. As Leijonhufvud (1968) argued

Keynes' definition of 'money' is much broader than that used by later Keynesians. Not only are all kinds of deposits generally included, but Keynes was also willing to draw the line between 'money' and 'non-money assets' more or less wherever analytical convenience dictates in dealing with a specific problem. This flexibility with regard to the definition of 'money' is a natural concomitant of the attempt to compress the essentials of the liquidity preference theory within the simplified framework of a two-asset system. (p. 327)[11]

With that flexibility of definition in mind, it is difficult to establish a single definition of money used by Keynes. But quotes such as viewing 'the quantity of money as determined by the action of the central bank' and 'in the case of money — postponing for the moment, our consideration of the effects of reducing the wage-unit or of a deliberate increase in its supply by the monetary authority — the supply is fixed'

(Keynes, 1936, p. 247), and the discussion of savings and investment (Chapter 7) seem to imply an essentially exogenously determined money supply. The role of expansion of loans and credit money in the working of the multiplier process was acknowledged by Keynes later (Keynes, 1937b) in his introduction of the finance motive in response to the criticisms of Ohlin (1937).

I would argue that the impact of *The General Theory* has been to impose a characterisation of the financial system in terms of two assets, with money regarded as outside money representing net worth and yielding zero interest, and in which profits do not influence investment either through availability of finance nor in terms of expectations of future profitability of investment.

A third difference between Kalecki and Keynes revolves around the usefulness of equilibrium analysis. Much post-Keynesian literature has stressed the importance of uncertainty, historic rather than logical time and the limitations of equilibrium analysis. The style of analysis used by Keynes is essentially one of short-run equilibrium analysis in the Marshallian tradition, whereby certain factors which vary in the longer term (notably the capital stock, state of expectations and confidence) are assumed constant and the equilibrium levels of the endogenous variables investigated. The 'Notes on the Trade Cycle' (Chapter 22) indicates that 'the trade cycle is best regarded ... as being occasioned by a cyclical change in the marginal efficiency of capital' (Keynes, 1936, p. 313). It would appear, then, that Keynes used equilibrium analysis and regarded equilibrium as a position which the economy could achieve, albeit possibly only for a short period of time. There is also the acceptance by Keynes of the equilibrium analysis of Hicks (1937), which introduced what later became known as the IS–LM analysis.

Davidson (1981) argues that whilst neoclassical general equilibrium analysis uses equilibrium to signify market clearing situations, Keynes and post-Keynesians use the term equilibrium more broadly to signify a situation when 'given an initial set of conditions, the market price is such that neither buyers nor sellers wish to alter their market offers' (p. 153).

In contrast, Kalecki did not use equilibrium analysis as a general tool. It can be noted that the word equilibrium does not appear in the index of Kalecki (1971).[12] Some of his discussion uses elements of equilibrium analysis (e.g. discussion of the multiplier process — Kelecki, 1971, p. 29). In general, however, he placed considerable emphasis on the role of investment and the cyclical nature of investment, leading to the business cycle. Further, as investment proceeded it built up the capital stock, and determined the long-run evolution of the economy. Kalecki (1971, ch.15) sets this out quite clearly. Having noted that the theory of growth usually worked in terms of moving equilibrium, he argued that the problem of the trend growth of the economy should adopt

an approach similar to that applied in the theory of business cycles. [This] consists of establishing two relations: one based on the impact of effective demand generated by investment upon profits and the national income; and the other showing the determination of investment decisions by, broadly speaking, the level and the rate of change of economic activity. The first relation does not involve now particularly intricate questions. The second, to my mind, remains the central *pièce de résistance* of economics. The long-run trend is but a slowly changing component of a chain of short-period situations. (p. 165)

The final difference which I want to mention briefly 'between Kalecki and Keynes concerned the relative weights attached by them to institutional and political factors as compared with pure knowledge or ideas, in determining economic policy and development' (Eshag, 1977). Keynes' view is much quoted, that 'the power of vested interests is vastly exaggerated compared with the gradual encroachment of ideas' and that 'the world is ruled by little else [than the ideas of economists and political philosophers]' (Keynes, 1936, p. 383). Whilst the analysis of Keynes implicitly assumes a particular institutional arrangement (it could not do otherwise), which has been partially sketched in above, he rarely discusses the influence of particular institutional arrangements.[13] Corporations, financial institutions and trade unions might as well not exist for the attention given to them by Keynes.

In contrast, for Kalecki 'the institutional framework of a

social system is a basic element of its economic dynamics' (Kalecki, quoted in Brus, 1977). In his much quoted 1943 paper, Kalecki wrote:

the maintenance of full employment through government spending financed by loans has been widely discussed in recent years. This discussion, however, has concentrated on the purely economic aspects of the problem without paying due consideration to political realities. The assumption that a Government will maintain full employment in a capitalist economy if it only knows how to do it is fallacious.

In this connection the misgivings of big business about maintenance of full employment by government spending are of paramount importance. The misgivings arise from '(i) the dislike of Government interference in the problem of employment as such; (ii) the dislike of the direction of Government spending (public investment and subsidising consumption); (iii) dislike of the social and political changes resulting from the *maintenance* of full employment' (p. 139). Kalecki's belief in the importance of institutions and of interest groups on economic policy and performance is well indicated by his essays on development (Kalecki, 1976).

Many Keynesians have followed Keynes in a belief in the importance of ideas and in the unimportance of vested interests. The resurgence of monetarism and in the adoption of monetarist policies has left many Keynesians in the awkward position of being unable to explain those changes except in terms of the stupidity or misguidedness of monetarists and their political advocates. Kaleckians, on the other hand, find it foreseen and explained in Kalecki (1943). For, as he wrote there, high levels of employment lead to a situation where

[t]he workers would 'get out of hand' and the 'captains of industry' would be anxious to 'teach them a lesson'. ... In this situation a powerful block is likely to be formed between big business and the *rentier* interests, and they would probably find more than one economist to declare that the situation was manifestly unsound. (p. 144)

In terms of these four sets of differences, it is my view that Kalecki adopts the more appropriate approach. Below I hope to sketch out a post-Kaleckian approach. For the present, I wish to note that, in line with Kalecki's view that the institutional arrangements are important, it is necessary to amend his work to take account of recent developments. I would stress the importance of the development of financial institutions (particularly pension funds and insurance companies) and the growth of multinational companies. In both cases, these institutions, besides heavily influencing the course of the economy, are essentially oligopolistic in nature. Whilst Kalecki paid much more attention to international trade than Keynes did, nevertheless it remains underdeveloped. Some interesting work along those lines is contained in Cowling (1982).

THE MONETARIST REVIVAL

The one advantage of the monetarist revival — to be offset against the numerous disadvantages — has been the highlighting of three features which have been ignored or underplayed by mainstream Keynesians. These are the underplaying of the supply side of the economy, the neglect of the role of money, and of expectations. But in all three respects monetarists have fallen back on pre-Keynesian solutions, rather than advancing to post-Kaleckian or post-Keynesian ones. On the supply side, the monetarist revival indicated that when Keynesians had considered the labour market, the atomistic competition assumption was made. The retention of atomistic competition means that the explanation of unemployment rests on a lack of price flexibility. The departure from the assumption of price rigidity by Keynesians embodied in the Phillips curve opened up the way, once Lipsey (1960) presented wage adjustment in terms of the Walrasian adjustment mechanism, for the monetarist revival. With economists' aversion to assumptions of money illusion and with the experience of inflation, it is not surprising that full employment equilibrium under the guise of the 'natural' rate of unemployment was soon back in business.

Monetarists have stressed the role of money, but in their scheme of things have left little role for money. It is often said that monetarists differ from Keynesians in their belief that only money matters. But that should be amended to only money matters, but not very much. In particular, money only matters in respect of inflation, and there is virtually no inter-action between the real and monetary sectors, with the classical dichotomy revived. Keynes, post-Keynesians and Kalecki provide a much more central role for money, with real and monetary disturbances intimately linked, and expansion of demand relying on an expansion in the money supply, and vice versa. The infamous helicopter money introduced by Fried-man (1969), and his theoretical reasoning there, vividly indi-cates the exogenous net worth nature of money in the mone-tarist framework.

The notion of 'rational' expectations is also closely asso-ciated with the monetarist approach and the stability of the private sector. Indeed, it can be argued that whilst 'the only thing which Keynes "removed" from the foundation of clas-sical theory was the *deus ex machina* — the auctioneer which is assumed to furnish, without charge, all the information needed to obtain the perfect coordination of the activities of all traders in the present and through the future' (Leijonhufvud, 1967, p. 410), monetarists have put back the *deus ex machina* in the form of 'rational' expectations. It is noticeable that 'rational' expectations provide everything that the auctioneer was be-lieved to provide. In doing so, the monetarists have not tackled the challenge thrown down by Keynes in terms of the problems of coordination in a decentralised economy, nor in terms of the problems arising from uncertainty and the unknowability of the future. They have merely asserted that the problems do not exist.

Whilst an equilibrium approach is maintained, hypotheses similar to 'rational' expectations will have an appeal, in that the logic of equilibrium requires that expectations are fulfilled and that people are not systematically fooled. In that context, the only question is whether in situations of disequilibrium, economic agents are to be assumed to have knowledge of the equilibrium situation on which they act, leading the system quickly back to equilibrium, or whether knowledge is assumed to be acquired adaptively.

But, as indicated above, a Kaleckian approach rejects the usefulness of the analysis of equilibrium as a situation which could ever exist, and stressed the evolution of the system over time. Thus, each 'play of the game' is a unique event, and non-equilibrium pervasive.[14] Whilst the formation of expectations remains an underexplored area in post-Kaleckian (and post-Keynesian) economics, 'rational' expectations loses further appeal in the context of an evolving economic system.

A POST-KALECKIAN MACROECONOMICS

The approach to macroeconomics which I sketch out below has two origins. The first, as indicated above, is the work of Kalecki. The second is to draw on key features in models of price determination, wage change, money supply, investment and savings behaviour which have been used by some practitioners in the relevant areas, for which there is good empirical backing and which draw on the general notion that the developed capitalist economy is an oligopolistic one. I would stress this second source as the driving force, though I find that much is consistent with the work of Kalecki, which also provides a source of fruitful ideas. Thus the basic 'vision' of the world is one in which oligopolistic managerial firms, and trade unions are credited economic organisations, in which money is largely credit money and financial institutions are important in influencing the allocation of finance. The approach is a mixture of building up a macro theory of the economy based on 'realistic' assumptions and building-blocks which conform with empirical evidence.[15]

I begin with the price–wage nexus. On the price side, the view is taken that the price level prevailing in an industry, p, is determined by the marginal costs and the degree of monopoly, i.e. $p = \lambda (X)mc$ where mc is marginal cost, X is a vector of factors determining the degree of monopoly (such as concentration, extent of collusion), and λ is the mark-up of price over price over marginal cost. The mark-up is seen as a function of the elements entering the degree of monopoly, and is an indicator of the degree of monopoly. Cowling (1982, 1982) has shown that a generalised theory of oligopoly leads to this conclusion (and contains the Cournot theory and joint profit maximisation as special cases), where the factors entering X are level of concentration, extent of collusion and the elasticity of demand (which can be manipulated via advertising, etc.). These factors are close to the list given by Kalecki. It is based on short-run profit maximisation, where it is assumed (by Cowling) that excess capacity provides barriers to entry. This equation is interpreted, rather as Kalecki did, as indicating the typical outcome under oligopoly, without implied precision of short-run profit maximisation.

There are many aspects of this price equation, and here there is space only to highlight a few. First, it may be expected that the mark-up and marginal costs under conditions of excess capacity vary little with the level of demand and output, leaving input cost changes as the predominate proximate cause of price changes. These were effectively the assumptions made by Kalecki, and the insubstantial nature of output effects on price changes and the importance of cost changes is now widely accepted.[16] Second, it can easily be translated into a price–cost margin equation, *viz* $(p - mc)/p = (\lambda(X) - 1)/\lambda(X)$, which indicates that the margin depends on the factors entering X. Structure–profitability relationships in industrial economics have focused on this type of relationship. Thus the claim that Kalecki's degree of monopoly theory is a tautology is seen as false, as is the claim that it cannot be tested. The testing is difficult and the estimation of structure–profitability relationships has often been undertaken on a very *ad hoc* basis (as I have argued in Sawyer, 1982c). Nevertheless, despite the difficulties, there is substantial evidence for the impact of concentration and advertising intensity on price–cost margins (Sawyer, 1981, ch.6).

Third, rewriting the above equation yields the ratio of the surplus of revenue over variable costs $S/pq = (\lambda(X) - 1)/\lambda(X) + (mc - avc)/pq$. The surplus is composed of profits and costs which are not marked up by the firm. In usual parlance, the surplus is equal to profits plus fixed costs. It is conventional to divide costs into variable and fixed (with respect to the decision period concerned). In this context I prefer the division into marked-up costs and non-marked-up ones. The reasons for this preference include that the former terminology suggests that the division of costs depends on technical factors (that is, which inputs can be varied and which cannot within the decision period). The latter terminology is suggestive of the idea that there are costs which controllers mark up, leaving a surplus out of which payments to members of the controlling coalition are made. Thus, for a large managerial corporation, the surplus could be seen as determined by surplus maximising considerations, and the division of the surplus between managerial income and perks, retained earnings for investment and dividends depends on the power of the interest groups involved. Reported profits may well move pro-cyclically in that the other payments out of the surplus may change little in response to the movements of the trade cycle, and the degree of monopoly may tend to move pro-cyclically.

The fourth point is to note that there is a difference of view on the direction of causation between profits and investment between a Kaleckian approach and some post-Keynesian approaches. Specifically, whilst some post-Keynesians (notably, Eichner, 1973, 1976) view the investment finance requirements of firms dictating price and profit decisions, a Kaleckian approach would adopt more of a profit-maximising approach, with the investment decision influenced by profitability, growth prospects, etc. In advocating a profit-maximising approach, there is an awareness that firms operate in an uncertain and changing environment so that firms are unlikely to be able to calculate exactly optimal price and output.

Appeals to oligopolistic pricing, especially of the administered-pricing form which stresses price inflexibilities, are often made by Keynesian economists (e.g. Meade, 1981, p. 49) as part of the explanation (alongside inflexible money wages) of price rigidities. Our argument here is that this *ad hoc* introduction of oligopolistic elements into an otherwise competitive market situation is unsatisfactory and misleading, and that if oligopolistic pricing is important then it must be fully incorporated.

The final point on this price approach is that the real wage is strongly influenced by the product market situation. Applying the price equation at the aggregate level, and assuming marginal cost = average variable costs, then average costs equal $(wL + fF)/Q$ where w is money wage, L is employment, F the input of imported materials, f their cost and Q output. Rearrangement yields:

$$w/p = (1/\lambda) (Q/L) - (f/p) (F/L) \qquad (7.1)$$

The interesting points about this equation are that it emphasises the relevance of the relative cost of imported materials and of the degree of monopoly on the real wage. In conventional macroeconomics, the real wage is portrayed as basically determined in the labour market (by interaction of the demand for and supply of labour), though it is recognised that in an interdependent system it is not possible to identify one specific market with determination of a particular price. An important feature of the post-Kaleckian (and post-Keynesian) approach is the stress laid on the role of product markets in the determination of the real wage.

This leads us onto consideration of the labour market. It is at this point that I diverge most sharply from the writings of Kalecki. Kalecki, as indicated above, stressed the role of the bargaining power of trade unions, but saw it working through shaping the degree of monopoly. Essentially, he argued that when unions push for higher money wages (arising from, say, increased militancy or from an observed high profit share), firms are restricted in their ability to pass on the wage increases as price increases. The argument is a modified version of the kinked demand curve approach (see Cowling, 1982, p. 100).

The approach which I wish to sketch here has two basic strands. First, the aspirations and the economic and political power of workers are highly relevant to the determination of wages, and in this respect there is little divergence from Kalecki. The existence of trade unions may modify aspirations of workers, but as Routh (1980) argued 'it is a mistake to imagine that there is a sharp division between unionized and un-unionized workers, for trade unions cannot do much more than institutionalise and direct drives and aspirations that are already present in the individual workers' (p. 203). The discussion is laid out in terms of unions, but many of the arguments would carry over into a non-union situation, though workers' ability to achieve their goals would be less.

Second, the aspirations of workers are described in terms of a target wage. At the aggregate level, the emphasis would be on the target real wage, but for each bargaining group there would be emphasis on relative wages and differentials. The target wage is seen as arising from notions of fair pay and a 'just' wage. Wood (1978) labelled these as 'normative pressures', and divided them into '*real* norms (implying that beliefs about fair pay in money terms are revised in response to change in prices) and *relative* norms (implying that beliefs about fair pay in money terms for particular people or jobs are revised in response to changes in other rates of pay)' (p. 22). The ideas of fair pay and 'just' wage have, of course, a long history.[17] Of particular relevance here is that the power of the idea of fair pay, maintenance of differentials, etc. has strongly influenced wage settlements, particularly those which go to arbitration.

The notion of a target real wage bargaining proved a useful analytical device in research into wage inflation. It has received a good deal of empirical support (see e.g. Henry, Sawyer and Smith, 1976; Artis and Miller, 1979; Henry, 1981) and is now used in two major macroeconometric models of the British economy (Cripps and Godley, 1976; National Institute of Economic and Social Research, 1983). So far very simple assumptions have been made on the determination of the target real wage (typically that it grows exponentially) and research is required to be able to better model target real wages. It can also be noted that a theory of wage bargaining which omits mention of a target real wage (or related concept) is likely to be deficient. For simply if on one round of negotiations workers lose ground (whether from a weak bargaining position or from underestimation of the rate of inflation), then in the absence of a target real wage the mechanism for seeking to restore lost ground is missing. For example, interpreting the expectations augmented Phillips curve of $\dot{w} = f(U) + \dot{p}^e$ (where

$\dot{w}$ is the rate of change of money wages, $\dot{p}^e$ the expected change of prices, and U level of unemployment) as relating to the outcome of bargaining (rather than from a competitive market), then high levels of U reduce $\dot{w}$ below $\dot{p}^e$ leading to falling real wages. The maintenance of high levels of U would lead to continually falling real wages.[18] The introduction of a target real wage (see below) limits that fall.

In the simplest form,[19] the target real wage approach leads to:

$$\dot{w} = a_1 + a_2 \dot{p}^e + a_3 U + a_4 (T - w/p)$$

where T is the target real wage.

In a no productivity change situation, an inflationary 'equilibrium' ($\dot{w} = \dot{p}^e$) leads to:

$$(w/p) = a_4^{-1}(a_1 + (a_2 - 1) \dot{p}^e + a_3 U + a_4 T) \qquad (7.2)$$

This equation serves to illustrate the simple point that the role of unemployment in models such as this is to restrain real wages. The real wage equation based on price behaviour (equation 7.1) can be brought together with this real wage equation (7.2) based on wage behaviour. The real demands from the two sides can be 'reconciled' through a number of routes. The first is through the levels of output and unemployment. Thus we treat these two equations as involving two unknowns — the real wage and output (with unemployment as a function of output). The output variable enters the equation above through influence on labour productivity and on the degree of monopoly, and the wage-side equation through determining unemployment. Thus, the sharper the disagreement over the real wage between firms and employees, the lower will be the level of output (and higher unemployment) needed to restrain profits and real wage demands such that they become consistent.

The other routes would include government policy designed to reconcile these real wage claims at high levels of output by reductions in the degree of monopoly, changes in the relative price of imported inputs, and more usually attempts (via incomes policy, exhortation, etc.) to reduce the target real wage and (via trade union legislation) unions ability to obtain wage increases (i.e. modifying values of the coefficients in the above equation).

I believe that our understanding of how the macroeconomy moves through time would be much increased if research could throw light on how T changes over time. This would include investigations into how T is modified in response to experience of unemployment, real wages, government expenditure, etc. In view of the preceding paragraph, we also need to know how various political activities interact on the target real wage.

The one point to be made here is that the target real wage is expected to evolve over time as productivity grows and real wages rise. It is clear that the target real wage approach requires something to be said about the evolution of the target over time. What has been less clear is that this highlights a major problem with the neoclassical approach and the 'natural' rate of unemployment. Simply, with given 'tastes', the supply of labour curve is fixed, so that shifts in the demand for labour curve (as a function of the real wage) arising from productivity growth would lead to a rising 'natural' level of employment and falling 'natural' level of unemployment.[20] A constant 'natural' rate of unemployment requires that the supply curve shifts to the right at the same pace as the demand curve.[21] The shifts in the supply curve can only come from 'taste changes' (which have to be assumed exogenous in a neoclassical approach) such that the willingness to supply labour is closely linked with labour productivity.

The discussion of the aggregate demand aspects focuses on three elements — investment, savings and money. One consequence of the neoclassical monetarist resurgence has been a tendency to neglect investment as a crucial part of aggregate demand. The IS–LM framework includes investment as the part of aggregate demand which is a function of the rate of interest, but otherwise does little to distinguish investment from other parts of aggregate demand. The monetarist approach may go further and picture aggregate demand as determined by the level of the money supply. The neoclassical growth model also removes the demand for investment from the scene, with the assumption that desired savings leads to corresponding changes in the capital stock. Thus our discussion of investment in some respects is a return to ideas which were common currency in the late 1940s (reflected by, for example, Harrod, 1936; Samuelson, 1939; Domar, 1947). It emphasises the key role of investment in aggregate demand, and particularly that fluctuations in investment are a major determinant of fluctuations in aggregate demand and output. Further, since investment adds to the capital stock, it serves to condition the long-term growth path.

The latter point is taken up briefly first. Much popular discussion of economic growth links the level of investment with the rate of growth. There may be some doubts on the strength of the links (especially how far variations in growth of countries can be explained by variations in investment). But, as is well known, the equilibrium growth rate in neoclassical models is determined by growth of labour force and (exogenously given) technical change. The view of Kalecki is quite different and, as indicated above, he viewed the long run as built up of successive short-run situations.

The theory of investment demand for an oligopolistic economy has not been well worked out. We would expect that when it has it will involve some of the following elements. First, changes in output, expected changes in output and the general growth climate will be important, arising from accelerator components of investment. Second, profits will be seen as much more important than in more conventional treatments, where interest rates and other costs of capital and changes in output are stressed. This arises from many considerations. The imperfect capital market view indicates the importance of profits as a source of finance and as an influence on the availability and cost of external finance. In an uncertain world, future profitability may be gauged in part by current profitability.[22] Further, on an accelerator-type argument, changes in profitability, leading to changes in desired capital stock, leads to investment. Whilst during the course of the trade cycle outputs and profits may move close together, Kalecki points to changes in profits, rather than output, as influencing invetment (e.g. Kalecki, 1971, ch.15) which leads to the view that a downturn in profits is one of the causes of downturns in investment. Third, although this is not specific to an oligopolised economy, there is an intimate link between investment and technological change, with bursts of techno-logical change leading to relatively high levels of investment, and with new capital equipment often required to embody technological change (Kaldor, 1961).

The major proposition concerning savings is the familiar one that the propensity to save out of labour income is substantially below that out of non-labour income. For con-venience, call the former wages (W) and the latter profits (P), and write savings $S = s_w W + s_p P$. It is well known that such a formulation (for a closed private sector economy) leads to the view that the distribution of income between wages and profits at full employment is determined by the level of investment (Kaldor, 1956). This differential savings propensity hypothesis was also advanced by Kalecki, but without the full employ-ment assumption made by Kaldor. In the version of Kalecki essentially the distribution between wages and profits is deter-mined by the degree of monopoly, leaving investment demand to determine the level of output, etc.[23] In the view I advanced above, the level of output and of real wages (and hence of wages in total and profits) are heavily influenced by the interaction of wage demands and profit demands. If that view is correct, then the impact of differential savings propensities is further reduced, and at the limit those propensities merely serve to translate wages and profits into levels of savings and consumption.

The differential savings propensity approach does incor-porate elements of an oligopolised economy where institu-tional arrangements are important. In a neoclassical world, households own firms, and savings decisions are effectively made by households based on utility maximisation considera-tions. In the post-Kaleckian world, whilst there may be some savings out of wages (contrary to the assumption often made by Kalecki that $s_w = 0$), they may be undertaken compulsorily (through occupational pension schemes) or semi-compulsorily (in order to provide housing in the absence of rented accom-modation, etc.), and may yield little net savings over a lifetime.[24] Thus Kalecki's zero savings assumption may be replaced by Modigliani's zero lifetime savings assumption. But the important assumption is that much of savings is made by firms in pursuit of their objectives (survival, profits, growth, etc.) with little reference to the utility of households who are the nominal owners of the firms.

The propensity to save out of non-labour income (some but not all of which appears as profits) is likely to depend on the phase of development. For example, Cowling (1982) argues that '[u]nder competitive capitalism it may be reasonable to assume that Marxian imperative to accumulate in order to survive, but in a world of monopoly or oligopoly this condition must be severely qualified' (p. 48). The competitive pressures on firms for accumulation may be lessened [under managerial capitalism] and the managers, in effective control, siphon off some of potential profits as managerial income (broadly defined).

The post-Kaleckian view of money probably departs little from the general post-Keynesian view. Money is seen as largely credit money, created alongside spending decisions. When an expansion of injections into the economy is desired (whether investment, government expenditure, autonomous consumption) then in the short run that expansion can only come to fruition when money is available to make the increased demands effective. The extra money may come from money previously (intentionally or unintentionally) hoarded, from the printing of money by governments, or through increased loans from the banking sector. Kalecki (1971) and Keynes (1937b) both describe the process involved. The creation of money in this sense is essentially a disequilibrium phenomenon, in the sense that some economic agents in the system must be seeking to expand their expenditure (at least in nominal terms) in order that money be created. Whilst as a working assumption it may be reasonable to suppose that increased expenditure plans lead to increases in the money supply, it is also necessary to acknowledge that there may be times when, by choice or government decree, banks restrict the expansion of the money supply whether through rationing by quantity or by price. This can arise through banks coming close to their ceilings so far as money multipliers are concerned, through firms seeking further loans and be judged too risky, etc.

Some brief points need to be added here. First, money can be destroyed as well as created under this system. Since loans carry an interest charge, economic agents will be keen to extinguish them where possible. Thus, following Kaldor and Trevithick (1981), if there were an excess supply of money, then those with loans outstanding would seek to use the excess deposits to pay off the loans thereby reducing the money supply. There may be limitations to this (e.g. fixed-term loans) which require the excess supply to pass to those with loans outstanding. Second, there can be further dimensions to the impact of changes in uncertainty. Specifically, the extent to which the money supply is part of a credit pyramid, and rests on a multiple of outside money held by the banks, permits uncertainty on the viability of the banking system to be transmitted into withdrawals of cash from banks and a reduction in the money supply. Third, since aggregate demand fluctuates, partly from the accelerator component of investment and the interaction of wage and price determination, this leads to an explanation of fluctuations in the money supply. In Friedman and Schwartz's (1963) study, the fluctuations in the money supply, which are postulated to lead to output and price fluctuations are, in any other than an accounting sense, left unexplained.

Because of arguments along the lines sketched above, the post-Kaleckian approach (as well as the post-Keynesian one) places rather more emphasis on the role of money and the interrelationships between the real and monetary sectors than either the monetarists or the orthodox Keynesians.

A post-Kaleckian view on inflation follows quite easily from the above. Like Rowthorn (1977), the analysis of inflation focuses on the conflict over income shares between four groups — labour, capital, government and the foreign sector. Attempts by any group to raise their income by increased wages, prices, taxes or import prices generates losses elsewhere in the system. When other groups seek to recoup their losses, the mechanism by which they do so is the raising of their prices.

Thus an attempt by capital to raise profits shows up initially as an output price rise. This leads to a fall in real wages and (under a flexible exchange rate regime) a fall in the exchange rate. Workers seeking to maintain real wages in the face of those price rises pursue higher money wage claims. The response of the government sector may be partially automatic, with taxes rising with or faster than nominal income rises and partially 'discretionary' response of tax rises to deflate inflation out of the system. With the interdependence of the economic system, which would be heightened if a more disaggregated picture were used, price rises can become embedded into the system, and much of the continuation of inflation is basically of a cost-push variety. An upsurge in inflation generates to some extent the money supply increases necessary to finance it. Notably, increases in costs of firms (arising from increases in prices by other firms, in wages and in imported inputs) would require increased finance by the firm, obtained in the short term by borrowing and in the longer term recouped by higher prices. Indeed, so far as the firm is concerned, an increase in outgoings on inputs would need to be met by borrowing during the period of production whether the increase arose from a desire to increase output or from increased input prices.

Thus a post-Kaleckian view of inflation would focus on the conflict between different groups and the response of the money supply to the existence of inflation. The anticipation of future inflation, particularly by firms, removes some of the inhibitions on firms from raising prices through fear of loss of market shares. But, in contrast to the monetarists view, there will be a far greater element of inflation responding to previous inflation. Thus, it is past changes in wages and prices which generate changes in the real wage to which workers respond. It is past cost increases to which firms respond. In any on-going inflation, there will be an inflationary climate which makes it difficult to separate previous inflationary forces from anticipatory ones. An inflation which is largely driven by the expectation of inflation may be seen as relatively easy to stop, since it only requires those expectations to be changed. At the limit, this led some of the 'rational' expectations school to adopt the short-sharp-shock treatment of an announced determination by government to reduce the rate of increase of the money supply, leading to a sharp downward revision of expected inflation followed by a fall in actual inflation. An inflation largely driven by the past experience of inflation is much more difficult to bring to a halt, with a deflation of demand through monetary or fiscal measures leading mainly to output falls.

One reaction to much of the above is that it says nothing new, and that many of the propositions are widely accepted. In some respects it is a reaction which I share. Indeed I would argue that a strength of the post-Kaleckian approach is that it draws on 'building-blocks' which are widely used and accepted. I have already pointed to the use in industrial economics of structure–profitability models akin to Kalecki's degree of monopoly model, in labour economics to the use of approaches based on union bargaining, wage comparabilities and the like, and in monetary economics of endogenous money supply. This line of argument can be extended to macroeconometric models.[25] In many models, we find the use of (i) prices based on a mark-up over costs; (ii) wage change equations based on a target real wage; (iii) investment functions which involve accelerator components, profitability, etc.; and (iv) consumption linked to personal disposable income (e.g. Davidson *et al.*, 1978) which imposes the view that retained profits are not included as part of personal income, and hence that the propensity to save and consume out of wages and profits are different. This points to substantial empirical support for the Kaleckian approach, and stresses the need for these building-blocks to be placed together in a theoretical framework, so that their consequences can be worked out. So far the macroeconometric models have been largely used for forecasting purposes and not for analysis. Forecasting and simulation clearly have their place in understanding how the macroeconomy works. But analysis can be clearer in indicating the interrelationships involved.

It is also the case that most macroeconomic discussion revolves around theoretical rather than econometric models. Thus, there is a need to present the post-Kaleckian approach in that mode. Further, despite what I have said about the implicit approval given to the post-Kaleckian approach by macroeconometric models and other areas of economics, it is difficult to find any evidence of that approach in conventional macroeconomic texts. First the Keynesian orthodoxy, and then the Keynesian–monetarist debate have effectively sealed off macroeconomic debate from a consideration of the oligopolistic nature of the economy.

Another reaction is that in so far as it says anything different, it is wrong. Although there is not space to develop fully the response to this, I can summarise it briefly as (i) there is substantial empirical support for various aspects of a post-Kaleckian approach, partly evidenced by what I have said in the last few paragraphs;[26] and (ii) the basic assumptions of a post-Kaleckian approach are more realistic than those used by Keynesians and monetarists.[27] The high levels of industrial concentration, the importance of multinational corporations, the degree of unionisation, the extent of firms' finance provided by retained earnings and bank borrowing, are all indicators of the superiority of the oligopolistic view over the competitive view as a starting-point.

CONCLUDING REMARKS

This chapter has only been able to deal briefly with some aspects of a post-Kaleckian macroeconomics. There are two particular areas on which I have said nothing and which are in urgent need of development. The first relates to the foreign sector. In this area, there is the question of the determination of the exchange rate, even if it is accepted that foreign exchange markets may be closer than most to being atomistic competitive. Further, there are questions of the restrictions placed on domestic prices by international competition, and the degree to which any 'law of one price' effect operates. Discussion of international competition has to involve the role of multinational corporations and the extent of effective collusion across national boundaries. Cowling (1982) has argued that the effect of international competition does not apply a competitive squeeze on domestic prices in that the domestic degree of monopoly appears largely unaffected by international competition, though there is a major impact on domestic output and capacity utilisation.

The second area relates to financial institutions. In the British context, the evolution of pension funds and insurance companies dealing with a large proportion of personal savings, financing a considerable part of the public sector borrowing requirement, expanding ownership of non-financial corporation have macroeconomic effects which require incorporation. Further, much savings through pension funds is not optional as far as the individual is concerned.

In the preface of *The General Theory*, Keynes spoke of 'a struggle of escape from habitual modes of thought and expression'. Yet, as Okun (1981) noted,

Keynes had to modify the classical framework because the persistence of underemployment was inconsistent with full microeconomic equilibrium in both product and labour markets. He altered it in the most conservative way possible, amending only one of the four functional relations that underlie labour and product market equilibrium. Only the classical supply curve of labour had to be overhauled. (p.12)

A post-Kaleckian approach offers a much sharper break with a neoclassical framework and its derivatives which have dominated economics this century. It offers liberation from the sterility of the Keynesian–monetarist debate over the role of price flexibility and degree of price rigidity in the system, and offers an explanation of unemployment which does not rest on failure of prices to adjust. It also offers a macroeconomics which is consistent with a considerable amount of evidence and with many aspects of non-neoclassical economics. Drawing on the field with which I am most familiar — industrial economics — few there would argue that perfect competition gives an adequate view of how industrial markets operate or that price changes respond to excess demand. Instead, the discussion involves different theories of oligopoly, and the determinants of the mark-up of price over costs. Yet in macroeconomics, the perfect competition view is generally preferred to an oligopolistic one. Clearly, macroeconomics cannot deal at the same level of detail as specialisms, such as industrial economics, but one would hope for some degree of coherence between macroeconomics and the various specialisms.

NOTES

*   This is a revised version of a paper given at a conference on *Post-Keynesian Economics* held at Thames Polytechnic, 28 May 1982.

1   By the work of Keynes, I mean for the purpose of this paper *The General Theory* (Keynes, 1936), and I seek to avoid comparisons between that and earlier work (especially Keynes, 1930). The work of Kalecki relevant to this paper is mainly contained in Kalecki (1971). I am also accepting that there is a distinction between the work of Keynes and the Keynesian neoclassical synthesis. I have argued elsewhere (Sawyer, 1982a) that there is a basic similarity between Keynesian macroeconomics and monetarism which allows us to talk of the Keynesian–monetarist orthodoxy.

2   Klein (1975), for example, wrote that: 'Kalecki's greatest achievement, among many, was undoubtedly his complete anticipation of Keynes' *General Theory*', whilst Robinson (1975) writes that: 'Michal Kalecki's claim to priority of publication is indisputable'.

3   For example, Kalecki (1971), ch.10 on investment, ch.7 on savings.

4   Reading the literature in this area, I am tempted to say deliberately misunderstood. A few examples: Bronfrebrenner (1971) discusses Kalecki's theory in its 1938 version, and does not mention the revised and much improved version of 1954 (Kalecki, 1938, 1954). Ferguson (1969) accuses Kalecki's degree of monopoly theory of being a tautology and of having been rejected empirically. Johnson (1973) discusses Kalecki, without providing any references for his readers (which is particularly strange since that book comprises edited lecture notes), in terms of a simple profit-maximising monopoly model, when it is clear from reading Kalecki that that was not his approach.

5   It must be added that some of the confusion arose from Kalecki (1938), and discussion there. There is also a tendency in the discussion of statistics to describe the actual mark-up of price over cost as the degree of monopoly, when strictly it should be that the mark-up moves in response to changes in the degree of monopoly.

6   This alludes, of course, to Robinson (1969).

7 One interesting point arises here. With implicit contracts, how is the contract enforced? Clearly legal remedies are ruled out. The firm is presumably constrained as far as the whole labour force is concerned to keep to the contract, for otherwise the reputation of the firm will be damaged such that workers will be unwilling to make future implicit contracts with that firm. But the individual worker has little protection, unless fellow workers help in any attempt to break the implicit contract. This would lead into the formation of trade unions (or their unofficial equivalent).

8 Some of the arguments on price rigidity rest on oligopolistic elements such as administered prices. Further, much of the recent work on implicit contracts, fixed-price markets, etc. would seem to offer explanations on why prices are relatively inflexible during the course of relatively small fluctuations of aggregate demand such as those generally experienced in the 1950s and 1960s. But deep depression, such as the inter-war period in Britain, and the period since 1974, do not fit that picture.

9 It may be that the household sector is defined in terms of the economic agents who save, whilst firms (or entrepreneurs) are those agents which undertake investment. Thus, a single economic agent could be regarded as both a household and a firm.

10 'Keynes' basic model treats capital goods and "bonds" as aggregate', and 'Keynes' representative non-money asset is a long-term asset' (Leijonhufvud, 1968, p. 135).

11 'We can draw the line between "money" and "debts" at whatever point is most convenient for handling a particular problem' (Keynes, 1936, p. 167, n. 1).

12 This was pointed out in the discussion following the paper by Asimakopulos in Harcourt (1977). There is the caveat that the index was not prepared by Kalecki himself since he died whilst the book was in the course of preparation for publication. The index was prepared by Mario Nuti, who notes that the omission of the word equilibrium from the index reflects Kalecki's approach.

13 For discussion of the institutional arrangements assumed by Keynes, see de Cecco (1977).

14 I use the term non-equilibrium rather than disequilibrium, since the latter implies a system out of equilibrium but adjusting towards equilibrium.

15 I have sought to justify this statement in Sawyer (1982a), ch. 5 (on realistic assumptions) and ch. 7 (on empirical evidence).

16 For example Coutts, Godley and Nordhaus (1978); Sawyer, Aaronovitch and Samson (1982); Sawyer (1983).

17 Monetarists have sometimes argued that their ideas have a long pedigree in economic discussion. But, as Desai (1981) points out, so do many of the counter-arguments to monetarism. Many of the arguments in this chapter could similarly be traced back.

18 The same argument does not apply with the expectations-augmented Phillips curve applied to a competitive market with unemployment as a (negative) proxy for excess demand. A fall in the real wage would lead to a rise in excess demand, and hence a fall in unemployment in subsequent period.

19 For a detailed development and discussion of variations on this, see Sawyer (1982a).

20 Assuming conventionally that the supply curve of labour is upward-sloping. The reduction in hours worked as real wages have risen over time may cast doubt on that assumption.

21 Abstracting from changes in participation rate.

22 This indicates a further difference between Kalecki and Keynes in that, whilst Keynes points to the importance of uncertainty, he rarely indicates how economic agents cope with it, and what rules-of-thumb, etc. are devloped. On the other hand, Kalecki often proceeds to try to establish possible relationships between variables of interest.

23 This simple view assumes that the degree of monopoly and marginal costs are constant with respect to the level of output. Allowing them to vary prevents the simple dichotomy indicated in the text.

24 Though personal savings as a proportion of disposable income rose during the 1970s in the UK to figures of the order of 13–15 per cent, savings in real terms (after allowing for impact of inflation on assets denominated in money terms, etc.) may have been close to zero (Taylor and Threadgold, 1979).

25 The macroeconometric models, such as the CEPG, NIESR, which are often described as neo-Keynesian should perhaps be labelled neo-Kaleckian. The relevance of the work of Kalecki for macroeconometric models was recognised by Klein (1964) when he wrote: 'whilst it should not be said that all the basic ingredients of modern econometric systems stemmed from Kalecki's model, it can be said that all the components of Kalecki's model are finding their way into strategic places in modern econometric models. His theories of the early 1930s are seen to be intellectual *tours de force* in the light of modern developments' (p. 191).

26 I have argued this at much greater length in Sawyer (1982a), ch.7.

27 Despite the Friedman-style methodology ignoring the realism of assumptions, I would argue for this as a relevant criterion for a theory. First, offered two theories then, *ceteris paribus*, more realism is

preferred to less. Although the degree of realism of a particular theory is difficult to measure, the derivation and measurement of predictions is not without its problems (Desai, 1981, pp.96–8). Second, econometric and other testing of theories has proved difficult and often controversial and has not lead to the rejection of theories and to a clear indication of a preferred theory. Before the happy day arrives when one theory (in macroeconomics) is clearly empirically superior to rivals some theoretical perspective has to be used.

8 The Political Economy of Rapid Industrialisation

T. Skouras

INTRODUCTION*

This chapter attempts to provide a simple conceptual framework in which the social and political tensions that accompany industrialisation can be focused on. The analysis of the socio-political stresses caused by rapid industrialisation is of interest both for the insights it may afford to historical cases of successful industrialisation and, more importantly, for the light it throws on some of the most serious resistances and obstacles to economic development. If a general conclusion may be drawn from this analysis, it is that the existing relations of production and initial political conditions not only shape the process of development, but are also crucial for its initiation and continuation. In other words, they are an integral part of the development process and cannot be validly abstracted from the study of development.

Kalecki's work,[1] which consistently takes into account the political implications of the transformation of the economic structure in the course of industrialisation, is the major influence on the construction of the simple model that is presented below. In our analysis, we shall distinguish three types of political regime and three types of property relations in agriculture. The political regimes are (i) socialist, (ii) capitalist, and (iii) 'intermediate'. The agricultural relations of production are characterised by (i) strong feudal elements, (ii) free peasant families cultivating their own small landholdings;

and (iii) commercial farming with hired agricultural labour. Inevitably, such a scheme operates at a quite high level of abstraction and there may well be historical cases which do not neatly fit its categories. Nevertheless, it serves well the basic heuristic objective of bringing out and demonstrating the role and importance of political conditions in the development process.[2]

Other categories or general assumptions concerning the setting of the analysis are presented below. Employment in the economy is divided into two sectors: the traditional and the mechanised (ignoring, for the time being, administrative employment by the state). Production in the traditional sector consists principally of agricultural produce, the largest part of which is food. Machinery is not used and whatever primitive tools are in use come from within the peasant household.

Labour productivity is very low in this sector. On the other hand, production in the mechanised branch is carried out by means of machinery and consists of a variety of investment and consumption goods. Traditional employment is rural; mechanised employment is mostly urban, but can also be rural to the extent that agricultural production is mechanised. Given this distinction, economic development can be viewed simply as the substitution of traditional by mechanised employment (or, alternatively, the substitution of high-productivity for low-productivity employment).

POLITICAL PROBLEMS OF DEVELOPMENT UNDER A SOCIALIST REGIME

Let us begin by considering the problems faced by a socialist regime in its attempt to industrialise rapidly. By 'socialist' we mean that the industrial means of production (or, in terms of our model, all machinery and equipment in the mechanised sector) are owned and controlled by the state. We do not restrict the term more than this and it thus follows that it can cover most regimes that call themselves socialist or people's republics. It must be emphasised that the term does not necessarily correspond to a specific accepted usage (if it can be argued that such agreement on usage has been or could be established) but must be understood in the sense of our basic definition.[3]

We shall take the task of an industrialising regime to be the expansion of the output of investment goods *at the fastest possible rate*. This will bring out in sharp relief the issues involved and will demonstrate the problems in their most acute form. A less ambitious policy will, at the cost of a slower industrialisation, attenuate the difficulties but will not alter their fundamental nature and direction. To examine what exactly is involved in this task, we shall use Figure 8.1 for the purposes of clarity and conciseness.

OC is labour employed in the consumption goods industry and DI is employment in the investment goods industry. OC + DI is the total employment in the mechanised sector (production of raw materials and intermediate goods is allocated between the two industries according to the proportions in which they are used in the production of investment or consumption goods). CD is the labour force in the traditional sector where most of the population is employed. OW is the average hourly industrial wage and OW × (OC + DI) is the total wage bill which in a socialist regime is paid by the state.

Assuming that saving out of wages is insignificant, the total wage bill will be spent and will be, therefore, equal to the aggregate effective demand for consumption goods. The supply of consumption goods can be represented as OC (like the labour employment in the consumption goods industry) by the simple expedient of defining the unit of consumption goods as the amount produced by one man-hour of employment (or, equivalently, by defining the employment unit in terms of the man-hours required to produce one unit of consumption goods). The total demand for consumption goods can then be represented by OP×OC; WP×OC being equal to OW×DI and representing the demand originating from the wage bill of the investment goods industry. It follows then that OP is the market-clearing price that, if ruling, would equate the demand and supply of consumption goods.

Employment in the mechanised sector is limited by the

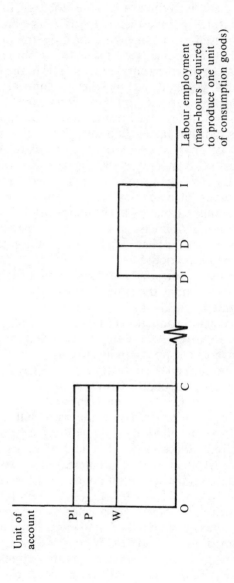

Figure 8.1

number of machines available and the technology underlying their use. Given the available technology, in order to increase the output of investment goods it is necessary to expand mechanised employment in the investment goods industry. But that, of course, requires spare machine capacity.

With the existing employment (DI) in the investment goods industry, enough machines, let us suppose, are produced to expand the capacity of both consumption and investment goods industries at a certain rate. To expand the investment goods industry faster than this, production within the investment sector must be reorganised so as to reduce the rate of expansion of machines suitable for the consumption goods industry to the benefit of machines suitable for further production of machines. So, if we exclude the possibility of initial unused capacity or the importation of foreign-produced machines, an increase in the rate of expansion of investment goods output implies a reduction in the rate of expansion of consumption goods.

Let us assume that, in its pursuit of the fastest possible industrialisation, the state increases the rate of expansion of investment goods to the maximum extent allowing only replacement production of machines used by the consumption goods industry. As a result, in the next period, employment in the investment goods industry can be, say, D^1I while in the consumption goods industry it remains OC. What is the effect of this on prices and real wages?

Money wages can be expected to be fully spent on consumption goods. Since the wage bill has now increased while the production of consumption goods has remained unaltered, prices must rise and real wages fall. Referring to Figure 8.1, the wage bill has increased by $OW \times D^1D$ and total spending on consumption goods has risen from $OP \times OC$ (= $OW \times (OC + DI)$ to $OP^1 \times OC$ (= $OW \times (OC + DI + DD^1)$)). The price of consumption goods produced by one hour's labour has gone up from OP to OP^1.[4] Since money wages have remained unchanged at OW, real wages have fallen.

The inflationary impact of the attempt to accelerate industrialisation can only be avoided if money wages are drastically cut, but the fall in real wages is, in any case, inevitable. It is this, of course, that is of primary political importance. A reduction in the standard of living of the industrial workers is likely to create among them dissatisfaction with the government. This will engender a dangerous social and political climate that any government, however firmly in control, will wish to avoid — the more so since the industrial working class usually provides the main political support for a socialist regime. In a less developed country, this class will inevitably be numerically small compared with the peasant class, but nevertheless of crucial political significance. It is likely to be better organised, urban rather than rural, and because of its importance in the development process and the socialist ideological emphasis on its vanguard social role, it will exert a political influence far beyond its size. In addition, for the development process to proceed reasonably smoothly, with a voluntary transfer of workers from the traditional to the mechanised sector, it is not unwise to sustain a differentially higher standard of living for the industrial workers. The absence of an economic incentive and reliance on compulsion for the transfer of labour from the village to the factory is beyond the contemplation of even the most powerful government. This, of course, means that the industrial working force is even economically a privileged section of the working population. It also means that even if a government is prepared to risk the dissatisfaction of the industrial workers, there are relatively narrow limits to the extent to which it can reduce their real wages in the effort to industrialise.

The implication of all this is that if industrialisation is to proceed at the fastest possible pace, it is necessary for the peasantry to carry a large share of the burden. The downward pressure on the industrial workers' standard of living must be relieved by supplies, especially of food, from the traditional sector. To analyse the conditions and political consequences of such a release and transfer of output from the numerous and relatively poor traditional to the mechanised sector, we must take into account the relations of production characterising traditional agriculture.

Let us begin by supposing that agricultural production is carried out by free peasant households owning small plots of

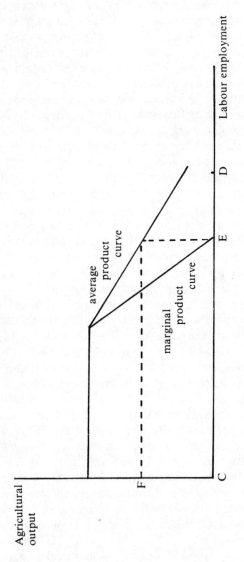

Figure 8.2

land. As an initial condition, this should produce the least political stress as it is clearly (among our alternatives) the most contiguous and in least opposition to a socialist regime. To develop the argument, we can refer to Figure 8.2, which illustrates the technical conditions of traditional agriculture.

We start by assuming the marginal product of labour to be zero; a condition which will be shown to be the least stressful for the initiation of the industrialisation process. With labour force (measured in man-hours) equal to CD, there is underemployment of ED. This should be understood as the shortfall of man-hours worked from the socially accepted norms. It is, in other words, the difference (= ED) between the hours that this labour force would have performed in the mechanised sector (CD) and the hours that it actually works in the traditional sector (CE). Given that production is carried out within households, it is not necessary that any member of a household is unemployed — they can all work less. So unemployment may be 'disguised' rather than open.

The average standard of living in the traditional sector is equal to the total product divided by the number of people it supports. We take this to be lower than that in the mechanised sector so that there is an economic incentive for peasants to seek mechanised employment (we shall see below what the problems are when this condition becomes difficult to satisfy). The standard of living can be represented in Figure 8.2 as total product divided by the whole labour force, (CF × CE)/CD, and this is less than the real income of workers in the mechanised sector.

If the differential is so large that peasants leave their villages in search of industrial work at a much faster rate than mechanised employment becomes available, a socialist government is likely to ban emigration to towns. This will be justified on the grounds of the harmful effects that such emigration has both on town and village communities. The absence of the appropriate urban infrastructure and housing, coupled with unemployment, creates the preconditions for urban slums and crime while back in the villages the rural exodus causes demoralisation and dislocation in the lives of those who remain behind. This 'external diseconomies' argument can be used to institute a system of controls on rural emigration. But then a system of permits discharged by the state machinery as a prerequisite to desirable urban employment can also be used as a means of increasing the state's social control over the peasantry. This effect, especially if the peasantry is initially hostile to the regime, may be judged so important that intentionally excessive differentials may be instituted (through taxation or fixing of relative prices) for purely political reasons.

The transfer of labour from the traditional to the investment goods industry of the mechanised sector is, as we have seen, accompanied by a downward pressure on the standard of living of the workers in that sector. What is the effect on the traditional sector?

As long as the transfer to the mechanised sector does not exceed ED man-hours, it would seem that the output of the traditional sector will remain unchanged. But this presupposes that the labour force staying in the traditional sector will increase the hours of work it performs to the level that is customary to the mechanised sector. If this happens, and it is by no means certain that the hours worked *will* increase to the required extent, then an unchanged output will be available to a smaller population and average consumption in the traditional sector will clearly rise. If hours worked increase less than this (or not at all), then the total output of the traditional sector will diminish though, of course, the remaining population will not, in any sense, be worse-off. But from the viewpoint of the state this latter possibility would be less than welcome. In the interest of rapid industrialisation, the state is, as we have seen, interested in relieving the downward pressure on the industrial workers' standard of living. For this purpose it must, in one way or another, tax away part of the traditional sector's output and secure it for the workers' consumption. It is clear that such an operation is politically easier the smaller the reduction in the consumption of the agricultural population that it entails. It is for this reason that an unchanged agricultural output associated with an outflow of labour to industry is a favourable (and a diminished output an unfavourable) outcome for the process of industrialisation.

Nevertheless, even in the best of cases, when output does not fall, the dilemma between the reduction in the standard of living of workers or peasants does not completely disappear. The new recruits to the mechanised sector must share the higher standard of living of the industrial workers; it follows that more than what they used to consume must be provided for them from the unchanged agricultural output, and consequently less will be left for the consumption of the remaining agricultural population. Obviously the dilemma becomes more pronounced if agricultural output in fact falls.

It is, therefore, clear that a transfer to the mechanised sector that exceeds ED man-hours and diminishes the traditional sector's output will intensify the problem. Every man-hour transfer from this point will reduce output and will require increasingly larger reduction in the consumption of the remaining agricultural population. Despite, then, the increase in productivity, as less labour-intensive techniques lead to an increase in the average product per man-hour, the drop in agricultural output makes increasingly more problematic the continuation of the industrialisation process. Inevitably, the day will come when consumption in the traditional sector cannot be squeezed further; alternatively, if such a ruthless policy towards the peasants is not pursued, the standard of living of industrial workers will rapidly fall to the level of the traditional sector and further voluntary transfer of labour will cease. In either case the technical limits of rapid industrial-isation will have been reached.[5]

But a host of problems will have arisen long before these technical limits have been reached. So far we have treated production in the traditional sector and diversion of its product to the benefit of the industrial workers as issues that are independent of each other. In fact, it is not unlikely that, faced with a policy that is hostile to their interests, the peasants will react by all means at their disposal including reduction in production below the levels that are technically feasible.

Let us briefly elaborate on this. The state can normally use, for its purposes, a variety of taxes or a system of regulated agricultural prices or some combination of these; its policy will be determined, among other things, by the extent to which production of the traditional sector is marketed or is consumed within the producing family units. Without entering into technical detail, it is clear that the state will have an interest in devising a policy that will, on the one hand, encourage the peasants to produce the maximum possible output and, on the other hand, to squeeze their level of consumption to as low a level as is feasible. It should be evident that such a policy is not an easy task either to devise or to implement, and that peasants are bound to react by withdrawing from the market as far as it is practicable for them to do so, by cheating and resisting the tax-collector as much as they can, and finally by reducing their effort and production. If the state then insists on breakneck industrialisation, it will attempt to control directly production in the traditional sector. It will thus be led to reorganisation of production with state-run collectives that impose work discipline and ensure that a substantial part of the output is siphoned off to the mechanised sector. Concurrently, it will attempt by various means (propaganda, prohibition of political activities, replacement of elected representatives by state employees, etc.) to increase the degree of social regimentation and control over the peasant communities. The success of these methods is doubtful as they immediately give rise to new problems created by the lack of a well-trained, public-spirited and conscientious bureaucracy. Inevitably, even with a relatively able civil service, the unpopular concentration of power in the hands of state-appointed local officials will soon lead to arbitrariness and corruption. In a longer perspective, the peasants' estrangement from and unwillingness to collaborate with the state will be a retarding factor at a later stage when new techniques become available and popular initiative is required for their learning, adoption and successful application. In addition, it will be impossible to contain these practices to the traditional sector only; when the majority of the population has to undergo such huge sacrifices in the interests of rapid industrialisation, it will be at least out of place to permit industrial democracy in the mechanised sector.Strikes and stoppages will be banned and there will be an effort to control fully whatever workers' organisations are allowed to operate. As a result, not only agriculture can be crippled in the future but, more importantly, the people as well as the state apparatus will be respectively conditioned to practices and will form attitudes that will make democratic processes impossible to operate for a long time in the future.

In conclusion, the price that has to be paid for industrial-isation to proceed at the fastest possible pace can be very heavy in terms of political freedom. If the development of partici-patory politics, political representation and democratic procedures is valued, as it should be in a socialist regime, then the process of industrialisation must be subjected to democratic control and not be allowed to dictate and compromise the development of democracy. But these concomitants of a rapid industrialisation policy may be of diminished importance in the context of widespread famine and misery. Then the immediate construction of the preconditions for the alleviation of misery may arguably be considered to take precedence over popular participation in political decision-making.

Our analysis and the ensuing conclusions are not materially affected under the alternative assumptions about agricultural relations of production. These will now be briefly considered. It can be argued that a free smallholding peasantry presents the least troublesome conditions for a socialist regime bent upon rapid industrialisation. It is to be expected that a rich peasantry or a feudal aristocracy will be, from the outset, opponents of a socialist regime. But their opposition will be of unequal strength and will assume a different form.

Let us first examine the feudal case.[6] In a country in which central government and administration are firmly established and in which religious, racial, linguistic and tribal differences are not pronounced, it is relatively easy to deal with the feudal elements. A radical land reform with distribution of feudal land to its cultivators will be a popular measure that will rally the peasantry to the side of the government and will probably create lasting goodwill for the regime. This will, in its turn, create a very important breathing space for the policy of rapid industrialisation as the sacrifices demanded from the peasantry will be tolerated at least for a while and certainly longer than in the case of a long-established free peasantry. Assuming, then, that central government (and, of course, the army) is firmly under the control of the socialist regime, it is possible that a feudal structure can be more propitious to rapid industrial-isation than not only a *kulak*-type peasantry but even a free, small peasantry.

On the other hand, the existence of religious, tribal or other differences when linked to a feudal (or semi-feudal) structure can present formidable opposition to a central government attempting to industrialise without regard for sectarian inter-ests. In these circumstances, a radical land reform without expropriation of the landlords and redistribution of the land may be a very risky operation that can even result in the downfall of the government and a drastic change of regime. This is because the landlords are not simply the owners of land to whom a tithe is paid but are also the religious or tribal leaders who, on this account, command the support of their people. In such a case, land reform not only may not find the peasantry on the side of the central government but may even be taken as an attack on the peasant community. This may particularly be so when the composition of the government is predominantly of a different tribal or religious denomination. In any case, it is highly unlikely that such traditional leadership will be adequately represented in an industrialising socialist government which has most probably emerged from within the army ranks. In such circumstances, land reform offers practically no advantage even if it is pushed through without loss of power. As long as the reform is seen as a defeat by the sectarian forces, the peasantry will be discontented and, especially when also faced by the strains and required sacrifices of rapid industrialisation, very likely rebellious. Such a situation, even with the certainty (which is of course quite an assumption) that revolts can be easily suppressed, is bound to have adverse effects on agricultural production and therefore also set back the industrialisation process.[7]

But it must not be thought that the obvious solution in such a case is for the government to forget land reform (however much it may ideologically be in favour of it) and to accept 'realistically' and accommodate the feudal elements in the interests of industrialisation. The process of industrialisation cannot fail to hurt feudal interests. The feudal tithe is usually a fixed proportion of the total product; as the population in the traditional sector is reduced and average product rises, total product and feudal income will inevitably fall.

Even if population growth is very fast and total product does not fall, the needs of the expanding body of industrial workers will dictate a tax or other policy that will divert to them a continuously increasing proportion of the product. Such a policy will have as its prime target the feudal income since there is a floor below which the peasants' consumption cannot be pushed. So inevitably the pursuit of rapid industrialisation will bring the government into a confrontation with feudal interests. The only choice that an industrialising government might be given is between having the confrontation sooner or having it later.

Let us now turn to the case of the *kulak*-type peasantry. The complement of this is the existence of landless agricultural workers and small land proprietors who work for a wage in the fields of the *kulaks* either wholly or for part of their working week. The greater the number of the agricultural workers, the lower will the wage tend to be and the larger the product and the incomes of the rich peasants. The total product, before the industrialisation policy begins, is less than the maximum possible since labour will not be hired beyond the point where the value of its marginal product falls below the wage. A situation of this kind implies a certain degree of commercialisation of production with the big owners interested in selling their product and making a money profit.

A policy of *rapid* industrialisation will not avoid coming into opposition with the interests of the commercial peasants. The tax and pricing policies necessary to divert the product for the payment of the new industrial workers will inevitably reduce the net incomes of the commercial peasants. Nevertheless, the complex of taxes, whether on goods they buy or goods they sell, is quite likely to have a regressive incidence (given the difficulties and probable inability of the civil service to administer a progressive income tax). As a result, the small proprietors may well be relatively worse affected and may have to carry the main burden of the industrialisation effort. It is even conceivable that, in their attempt to preserve their standard of consumption, they may increase their supply of wage labour and thus become even more dependent on the rich peasants. Whether the latter will find the wage they have to pay reduced or not will depend not only on the increased supply of wage labour (which will tend to reduce wages) but also on the rate of labour absorption in mechanised employment (which will tend to increase wages) and finally on the rate of population growth. In any case, inequalities are likely to increase and embarrass a 'socialist' government. In addition, dissatisfaction with the government will be widespread and resistance, in various forms, against the government and the tax-collectors will spread. Such acts will often be organised by the rich peasants who, due to their economic power and their position as village notables, will probably lead the resistance against the government. In a situation of this kind, it might be tempting for a determined government to attempt to deal with the resistance to its policies by smashing commercial farming. The *kulaks* will then be used as scapegoats and all the problems that the peasants are experiencing will be attributed to the 'capitalist', 'treasonous' and 'unpatriotic' activities of the commercial peasantry. By successfully shifting popular dissatisfaction with the hardships of rapid industrialisation and channelling them against the *kulaks*, the government can succeed not only in gaining a measure of respite but also in neutralising its political enemies. But to hold a balance in such matters is practically impossible and it can be argued that, once embarked on such a dangerous policy, Stalinist-type excesses become inevitable. The inhumanity thus entailed certainly outweighs any benefits that industrialisation may bring to future generations.

In conclusion, rapid industrialisation in this case is probably more difficult than in both cases previously considered. Unlike the case of the small, independent peasantry, an industrialising socialist government has here to face a class that is hostile to it right from the start and which is in a better position in terms of economic power and political consciousness to organise its opposition effectively. Again, unlike the case of feudalism, the *kulaks* are deeply involved in the process of production and are often the most enterprising, innovating and successful agricultural producers. They are therefore in a much stronger position to resist the government than feudal elements that are estranged from production.[8] Even a so-called Stalinist policy with no compunction for human suffering, and even intent on their extermination, has to deal with the ravages this would cause both on the volume of agricultural production in the short run, and on the general development of agriculture in a longer perspective.

POLITICAL PROBLEMS OF DEVELOPMENT UNDER A CAPITALIST REGIME

In contrast to the socialist regime previously considered, we shall take the capitalist regime to mean that the industrial means of production are predominantly privately-owned. In such a regime, most investment is carried out by private firms and industrialisation is the task of private enterprise. The role of the government is to provide the incentives and the appropriate environment for private enterprise to operate in. Even though the state may control certain firms or even sectors of the economy, this is done in aid of, or as a spur to, the private sector and it is not meant to endanger the principle of private enterprise.

It is clear that in such a context the government cannot directly determine the rate of industrialisation but can only indirectly influence the investment decisions in the private sector. It is also clear that in order to encourage industrial investment, it must create favourable profit prospects. There is therefore a series of measures which the government can take to improve the profitability of the private industrial sector. In this respect, the importance of the tax and subsidy structure (including the tariff structure) is quite obvious and has been often discussed in the development literature. But the effort to improve the gross profitability of private industry can be extended in other important directions. More specifically, there are two main areas of government action. The first has to do with the control of the labour force. If a trade union organisation is already in existence and operating effectively, an attempt will be made to reduce its power, while if such an organisation is non-existent its setting-up will be promoted. In both cases the objective is control of the workers' organis- ations,[9] in the pursuit of which all possibilities of the legal apparatus will be fully used. It is, of course, clear that a docile and controlled labour force, and especially one that has given up the right to strike without due notice and procedure, is an excellent precondition for the making of profit.

The second area of government action is in the domain of credit creation. Investment in industrial capacity will be given highly preferential treatment, and credit will be made available to industrial investors easily and at a low cost. If the banking system does not cooperate fully in the provision of cheap credit for industrial investment, the government will be tempted to nationalise, or find some other way to control the recalcitrant banks. Of course, the extent to which a capitalist government is prepared to move along this road depends on a number of factors, the most important of which is the structural configuration of political forces and the position within it of pro-business rival parties. A coalition government of the right will find it more difficult to pursue a policy of nationalisation than a strong one-party government that has no significant rival on its right. Other factors will be the cohesion of the banking interests, the support that the main industrialists afford them, and the strength and stand on this issue of the socialist opposition. As a result of these and other special factors that may be relevant in a specific context, national- isation of credit becomes an unlikely policy in a capitalist regime. Nevertheless, our point is that such a policy is in the logic of an industrialisation programme by private enterprise. After all, modern banking systems are, first, heavily regulated; second, they are not supposed to be motivated solely by the pursuit of profit; and, third, they are crucial in determining the conditions of profitability for the rest of the system. As long, therefore, as this is not a first step in the abolition of private property by a hostile government but an attempt to improve profitability and encourage investment by a government that is fully committed to private enterprise, nationalisation of credit is a measure of rationalisation that can greatly contribute to the better functioning and growth of a capitalist economy.

Supposing, then, that private investors are sufficiently motivated and are successfully increasing the productive capacity of the economy at a satisfactorily high rate, the government has to ensure that their buoyancy is kept intact and the problems arising out of rapid industrialisation are contained as far as possible. The main problem, of course, is the downward pressure on the consumption of the workers and the shifting of this burden from the workers in the mechanised sector to the traditional sector. This shifting, as we have seen, is necessary in order to maintain a continuous voluntary flow of labour from the backward to the mechanised sector and thus enable the industrialisation process to go on. An uninterrupted and adequate flow is more crucial here than in the socialist case because a lot hinges on the existence of a plentiful supply of labour for mechanised employment. In the absence of a plentiful supply of labour, money wages will certainly rise and real wages may well also rise; the labour force will, in any case, be more difficult to control; and, as a result, the profit expectations and confidence of private industry may be adversely affected. Such an occurrence will depress the level of investment and may require considerable time and effort on the part of the government to restore confidence and step up again the rate of growth. It is because of this reliance on the, often sensitive, expectations of profit that a capitalist government will be greatly concerned about the availability of plentiful labour. It will therefore be eager to encourage a flow of labour out of the traditional sector and loth to take active measures to stop it even when it has acquired excessive dimensions. This may be the most important reason why urban unemployment and shanty towns are more prevalent in countries industrialising under a capitalist than under a socialist regime.

It should be noted that shifting the burden of industrialisation on the traditional sector which contains the majority of the population is an extremely difficult task if the government must also win elections. There is therefore a recurrent, if not permanent, temptation for an industrialising government to use whatever means it has in order to postpone, rig or, if possible, dispose altogether of elections. On the other hand, an outright dictatorial regime is very risky for right-wing politicians because they inevitably have to rely for its establishment and perpetuation on the army, with the danger that the military will eventually fully take over. A delicate balance has therefore to be kept between developing the repressive police and military apparatus to intimidate the voting population into forced electoral victories, and holding the repressive apparatus in check so that it doesn't seize power for itself.

If a dictatorship is established, the problems faced are not, at first sight, dissimilar to the ones we examined with respect to a socialist regime. This is because the government can, to a large extent, ignore the displeasure of the working population who have, in the main, to shoulder the burden of the industrialisation effort. But in other respects a regime of this kind has considerably more difficulties. Such a regime has a smaller base of support among the population; it is grossly deficient in ideological power; and, as a rule, it can draw on a much restricted pool of talent. Also, and more importantly, it is dependent for the success of its industrialisation programme on private investment and, consequently, on the satisfaction of the demands made on it by private enterprise. In particular, the demand for luxury consumption goods on the part of private property owners cannot be eliminated or severely restricted. As a result, to achieve a given rate of industrialisation, it has to demand a greater sacrifice on the part of the workers and the traditional sector. Furthermore, this must be done in the face of large inequalities of income and consumption, and in the absence of ideological conviction and popular support. It is then inevitable that repression will mount and that the regime will find its options increasingly restricted. If it slackens the industrialisation effort or, alternatively, attempts directly to control the rate of investment, it will, in both cases, find its sole ally, the business class, turning against it and right-wing politicians, who until then tolerated it, joining the resistance. Short of confrontation with the domestic and international business interests, for which it is generally ill-equipped, its only option is increasing repression in the pursuit of industrialisation. Such a regime is therefore, in a sense, a servant of business interests and often a dispensable one at that. In any case, the difficulties it has to meet are greater, and its chances of successfully keeping on a course of rapid industrialisation are considerably slimmer than those of a socialist regime.

It is now time to consider capitalist industrialisation under parliamentary rule. We shall examine the different types of obstacle and social strain (which, by assumption, do not reach the point of abandoning parliamentary rule) that accompany the process of industrialisation under different relations of production in the traditional sector. We begin then with the case of the free smallholding peasantry.

A smallholding peasantry can be given to subsistence farming or be part of a larger, even international, commercial network. The historical origin of such peasantry is of importance here. If it owes its existence to a land reform that has broken up feudal estates and has imposed limits on the size of land owned by any one family, it is more likely to be commercially-oriented than if it has persisted in this form for a long time. In both cases, a capitalist state will attempt to develop an orientation of production towards the market and extend monetisation of economic relations. The speed and success of this will, of course, depend on the historical experience and the actual state of the particular peasant society.

The means by which monetisation is promoted in a subsistence farming setting will include taxes payable in money and the introduction of consumption goods, such as cheap transistor radios and bicycles, which can only be obtained with money. By such stick-and-carrot methods production will be directed to the market. The intended results are (a) that the population becomes accustomed to the mentality of capitalist production; (b) that peasant production increases to the maximum, within its given technical possibilities, as the 'demonstration effect' of the new goods increases the consumption needs of peasants; and (c) peasants become specialised in order to increase their monetary income and, at the same time, they become dependent on the market even for their customary consumption. All these facilitate the industrialisation effort in that the 'pull' of mechanised, urban employment is augmented while the population remaining behind keeps its efforts and production as high as possible. In addition, once the peasantry becomes committed to production for the market, it becomes easier to effect the transfer of part of their produce to workers in mechanised employment by manipulating the relative prices of the mechanised and traditional sector's produce. This has the advantage over taxation that it is not universally understood as the government's doing and, therefore, the government can, to a considerable extent, evade the responsibility for it and thus avoid losing votes.

Once peasant production becomes integrated within the market economy, the rate of industrialisation can become quite rapid. A smallholding peasantry is unlikely to be effective in organising to defend itself against a capitalist, industrialising state. Its mode of production promotes an individualist (or rather 'individual family') outlook which, when linked to a regionalist chauvinism that, even in the unlikely case that it does not historically exist, can be promoted and cultivated by the state, makes its organising a broad and effective base quite improbable. In addition, their property in land tends to make them conservative and tie them to non-socialist politics. As a result, in view of their particular ideological blockages which make difficult any coherent political action, they are more likely to take the road of least resistance and channel their energy into competing among themselves for the fastest migration to the urban centres. In consequence, the peasant villages and way of life will suffer great ravages, but labour for mechanised employment will be plentiful and the transfer of produce from the traditional to the mechanised sector will proceed without serious opposition.

Agricultural production, characterised by large holdings and hiring of agricultural labourers, has the advantage over the previous case that production for the market and market relations exist right from the start. On the other hand, the disadvantages may well be more serious. First, the initial output will be, as we have seen, smaller than the maximum and not larger than the point where marginal revenue product of labour is equal to the money wage. Second, big farmers will be an important political force and their interests will have to be taken into account. In fact, it is unlikely that an industrialising government will be able to stay in power without their support. Their consent will have to be bought with measures such as protection against foreign competition, various tax allowances, and other prerogatives that result in a lower level of consumption for the working population and, consequently, a lower feasible rate of industrialisation. Nevertheless, at a larger stage of capitalist industrialisation, this form of agricultural organisation may prove, because of the large size of farms that is amenable to mechanisation, the most efficient and technologically progressive. Finally, another disadvantage from the viewpoint of a capitalist government is that the landless workers will be a radical element attracted to socialist politics. Their large number can give a strong impetus to the building-up of a communist party which can then act as a pole of attraction and thus further facilitate organisation and recruitment among the — for a considerable period — less numerous ranks of workers in mechanised employment.

So far we have examined the implications that various combinations of political regimes and relations of production in agriculture have for rapid industrialisation, without enquiring into the plausibility of an industrialising government. Our basic assumption, that the government wishes to industrialise rapidly, on which our analysis is built, is only a device in order successfully to abstract from all sorts of economic and sociopolitical interdependencies that, though of secondary importance at this level of abstraction, can prove to be crucial under particular historical circumstances. It was considered that the complex interdependency of economic and socio-political factors could be fruitfully broken at this point to provide a handle for our understanding, because though this particular condition (an industrialising government) has a determining influence on the other considered variables, it is itself relatively independent of them. It always determines them without being in most cases determined by them. That it is relatively independent is an empirical statement based on post-war historical experience. Since the war, we have witnessed attempts at industrialisation under all kinds of political and socioeconomic conditions. The wish, if not the will, to industrialise seems to be universal under whatever regime. This is the reason we feel that our procedure in making it the pivotal assumption and treating it as an independent variable is analytically justifiable.

It is, of course, not implied that empirical statements are not in need of theoretical explanation. It is obvious that they are, and such a theoretical explanation will, in fact, define the limits of validity of the present analysis. But such a task lies outside the scope of this work.[10] All that is hoped for here is that, given the historical conjuncture of the present and the recent past, the choice of the basic assumption (or pivotal independent variable) is analytically appropriate for the elucidation of some important economic and sociopolitical interdependencies in this period.

This methodological clarification could have waited until the end if it was not felt that in the remainder of this chapter the cases considered require both a consciousness of the crucial importance of this assumption and a critical stand towards it. This will become apparent in the remaining capitalist case to be considered, and in the examination of Kalecki's concept of the 'intermediate regime'.

The existence of feudal relations of production in agriculture is a particularly unfavourable circumstance for the programme of rapid industrialisation. The political power of the feudal class cannot fail to be substantial, and it will also not fail to be used against the industrialising government. Industrialisation will harm the feudal class economically, by reducing both its gross and net income, and also politically, by removing the labour force from the land and thus reducing feudal power and influence. A political compromise is difficult to strike as long as rapid industrialisation is the aim. Either the government will be dominated by the feudalist interests and rapid industrialisation will be abandoned, or the feudalist elements will have to be politically neutralised.

We have seen that in the socialist case there are circumstances when a radical land reform can both neutralise the feudal class and gain support for the regime among the peasants. The same is true for a capitalist regime but, of course, the determination for such a step becomes much more problematic for a government that probably depends politically on feudal support. But even if the determination exists, it is not clear that the attempt will be successful; the feudal structure may prove too strong for the reforming capitalist wing of the government. This is, therefore, a case when questioning of the plausibility of the industrialising government assumption becomes perfectly in order.

In the absence of a political defeat of the feudal class, industrialisation is possible only if the feudal class itself becomes divided and raises within its own fold the captains of industry and the bulk of the emergent business entrepreneurs. It is only such a transformation of the dominent class and its gradual adoption of capitalist, commercial values that can provide the basis for a state-supported policy of industrialisation.[11] The necessary equilibrium between the landed and the newly-emergent industrial interests of the class during the industrialisation period is likely to be fragile and necessitate the establishment, as arbiter and regulator, of a strong and — in the absence of effective opposition — possibly dictatorial state.[12]

THE 'INTERMEDIATE REGIME' AND DEVELOPMENT PROSPECTS

The notion of the 'intermediate regime' is due to Kalecki, who introduced it to account for what he considered to be a new historical phenomenon.[13] An 'intermediate regime' is neither strictly capitalist nor socialist, but is 'intermediate' in a number of ways. First, it is intermediate between capitalist and socialism in that though the state owns a large part of the means of production and is responsible for a great part of investment, private ownership of industrial means of production and the institution of private property is accepted by the state and can still be significant. Second, it represents the interests of lower-middle class and rich or medium-rich peasants, that is the strata that are intermediate between the upper classes which are the main owners of the means of production (big business and the remnants of feudalism) and the lower classes (poor peasants, agricultural workers and the urban poor). Finally, it is intermediate between the western and the Soviet blocs, in that it tends to be neutral and non-aligned. This last characteristic is a counterpart of the other two at the international level but it is not fundamental in the way that the other two are. So, in essence, the 'intermediate regime' is the rule of the lower-middle class through state capitalism.

It may be argued that this typology is somewhat vague and does not provide sufficiently refined criteria for differentiating among actual regimes. Indeed, it can be argued that it is too widely embracing and subsumes a variety of (especially capitalist) economies under the 'intermediate regime' label. Since nearly all economies are characterised by a combination of private and state ownership of the means of production, and the lower-middle class is, as a rule, highly represented in the state apparatus, very few countries can be immediately excluded from the intermediate regime classification. But Kalecki goes further than this and, in introducing the concept, he also provides the conditions for its historical genesis as well as the conditions for its survival or reproduction. Admittedly, this is not done in a systematic fashion and, in Kalecki's extremely laconic writing, it often tends to be implicit rather than explicit. In any case, it is worth examining the potential of the concept even if this carried us beyond a strictly textual interpretation of Kalecki's writings.[14]

The basic condition for the emergence of the intermediate regime is that at the time of a country's independence there is no developed native capitalist class. This is a necessary but clearly not a sufficient condition. Though it may be true that in the process of political emancipation — especially if this is not accompanied by armed struggle — representatives of the lower-middle class rise in a way naturally to power, overall power and political dominance can still rest with the land-owning, feudal class. Therefore, for an intermediate regime to emerge it must be both that there is no developed native capitalist class and that either the feudal class is insignificant or it is politically divided and ineffectual. This condition has been met for many countries at the time of their independence since the second world war. Nevertheless intermediate regimes can be established even in countries that became independent long ago and where a native capitalist class did not develop (Kalecki and Kula, 1976). In such a case, a *coup* or revolution, involving the army usually in alliance with other nationalist forces, can bring into being an intermediate regime. In short, an intermediate regime is the rule of the lower-middle class through its control of the state machinery: control that became possible because of the economic weakness of the traditional ruling class and which is used both to weaken this class even further and to keep the working class and the rural proletariat politically unorganised and ineffectual.

The important question is whether the rule of the lower-middle class through state capitalism can survive once established. Apart from the near non-existence of the native capitalist class and the weakness of the feudal class that make an intermediate regime possible, there are two favourable recent developments. Both of these tend to make the external environment more propitious for the appearance and survival of the regime. The first is that the state has assumed an increasingly large role in the economies of the developed capitalist countries.[15] As a result, their opposition to regimes that, in this respect, seem to resemble them has somewhat weakened. Second, the possibility of obtaining aid and credit from socialist countries makes dependence on developed capitalist countries less necessary for industrialisation. It is thus possible to reduce to a considerable degree political and economic pressure from foreign capitalist interests.

But the historical emergence of international conditions that are not inimical to its existence is not enough for the intermediate regime to survive. For the lower-middle class to keep in power, it must (a) Achieve not only political but also economic emancipation, i.e. gain a measure of independence from foreign capital. (b) Carry out a land reform. (c) Assume continuous economic growth. It is clear that the first two requirements are aimed at neutralising its opponents (*comprador* and feudal elements) and consolidating its victory. They are also important as preconditions for the third requirement. Economic growth is necessary in order to satisfy, above all, the aspirations of the lower-middle class. After all, it is the lack of rapid growth prospects under the traditional ruling class and the promise of such growth by the lower-middle class state that legitimises the emergence of the intermediate regime.

The pursuit and achievement of economic growth seem therefore, to provide the main ideological rationale of the intermediate regime. The pursuit of growth provides direction and cements together the various ideological tendencies of the lower-middle class, while the achievement of growth provides the economic and political legitimation of its rule. At a more concrete level, it also makes possible the expansion of the state machinery and the provision of jobs, career opportunities, and economic and social influence to the lower-middle class. These seem to be necessary conditions for the cohesion of the state personnel and for the identification of the lower-middle class with the state apparatus. It should be noted that it is the state apparatus that provides both the focus for lower-middle class's identity as a class and the instrument for its rule.

Are these requirements sufficient for the lower-middle class to keep in power? For an answer to this question one must consider the strength of the intermediate regime's opponents. These are, from above, the upper middle class allied with foreign capital and the feudal landowners and, from below, the small landholders and landless peasants, as well as the poor urban population. The former, though weak, are the main opponents, at least in the immediate period following the establishment of the regime, and the two first policies are meant to weaken them even further. The latter will be prevented, as far as possible, from creating the organisations that will politically represent them. But the 'native' (in contrast to the *comprador*) elements of the middle class will not necessarily come into conflict with the intermediate regime. On the contrary, given their lack of economic and political muscle (which disqualified them as challengers to the regime's power) and the dearth of managerial and entrepreneurial talent, they may even be relied upon in the effort for development. They can be used for development purposes in a variety of ways: as an alternative to the state machinery in various projects for which they may have superior expertise; as a competitive means of shaking up and improving the efficiency of the state bureaucracy, as a means of drawing in certain types of private foreign investment; and, finally, as a means of manoeuvering and signalling the regime's international position between the western and Soviet blocs.[16] On the other hand, by being used in these ways, they may grow in influence and strength to the point of eventually undermining the regime. Reliance on this class in the strategy of economic development could easily result in the repetition of a well-known historical pattern — the final submission of the lower-middle class to the interests of big business. It follows that the attitude of the intermediate regime towards the native upper-middle class is bound to be ambivalent: this class can be useful in the development effort and is worth preserving but it must always be kept under control and be economically ultimately dependent on the state.

Is economic development possible under an intermediate regime? What are the political and social strains created by a programme of rapid industrialisation? Or, to put it somewhat differently, is an intermediate regime a *stable* regime?

We have already argued that development is desirable in that it provides a focal point for the diverse ideological tendencies of the lower-middle class and it creates the potential for the further expansion and influence of the state apparatus which is necessary for the cohesion of the state personnel and the identification of the lower-middle class with the state machine. But does this mean that development is indispensable for an intermediate regime? It is possible to imagine circumstances in which both these functions of development are realised in its absence. For example, nationalism can replace development as the ideological focal point,[17] while the existence of natural wealth in the form of oil or some other asset can provide the revenue for the expansion of the state apparatus. Even the existence of the first alone, if it results in placing the society on a war footing, can be sufficient since it extends the influence and importance of the state apparatus. In any case, even if economic development is not a strictly necessary condition for the survival of the intermediate regime,[18] the achievement of 'continuous economic growth' clearly contributes considerably to its reproduction.

Let us now return to the question of the likelihood of such growth.

A programme of rapid industrialisation will almost certainly strain the alliance between the lower-middle class and the rich or medium-rich peasants. The required shift of resources (both product and labour) from the traditional to the mechanised sector is bound to affect adversely the wealthy peasants. Prices of agricultural products will have to be controlled, or wealthy peasants heavily taxed, for a transfer of product to the mechanised sector to be effected. In this game the wealthy peasants have a strong hand. First, they can withdraw their political support from the intermediate regime which, in certain circumstances, can seriously endanger its survival; and, second, they can react by cutting back their output and, in this way, reduce the potential rate of development and frustrate the rapid industrialisation effort.

The state has therefore, in such circumstances, to follow policies that will take into consideration the interests of the wealthy peasants and it must, right from the start, prudently abandon any plans for break-neck industrialisation. In addition, the demands — on the part of the lower-middle class — for the rapid creation of jobs in the state sector and expansion of the state apparatus will result in a considerable loss of labour power to potential productive employment and consequent reduction in output. It is also possible that the overmanned state apparatus will cause further setbacks to production and the rate of industrialisation through inefficiency and corruption.

In conclusion, it would seem that the achievement of 'continuous economic growth' at a rapid enough rate is a problematic task for an intermediate regime. In view of the above constraints and pressures (and these may be compounded by international geopolitical considerations and/or nationalist/chauvinist aspirations), it is to be expected that the industrialisation policy will not be stable and clearly-defined, but will be characterised by spasmodic starts and reverses. The temptation to use the upper-middle class and even, to a certain degree, foreign capital is understandable in periods when the other constraints are biting. Nevertheless, such a policy could make it more likely that the balancing act among the different interests will later become even more difficult and may even end in the final submission of the lower-middle class to the interests of big business. In that case the intermediate regime will have been only a brief, transitional phenomenon: an intermediate stage in the passage from colonial status to peripheral capitalism.

CONCLUSION

There are two lessons to be drawn from the above analysis. First, the importance of the political factors in the development process cannot be overstated and any analytical approach to development must take them into account. Second, rapid industrialisation is a rare and unlikely phenomenon under any political regime, because of the sociopolitical stresses that it inevitably gives rise to. It follows that a determined policy of rapid industrialisation should not be lightly embarked upon as it entails huge risks both for parliamentary regimes, which may not survive the experiment, and for socialist ones, which may abort their humanist aspirations and ideals. It is this consideration, rather than technical, economic or other deficiencies, which may explain why programmes of rapid industrialisation, though often proudly announced, are rarely pursued with vigour to a successful end.

NOTES

*   A version of this chapter was presented at the Annual Conference of the Association of Polytechnic Teachers in Economics, Sheffield City Polytechnic, April 1977.

1   A selection of Kalecki's writings on development is published in English (see Kalecki, 1976a).

2   Thus both the objective and the approach followed are quite different from Papandreou (1966). Papandreou's concern is with both positive and normative issues relating to the political aspects of plan formulation and implementation, and he neither makes use of an explicit model nor does he make 'relations of production' a central analytical category.

3   A strong argument can be made for using instead a term such as 'state capitalism' and reserving the term 'socialism' to signify a lot more beyond the form of ownership of the means of production. According to this view, socialism implies wide popular participation at all levels of economic and political decision-making and is associated with the elimination of all class distinctions and the full development of the means of production. Such a view of socialism presupposes a mature, industrialised economy and bears little relationship to the developing countries that call themselves socialist. For this reason, and also because it can be reasonably maintained that such socialism has never yet existed, we have decided not to make this distinction here though, undoubtedly, for different theoretical purposes a more complex definition of socialism (together with concepts such as state capitalism) may well be more appropriate.

4   This refers to the market-clearing price. If the state does not raise prices to OP^1, there will be scarcities, and the workers will not be able to spend all their income.

5   Foreign aid could, of course, prolong this process but this is not something a country can count on, and its scope is usually limited. It must not be forgotten that the whole analysis abstracts from technical progress which, in any case, is unlikely in the traditional sector that is defined by the absence of machinery.

6   It should be made clear at this point that we are not envisaging a feudal system in which central government is non-existent or so weak as to be ineffectual. In the contemporary world, the notion of a nation-state is inseparable from that of an operative central government. Feudal elements can, in certain circumstances, present a challenge to the cohesion of the nation-state and the power of central government but, in most relevant cases, feudal relations of production that continue in

agriculture are not in a position to dispute the political predominance of central government.

7 It should be noted that the (relatively) most favourable context for the government is provided by a low rate of population growth that results in an increased average product. In such an event, there is a decline in the economic power of feudal landlords and an increasing independence of the peasants. But this is probably a minor consideration compared with the weight of the traditional allegiance to the landlords as religious or tribal leaders.

8 We have seen that when a feudal structure is in conjunction with other deeply-rooted dividing forces, rapid industrialisation may become, in feudal case also, a very dangerous and difficult undertaking.

9 In the previously examined socialist case, it is taken for granted that workers' organisations will be state-controlled. It is also easier to achieve this given the pervasive involvement of the state with production and the ideological presentation of the state machine as a 'workers' state'.

10 A first step in this direction could be made by considering Gerschenkron's (1962, 1968) hypothesis (arising out of his historical study of European nineteenth-century industrialisation) according to which the greater the degree of relative backwardness, the greater are the intensity of the industrialisation 'spurt', the concentration on producers' goods, the pressure on the levels of consumption, and the role of the state in the industrialisation effort. It could be conjectured that the relative backwardness of non-industrial countries after the second world war made it necessary for the state to assume the leading role and responsibility for the huge task of rapid industrialisation. The degree of relative backwardness would then become the key explanatory variable in the fashion of Gerschenkron.

11 Given the long-established dominance of the feudal class and the absence of serious opposition from a new and separately constituted capitalist class, the reasons for such a transformation are more likely to be mainly external, relating to the international position and challenges facing this class, than arising from internal pressures.

12 The view that fascist regimes tend to arise out of industrialisation led by the landed class is supported by Moore's (1966) comparative study of six countries.

13 See Kalecki (1976b) and Kalecki and Kula (1976). Both papers are reprinted in Kalecki (1976a). A detailed treatment of industrialisation in the intermediate regime, based on this paper, can be found in Skouras (1978a and b).

14 It should be noted that there are only two papers on this topic in

English. There may well be other references or thoughts on intermediate regimes in his much more numerous Polish writings (for a full bibliography, see Feiwell, 1975).

15   It may be argued that, even in developed capitalist countries, the growth of state capitalism is a victory for the lower-middle class. Nevertheless, the role of the state in advanced capitalism is a contentious issue and, in any case, it is clear that in these societies the rise of the lower-middle class is neither due to the economic and political weakness of the capitalist and working classes nor is the 'lower-middle class state' directed against the economic interests and political representation of these classes.

16   The delicate act of balancing between the two blocs which often requires a move in the one direction followed by another, seemingly contradictory, one in the opposite direction, is not only necessary for independence from foreign interests, and thus for the survival of the regime, but is also functional in extracting aid.

17   It should be noted that nationalism/chauvinism can be used as an ideological rallying force by all kinds of regimes, but it is particularly well suited to lower-middle class regimes. The reason is that both capitalist and socialist ideology are relatively well formed and contain considerable internationalist undercurrents. On the contrary, lower-middle class ideology reflects, in its diffuseness and lack of definite orientation, the absence of clearly distinct economic or material class interests. It is only through the state, and in circumstances in which the state operates in a ruling-class vacuum, that the identity of the lower-middle class is constituted and merged with that of the state. Thus, the ideology of this class tends to be one (like nationalism) that involves the state and can best be expressed and pursued through the state apparatus.

18   It can be argued that the circumstances above are, in most cases, beyond the full control of any regime and are not properly speaking part of any planned action necessary for the survival and reproduction of the 'intermediate regime'. But this objection relies for its validity on the questionable assumption that the regime has full, or at least considerably greater, control over the achievement of 'continuous economic growth'.

Bibliography

Andersen, L.C. and Jordan, J.L. (1968), 'Monetary and fiscal actions: a test of their relative importance in economic stabilization', *Federal Reserve Bank of St Louis* (Monthly Review November).

Appelbaum, E. (1979), 'The labour market', in Eichner, A.S. (ed.), *A Guide to Post-Keynesian Economics* (Macmillan: London).

Arestis, P. (1979), 'The "crowding-out" of private expenditure by fiscal actions: an empirical investigation', *Public Finance (September)*.

Arestis, P. and Hadjimatheou, G. (1982), 'The determinants of the average propensity to consume in the UK', *Applied Economics* (April).

Arestis, P. and Karakitsos, E. (1980), 'Fiscal actions, optimal control and "crowding-out" within the NIESR model', *Greek Economic Review* (December).

Arestis, P. and Karakitsos, E. (1982), 'Crowding-out in the UK within an optimal control framework', *Journal of Public Policy* (Vol. 2, No. 1).

Arrow, K. and Hahn, F.H. (1971), *General Competitive Analysis* (Holder Day: San Francisco).

Artis, M.J. (1978), 'Fiscal policy and crowding-out', in Posner, M. (ed.), *Demand Management* (Heinemann: London).

Artis, M.J. and Miller, M. (1979), 'Inflation, real wages and the terms of trade', in Bowers, J.K. (ed.), *Inflation, Development and Integration – Essays in Honour of A.J.Brown* (Leeds University Press: Leeds).

Artis, M.J. and Nobay, A.R. (1969), 'Two aspects of the monetary debate', *National Institute Economic Review* (August).

Asimakopulos, A. (1978), 'The non-comparability of criteria for the choice of optimal technique', *Australian Economic Papers* (June).

Asimakopulos, A. (1980-81), 'Themes in a post Keynesian theory of income distribution', *Journal of Post Keynesian Economics* (Winter).

Asimakopulos, A. and Burbidge, J.B. (1974), 'The short-period incidence of taxation', *Economic Journal* (June).

Atkinson, A.B. and Stiglitz, J.E. (1980), *Lectures on Public Economics* (McGraw-Hill: Maidenhead).

Bacon, R. and Eltis, W.A. (1976), *Britain's economic problem: too few producers* (Macmillan: London).

Bacon, R. and Eltis, W.A. (1979), 'The measurement of the growth of non-market sector and its influence: a reply to Hadijmatheou and Skouras', *Economic Journal* (June).

Ball, R.J. (1964), *Inflation and the theory of money* (Allen & Unwin: London).

Ball, R.J., Burns, T. and Miller, G.W. (1975), 'Preliminary simulations with the London Business School macroeconomic model', in Renton, G.A. (ed.), *Modelling the economy* (Heinemann: London).

Ball, R.J., Burns, T. and Warburton, P.J. (1979), 'The London Business School model of the UK economy: an exercise in international monetarism', in Ormerod, P. (ed.), *Economic Modelling* (Heinemann: London).

Baran, P.A. and Sweezy, P.M. (1966) *Monopoly Capital* (Penguin: Harmondsworth).

Barro, R. (1974), 'Are government bonds net wealth?', *Journal of Political Economy* (November/December).

Barro, R. and Grossman, H. (1976), *Money, Employment and Inflation* (Cambridge University Press: Cambridge).

Bhaduri, A. and Robinson, J. (1980), 'Accumulation and exploitation: an analysis in the tradition of Marx, Sraffa and Kalecki', Cambridge Journal of Economics (June).

Bisham, J.A. (1975), 'Appendix: The NIESR model and its behaviour', in Renton, G.A. (ed.), *Modelling the Economy* (Heinemann: London).

Blackaby, F. (ed.) (1979), *British Economic Policy, 1960–74* (Cambridge University Press: Cambridge).

Blaug, M. (1976), 'Kuhn versus Lakatos on paradigms versus research programmes in the history of economic thought', in Latsis, S. (ed.), *Method and Appraisal in Economics* (Cambridge University Press: Cambridge).

Blinder, A.S. and Solow, R.M. (1973), 'Does fiscal policy matter?', Journal of Public Economics (November).

Blinder, A.S. and Solow, R.M. (1974), 'Analytical foundation of fiscal policy', in Blinder, A.S. *et al.*, *The Economics of Public Finance* (Brookings Institution: Washington, DC).

Blinder, A.S. and Solow, R.M. (1976a), 'Does fiscal policy matter?' A correction', *Journal of Public Economics* (January/February).

Blinder, A.S. and Solow, R.M. (1976b), 'Does fiscal policy still matter? A reply', *Journal of Monetary Economics* (November).

Board of Governors of the Federal Reserve System (1976), *Flow of Funds Accounts 1946–1975* (Washington, December).

Breton, A. (1974), *The Economic Theory of Representative Government* (Macmillan: London).

Bronfrebrenner, M. (1971), *Income Distribution Theory* (Macmillan: London).

Brunner, K. and Meltzer, A.H. (1968), 'Liquidity traps for money, bank credit and interest rates', *Journal of Political Economy* (February).

Brunner, K. and Meltzer, A.H. (1972), 'Money debt and economic activity', *Journal of Political Economy* (September).

Brunner, K. and Meltzer, A.H. (1976), 'An aggregative theory for a closed economy', in Stein, J.L. (ed.), *Monetarism* (North-Holland: Amsterdam).

Brus, W. (1977), 'Kalecki's economics of socialism', *Oxford Bulletin of Economics and Statistics* (February).

Buiter, W.H. (1977a), 'Crowding-out and the effectiveness of fiscal policy', *Journal of Public Economics* (June).

Buiter, W.H. (1977b), 'Short-run and long-run disequilibrium in dynamic macromodels', *Southern Economic Journal* (July).

Bullock, P. and Yaffe, D. (1975), 'Inflation, the crisis and the post-war boom', *Revolutionary Communist* (November).

Burbidge, J.B. (1979), 'The international dimension', in Eichner, A.S. (ed.), *A Guide to Post-Keynesian Economics* (Macmillan: London).

Butkiewicz, J.L. (1979), 'Outside wealth, the demand for money and the crowding-out effect', *Journal of Monetary Economics* (April).

Carley, M. (1980), *Rational Techniques in Policy Analysis* (Heinemann Educational Press: London).

Carlson, K.M. (1978), 'Does the St Louis equation now believe in fiscal policy?', *Federal Reserve Bank of St Louis* (Monthly Review, December).

Carlson, K.M. and Spencer, R.W. (1975), 'Crowding-out and its critics', *Federal Reserve Bank of St Louis* (Monthly Review, December).

Cebula, R.J. (1978), 'An empirical analysis of the "crowding-out" effect of fiscal policy in the United States and Canada, *Kyklos* (Vol. 31, Fasc. 3).

Cebula, R.J. and Curran, C. (1978), 'Giffen goods, IS curves and macroeconomic stability: a comment', *Metroeconomica* (January/December).

Chick, V. (1973), *The Theory of Monetary Policy* (Grays–Mills: London).

Chick, V. (1977), *The Theory of Monetary Policy*, revised edition (Basil Blackwell: Oxford); first edition (Gray-Mills: London, 1973).

Chick, V. (1978), 'The nature of the Keynesian revolution: a reassessment', *Australian Economic Papers* (June).

Choudhry, N.N. (1976), 'Integration of fiscal and monetary sectors in econometric models: a survey of theoretical issues and empirical findings', *International Monetary Fund, Staff Papers* (July).

Christ, C. (1968), 'A simple macroeconomic model with a government budge restraint', *Journal of Political Economy* (January).

Christ, C. (1978), 'Some dynamic theory of macroeconomic policy effects on income and prices under the government budget restraint', *Journal of Monetary Economics* (January).

Clower, R.W. (1965), 'The Keynesian counter-revolution: a theoretical appraisal', in Hahn, F. and Brechling, F. (eds), *The Theory of Interest Rates* (Macmillan: London).

Clower, R.W. (1969), 'Introduction', in Clower, R.W. (ed.), *Monetary Theory* (Penguin: Harmondsworth).

Clower, R.W. (1970), 'Is there an optimal money supply?' *Journal of Finance* (May).

Cornwall, J. (1972), *Growth and Stability in a Mature Economy* (Wiley: London).

Cornwall, J. (1978), *Modern Capitalism: Its Growth and Transformation* (St Martin Press: London).

Corrigan, E.G. (1970), 'The measurement and importance of fiscal policy changes', *Federal Reserve Bank of New York* (Monthly Review, June).

Council of Economic Advisers (1974), 'The full employment surplus', in Smith, W.L. and Teigen, R.L. (eds), *Readings in Money, National Income and Stabilization Policy*, third edition (R.D. Irwin: Homewood, Illinois).

Coutts, K., Godley, W.A.H. and Nordhaus, W. (1978), *Industrial Pricing in the United Kingdom* (Cambridge University Press: Cambridge).

Cowling, K. (1981), 'Oligopoly, distribution and the rate of profit', *European Economic Review* (February).

Cowling, K. (1982), *Monopoly Capitalism* (Macmillan: London).

Cripps, F. and Godley, W.A.H. (1976), 'A formal analysis of the

Cambridge Economic Policy Group model', *Economica* (November).

Crouch, C. (ed.) (1979), 'The state capital and liberal democracy', in Crouch, C. (ed.), *State and Economy* (Croom Helm: London).

Currie, D.A. (1978), 'Macroeconomic policy and government financing', in Artis, M.J. and Nobay, A.R. (eds), *Contemporary Economic Analysis, Vol. 1* (Croom Helm: London).

Currie, D.A. (1981), 'Monetary and fiscal policy and the crowding-out issue', in Artis, M.J. and Miller, M.H. (eds), *Essays in Fiscal and Monetary Policy* (Oxford University Press: Oxford).

Darby, M.R. (1976), 'Comments on Modigliani and Ando', in Stein, J.L. (ed.), *Monetarism* (North-Holland: Amsterdam).

David, P.A. and Scalding, J.L. (1975), 'Private savings: ultra-rationality, aggregation and "Dennison's Law"', *Journal of Political Economy* (Vol. 82, No. 2).

Davidson, J.E.H., Hendry, D.F., Srba, F. and Yeo, S. (1978), 'Econometric modelling of the aggregate time-series relationship between consumers' expenditure and income in the United Kingdom', *Economic Journal* (December).

Davidson, P. (1965), 'Keynes' finance motive', *Oxford Economic Papers* (March).

Davidson, P. (1967), 'The importance of the demand for finance', *Oxford Economic Papers* (July).

Davidson, P. (1978), *Money and the Real World*, second edition (Macmillan: London).

Davidson, P. (1980), 'Post Keynesian economics', *The Public Interest* (special issue).

Davidson, P. (1981), 'Post Keynesian economics', in Bell, D. and Kristol, I. (eds), *The Crisis in Economic Theory* (Basic Books: New York).

Davies, R.G. (1969), 'How much does money matter? A look at some recent evidence', *Federal Reserve Bank of New York* (Monthly Review, June).

de Cecco, M. (1977), 'The last of the Romans', in Skidelsky, R., *The End of the Keynesian Era* (Macmillan: London).

DeLeeuw, F. and Kalchbrenner, J. (1969), 'Monetary and fiscal actions: a test of their relative importance in economic stabilization: a comment', *Federal Reserve Bank of St Louis*, (Monthly Review, April).

Desai, M. (1981), *Testing Monetarism* (Pinter: London).

Domar, E.D. (1947), 'Expansion and exmployment', *American Economic Review* (March).

Easlea, B. (1973), *Liberation and the Aims of Science* (Chatto & Windus: London).

Eatwell, J. (1979), 'Theories of value, output and employment', *Thames Papers in Political Economy* (Summer).

Economist (1981), 5–11 September (London).

Economist (1982a), 20–6 March (London).

Economist (1982b), 16–22 October (London).

Eichner, A.S. (1973), 'A theory of the determination of the mark-up under oligopoly', *Economic Journal* (December).

Eichner, A.S. (1976), *The Megacorp and Oligopoly* (Cambridge University Press: Cambridge).

Eichner, A.S. (ed.) (1979), *A Guide to Post-Keynesian Economics* (Macmillan: London).

Eichner, A.S. (1983), 'Why economics is not yet a science', in Eichner, A.S. (ed.), *Why Economics is not Yet a Science* (Mac-Millan: London).

Eichner, A.S. and Kregel, J.A. (1975), 'An essay on post-Keynesian theory: a new paradigm in economics', *Journal of Economic Literature* (December).

Engellau, P. and Nygen, B. (1979), *Lending Without Limits* (Secretariat of Future Studies: Stockholm).

Eshag, F. (1977), 'Kalucki's political economy: a comparison with Keynes', *Oxford Bulletin of Economics and Statistics* (February).

Evans, H.P. and Riley, C.J., (1975), 'Simulations with the Treasury model', in Renton, G.A. (ed.), *Modelling the Economy* (Heinemann: London).

Faxen, K.O. (1957), *Monetary and Fiscal Policy under Uncertainty* (Almquist & Wiksell: Stockholm).

Federal Reserve Bank of New York (1965), 'The initial effects of Federal budgetary changes on aggregate spending' (July).

Feiwell, G.R. (1975), *The Intellectual Capital of Michal Kalecki: A Study in Economic Theory and Policy* (University of Tennessee Press: Knoxville).

Ferguson, C.E. (1969), *The Neo-Classical Theory of Production and Distribution* (Cambridge University Press: Cambridge).

Fetherston, M. and Godley, W.A.H. (1981), 'Fiscal and monetary policy in an open economy', in Artis, M.J. and Miller, M.H. (eds), *Essays in Fiscal and Monetary Policy* (Oxford University Press: Oxford).

Floyd, J.E. and Hynes, J.A. (1978), 'Deficit finance and "First-round" crowding-out: a clarification', *Canadian Journal of Economics* (February).

Forman, L. and Eichner, A.S. (1981), 'A post-Keynesian short-period model: some preliminary econometric results', *Journal of Post Keynesian Economics* (Fall).

Friedman, B.M. (1977), 'Even the St Louis model now believes in fiscal policy', *Journal of Money, Credit and Banking* (May).

Friedman, B.M. (1978), 'Crowding-out or crowding-in? Economic consequences of financing government deficits', *Brookings Papers on Economic Activity* (No. 3).

Friedman, M. (1953), *Essays in Positive Economics* (University of Chicago Press: Chicago).

Friedman, M. (1956), 'The quantity theory of money — a restatement', in Friedman, M. (ed.), *Studies in the Quantity Theory of Money* (Chicago University Press: Chicago).

Friedman, M. (1957), *A Theory of the Consumption Function* (Princeton University Press for the National Bureau of Economic Research: Princeton, NJ).

Friedman, M. (1959), 'The demand for money: some theoretical and empirical results', *Journal of Political Economy* (August).

Friedman, M. (1969), *The Optimum Quantity of Money and Other Essays* (Aldine: Chicago).

Friedman, M. (1972), 'Comment on the critics', *Journal of Political Economy* (September/October).

Friedman, M. and Meiselman, D. (1963), 'The relative stability of monetary velocity and the investment multiplier in the United States', *Commission on Money and Credit, Stabilisation Policies* (Prentice–Hall: Englewood Cliffs, NJ).

Friedman, M. and Schwartz, A. (1963), *A Monetary History of the United States, 1867-1960* (National Bureau of Economic Research, Princeton University Press: Princeton, NJ).

Fromm, G. and Klein, L.R. (1973), 'A comparison of eleven econometric models of the US', *American Economic Review* (May).

Garegnani, P. (1978, 1979), 'Notes on consumption, investment and effective demand: I and II', *Cambridge Journal of Economics* (December/March).

Garegnani, P. (1981), 'Alternative interpretations of Keynes: a reply to Kregel' (Mimeo: Trieste).

Gerschenkron, A. (1962), *Economic Backwardness in Historical Perspective* (Harvard University Press: Harvard).

Gerschenkron, A. (1968), *Continuity in History and Other Essays* (Harvard University Press: Harvard).

Godley, W.A.H. and Nordhaus, W.D. (1972), 'Pricing in the trade cycle', *Economic Journal* (September).

Goldfeld, S.M. and Blinder, A.S. (1972), 'Some implications of endogenous stabilization policy', *Brookings Papers on Economic Activity* (No. 3).

Goodhart, C.A.E. (1975), *Money, Information and Uncertainty* (Macmillan: London).

Gordon, R.J. (1976), 'Comments on Modigliani and Ando', in Stein, J.L. (ed.), *Monetarism* (North-Holland: Amsterdam).

Gough, I. (1979), *The Political Economy of the Welfare State* (Croom Helm: London).

Gouldner, A. (1976), *The Dialectics of Ideology and Technology* (Oxford University Press: Oxford).

Gramlich, E.M. (1971), 'The usefulness of monetary and fiscal policy as discretionary stabilization tools', *Journal of Money, Credit and Banking* (May).

Groenewegen, P.D. (1979), 'Radical economics in Australia: a survey of the 1970s', in Gruen, F.G. (ed.), *Surveys of Australian Economics, Vol. 2* (Allen & Unwin: London).

Hadjimatheou, G. and Skouras, A. (1979), 'Britain's economic problem: the growth of the non-market sector?', *Economic Journal* (June).

Hahn, F.H. (1969), 'On some problems of proving the existence of an equilibrium in a monetary economy', in Clower, R. (ed.), *Monetary Theory* (Penguin: London).

Hahn, F.H. (1971), 'Professor Friedman's views on money', *Economica* (February).

Hahn, F.H. (1973), *On the Notions of Equilibrium in Economics* (Cambridge University Press: Cambridge).

Hansen, A. (1949), *Monetary Theory and Fiscal Policy* (McGraw-Hill: New York).

Harcourt, G.C. (1969), 'Some Cambridge controversies in the theory of capital', *Journal of Economic Literature* (June).

Harcourt, G.C. (1972), *Some Cambridge Controversies in the Theory of Capital* (Cambridge University Press: Cambridge).

Harcourt, G.C. (ed.) (1977), *The Microeconomic Foundations of Macroeconomics* (Macmillan: London).

Harcourt, G.C. (1979a), 'Review of John Hicks, *Economic Perspectives, 1977*', *Economic Journal* (March).

Harcourt, G.C. (1979b), 'Review of Ian Steedman, *Marx after Sraffa, 1977*', *Journal of Economic Literature* (June).

Harcourt, G.C. (1980), 'Review of Donald J. Harris, *Capital Accumulation and Income Distribution, 1978*', *Journal of Economic Literature* (September).

Harcourt, G.C. (1981a), 'Marshall, Sraffa and Keynes: incompatible bedfellows?', *Eastern Economic Journal* (January).

Harcourt, G.C. (1981b), 'Notes on an economic querist: G.L.S. Shackle', *Journal of Post Keynesian Economics* (Fall).

Harcourt, G. C. (1982), 'The Sraffian contribution: an evaluation', in Bradley, I. and Howard, M.C. (eds), *Classical and Marxian Political Economy: Essays in Honour of Ronald L. Meek* (Macmillan: London).

Harcourt, G.C. and Kenyon, P. (1976), 'Pricing and the investment decision', *Kyklos* (September).

Harris, D.J. (1975), 'The theory of economic growth: a critique and reformulation', *American Economic Review* (May).

Harris, D.J. (1978), *Capital Accumulation and Income Distribution* (Stanford University Press: Stanford).

Harrod, R.F. (1936), *The Trade Cycle* (Oxford University Press: Oxford).

Hendershott, P.H. (1976), 'A tax cut in a multiple security model: crowding-out, pulling-in and the term structure of interest rates', *Journal of Finance* (September).

Henry, S.G.B. (1981), 'Incomes policy and aggregate pay', in Fallick, J.L. and Elliot, R.F. (eds), *Incomes Policy, Inflation and Relative Pay* (Allen & Unwin: London).

Henry, S.G.B., Sawyer, M. and Smith, P. (1976), 'Models of inflation in the United Kingdom: an evaluation', *National Institute Economic Review* (August).

Hicks, J.R. (1937), 'Mr. Keynes and the classics: a suggested interpretation', *Econometrica* (April).

Hicks, J.R. (1976), 'Must stimulating demand stimulate inflation?', *Economic Record* (December).

Hicks, J.R. (1977), *Economic Perspectives. Further Essays on Money and Growth* (Clarendon Press: London).

Hines, A.G. (1971), 'Alternative theories of the rate of interest', (Mimeo: London).

Ietto Gillies, G. (1978), 'Does the state produce luxuries? a critique of Bacon and Eltis', *British Review of Economic Issues* (May).

Infante, E.P. and Stein, J.L. (1976), 'Does fiscal policy matter?', *Journal of Monetary Economics* (April).

International Currency Review (1980), Vol. 12, Nos. 4 and 6 (London).

International Herald Tribune (1981a), Special supplement on Euromarkets (November).

International Herald Tribune (1981b), Special supplement on international finances (March).

Johnson, H.G. (1973), *The Theory of Income Distribution* (Gray Mills: London).

Kaldor, N. (1955), 'Alternative theories of distribution', *Review of Economic Studies* (No. 2, Vol. 23).

Kaldor, N. (1961), 'Capital accumulation and economic growth', in Lutz, F. (ed.), *The Theory of Capital* (Macmillan: London).

Kaldor, N. (1978), *Further Essays on Economic Theory* (Duckworth: London).

Kaldor, N. and Trevithick, J. (1981), 'A Keynesian perspective on money', *Lloyds Bank Review* (January).

Kalecki, M. (1938), 'Distribution of national income', *Econometrica* (April).

Kalecki, M. (1943), 'Political aspects of full employment', *Political Quarterly* (October).

Kalecki, M. (1954), *Theory of Economic Dynamics* (Allen & Unwin: London).

Kalecki, M. (1971), *Selected Essays on the Dynamics of the Capitalist Economy, (1933-1970)* (Cambridge University Press: Cambridge).

Kalecki, M. (1976a), *Essays on Developing Economies* (Harvester Press: Brighton).

Kalecki, M. (1976b), 'Observations on social and economic aspects of "intermediate regimes"', in Kalecki, M. *Essays on Developing Economies* (Harvester Press: Brighton).

Kalecki, M. and Kula, M. (1976), 'Bolivia — an "intermediate regime" in Latin America', in Kalecki, M. *Essays on Developing Economies* (Harvester Press: Brighton).

Katouzian, H. (1980), *Idology and Method in Economics* (New York University Press: New York).

Keran, M.W. (1969), 'Monetary and fiscal influences on economic activity — the historical evidence', *Federal Reserve Bank of St Louis* (Monthly Review, November).

Keran, M.W. (1970), 'Monetary and fiscal influences on economic activity: the foreign experience', *Federal Reserve Bank of St Louis* (Monthly Review, February).

Keynes, J.M. (1930), *A Treatise on Money* (Macmillan: London).

Keynes, J.M. (1936), *The General Theory of Employment, Interest and Money* (Macmillan: London).

Keynes, J.M. (1937a), 'The general theory of unemployment', *Quarterly Journal of Economics* (February).

Keynes, J.M. (1937b), 'Alternative theories of the rate of interest', *Economic Journal* (June).

Keynes, J.M. (1937c), 'The "ex-ante" theory of the rate of interest', *Economic Journal*, (December).

Keynes, J.M. (1971–), *Collected Writings, Vols. IV, V, VI, VII, XIV, XXII, XXIX* (Macmillan: London).

Keynes, J.M. (1972), *Collected Works, Vol. IX* (Macmillan: London).

Keynes, J.M. and Henderson, H.D. (1929), 'Can Lloyd George do it?', in Keynes, J.M. (ed.), *Essays in Persuasion* (Macmillan: London).

Kindleberger, C.P. (1973), *The World in Depression 1929–39* (Allen Lane: London).

Kitromilides, J. and Skouras, A. (1979), 'On a communication aspect of the relationship between theory and policy-making', *Kyklos* (Vol. 32, Fasc. 3).

Klein, L.R. (1964), 'The role of econometrics in socialist economics', in *Problems of Economic Dynamics and Planning: Essays in Honour of Michal Kalecki* (PWN-Polish Scientific Publishers: Warsaw).

Klein, L.R. (1968), *The Keynesian Revolution* (Macmillan: London).

Klein, L.R. (1973), 'Commentary on "the state of the monetarist debate"', *Federal Reserve Bank of St Louis* (Monthly Review, September).

Klein, L.R. (1975), 'Foreword', in Feiwell, G. *The Intellectual Capital of Michal Kalecki* (University of Tennessee Press: Tennessee).

Kregel, J.A. (1973), *The Reconstruction of Political Economy: An Introduction to Post-Keynesian Economics* (Macmillan: London).

Kregel, J.A. (1976), 'Economic methodology in the face of uncertainty: the modelling methods of Keynes and the post-Keynesians', *Economic Journal* (June).

Kregel, J.A. (1981), 'Effective demand: origins and development of the notion' (Mimeo: Trieste).

Kriesler, P. (1981), 'Kalecki's theory of income distribution', (Unpublished MEc Thesis: Sydney).

Kurihara, K. (ed.) (1955), *Post-Keynesian Economics* (Allen & Unwin: London).

Laidler, D.E.W. (1968), 'The permanent income concept in a macroeconomic model', *Oxford Economic Papers* (March).

Laury, J.S.E., Lewis, G.R. and Ormerod, P.A. (1978), 'Properties of macroeconomic models of the UK economy: a comparative study', *National Institute Economic Review* (February).

Leijonhufvud, A. (1967), 'Keynes and the Keynesians: a suggested interpretation', *American Economic Review* (May).

Leijonhufvud, A. (1968), *On Keynesian Economics and the Economics of Keynes* (Oxford University Press: Oxford).

Leijonhufvud, A. (1979), 'Review of John Hicks, *Economic Perspectives, 1977*', *Journal of Economic Literature* (June).

Lewis, G.R. and Ormerod, P.A. (1979), 'Policy simulations and model characteristics', in Cook, S.T. and Jackson, P.M. (eds), *Current Issues in Fiscal Policy* (Martin Robertson: Oxford).

Lindbeck, A. (1977), *The Political Economy of the New Left*, second edition (New York University Press: New York).

Lindblom, C. (1959), 'The science of muddling through', *Public Administration Review* (Spring).

Lipsey, R. (1960), 'The relationship between unemployment and the rate of change of money wages in the UK, 1862–1957. A further analysis', *Economica* (February).

Longstreth, F. (1979), 'The City, industry and the state', in Crouch, C. (ed.), *State and Economy* (Croom Helm: London).

Malinvaud, E. (1977), *The Theory of Unemployment Reconsidered* (Basil Blackwell: Oxford).

Marshall, A. (1920, 1961). *Principles of Economics: An Introductory Volume*, Vol. 1, Ninth (valiorum) edition (Macmillan: London).

McCallum, B. (1978), 'Price level adjustment and the rational expectations theory', *Journal of Money, Credit and Banking* (November).

McGrath, B. (1977), 'Implications of the government budget constraint', *Journal of Money, Credit and Banking* (May).

Meade, J.E. (1975), 'The Keynesian revolution' in Keynes, M. (ed.), *Essays on John Maynard Keynes* (Cambridge University Press: London).

Meade, J.E. (1981), 'Comments on the papers by Professors Laidler and Tobin', *Economic Journal* (March).

Meltzer, A.H. (1981), 'Keynes's *General Theory*: a different perspective', *Journal of Economic Literature* (March).

Meyer, L.H. (1975), 'The balance sheet identity, the government financing constraint, and the crowding-out effect', *Journal of Monetary Economics* (January).

Meyer, L.H. (1980), 'Financing constraints and the short-run response to fiscal policy', *Federal Reserve Bank of St Louis* (Monthly Review, June/July).

Minsky, H.P. (1974), 'The modelling of financial instability: an introduction', in Vogt, W.G. and Mickle, M.H. (eds), *Modelling and Simulation*, Vol. 5, Proceedings of the Fifth Annual Pittsburgh Conference (School of Engineering, University of Pittsburgh).

Minsky, H.P. (1975a), *John Maynard Keynes* (Columbia University Press: New York).

Minsky, H.P. (1975b), 'Suggestions for a cash flow-oriented bank examination', *Conference on Bank Structure and Competition* (Federal Reserve Bank of Chicago).

Minsky, H.P. (1977), 'A theory of systemic fragility', in Altman, E. and Sametz, A.N. (eds), *Financial Crises* (Wiley Interscience: New York).

Minsky, H.P. (1978), 'The financial instability hypothesis: a restatement', *Thames Papers in Political Economy* (Autumn); reprinted in this volume, chapter 2.

Minsky, H.P. (1982), 'Can it happen again? A reprise', *Challenge* (July/August).

Mitchell, D. W. (1981), 'Deficit and inflation in a post Keynesian model', *Journal of Post Keynesian Economics* (Summer).

Modigliani, F. (1944), 'liquidity preference and the theory of interest and money', *Econometrica* (January).

Modigliani, F. (1971), 'Monetary policy and consumption: linkages via interest rate and wealth effects in the FMP model', in *Consumer Spending and Monetary Policy: The Linkages* (Federal Reserve Bank of Boston, Conference Series No. 5, June).

Modigliani, F. (1977), 'The monetarist controversy or should we forsake stabilisation policies?', *American Economic Review* (March).

Modigliani, F. and Ando, A. (1976), 'Impacts of fiscal actions on aggregate income and the monetarist controversy: theory and evidence', in Stein, J.L. (ed.), *Monetarism* (North-Holland: Amsterdam).

Modigliani, F. and Miller, M. (1958), 'The cost of capital, corporation finance and the theory of investment', *American Economic Review* (June).

Moggeridge, D. (ed.) (1973), *The Collected Works of John Maynard Keynes Vol. XIV* (Macmillan: London).

Moore, B., Jr (1966), *Social Origins of Dictatorship and Democracy: Lord and Peasant in the Mating of the Modern World* (Penguin: Harmondsworth).

Moore, B.J. (1979), 'Monetary factors', in Eichner, A.S. (ed.), *A Guide to Post-Keynesian Ecnomics* (Macmillan: London).

Morrison G. (1966), *Liquidity Preferences of Commercial Banks* (The University of Chicago Press: Chicago).

National Institute of Economic and Social Research (1981), 'Monetary and fiscal policy in the National Institute model', in Artis, M.J. and Miller, M.H. (eds), *Essays in Fiscal and Monetary Policy* (Oxford University Press: Oxford).

National Institute of Economic and Social Research (1983), *National Institute Model 6* (Mimeo: August).

Neild, R.R. (1963), 'Pricing and employment in the trade cycle', *NIES Occasional Paper* (No. 21).

Ohlin, B. (1937), 'Some notes on the Stockholm theory of savings and investment I and II', *Economic Journal* (March/June).

Okun, A. (1981), *Prices and Quantities: A Macroeconomic Analysis* (Basil Blackwell: Oxford).

Papandreou, A. (1966), *The Political Element in Economic Development* (Wicksell Lectures, Almqvist).

Parenti, M. (1970), 'Power and pluralism: a view from the bottom', *The Journal of Politics* (August).

Pasinetti, L.L. (1970), 'Rate of profit and income distribution in relation to the rate of economic growth', in Sen, A.K. (ed.), *Growth Economics* (Penguin: London).

Patinkin, D. (1965), *Money, Interest and Prices*, second edition (Harper & Row: New York).

Peston, M. (1979), 'When is a problem of economic policy solvable?', *Thames Papers in Political Economy* (Spring).

Peston, M. (1981), 'An aspect of the crowding-out problem', *Oxford Economic Papers* (March).

Rasche, R.H. (1973), 'A comparative static analysis of some monetarist proposition', *Federal Reserve Bank of St Louis* (Monthly Review, December).

Redhead, K. (1978), 'Profits and crowding-out', *British Review of Economic Issues* (May).

Riach, P.A. (1981), 'Labour-hiring in post-Keynesian economics' (Mimeo: Adelaide).

Riach, P.A. and Richards, G.M. (1979), 'The lessons of the Cameron experiment', *Australian Economic Papers* (June).

Robinson, J. (1951, 1965, 1979), *Collected Economic Papers Vols I, III, V* (Basil Blackwell: Oxford).

Robinson, J. (1956), *The Accumulation of Capital* (Macmillan: London).

Robinson, J. (1969), *The Economics of Imperfect Competition*, second edition (Macmillan: London).

Robinson, J. (1971), *Economic Heresies* (Macmillan: London).

Robinson, J. (1974), 'History versus equilibrium', *Thames Papers in Political Economy* (Autumn).

Robinson, J. (1975), *Collected Economic Papers, Vol. 3*, second edition (Basil Blackwell: Oxford).

Robinson, J. (1977), 'Michal Kalecki on the economics of capitalism', *Oxford Bulletin of Economics and Statistics*, special issue (February).

Robinson, J. (1979a), 'Foreword', in Eichner, A.S. (ed.), *A Guide to Post-Keynesian Economics* (Macmillan: London).

Robinson, J. (1979b), 'Garegnani on effective demand', *Cambridge Journal of Economics* (June).

Rotheim, R.J. (1981), 'Keynes' monetary theory of value (1933)', *Journal of Post Keynesian Economics* (Summer).

Routh, G. (1980), *Occupation and Pay in Great Britain, 1906-79* (Macmillan: London).

Rowthorn, R. (1977), 'Conflict, inflation and money', *Cambridge Journal of Economics* (September).

Russell, E.A. (1978), 'Foreign investment policy — what role for the economist?', *Australian Economic Papers* (December).

Samuels, J.M., Groves, R.E.V. and Goddard, C.S. (1975), *Company Finance in Europe* (The Institute of Chartered Accountants in England and Wales: London).

Samuelson, P. (1939), 'Interactions between the multiplier analysis and the principle of acceleration', *Review of Economics and Statistics* (May).

Sawyer, M. (1981), *Economics of Industries and Firms* (Croom Helm: London).

Sawyer, M. (1982a), *Macro-Economics in Question* (Wheatsheaf Books: Brighton).

Sawyer, M. (1982b), 'Collective bargaining, oligopoly and macro-economics', *Oxford Economic Papers* (November).

Sawyer, M. (1982c), 'On the specification of structure–performance relationships', *European Economic Review* (March).

Sawyer, M. (1983), *Business Pricing and Inflation* (Macmillan: London).

Sawyer, M., Aaronovitch, S. and Samson, P. (1982), 'The influence of cost and demand changes on the rate of change of prices', *Applied Economics* (April).

Scarth, W.M. (1976), 'A note on the "crowding-out" of private expenditure by bond-financed increases in government spending', *Journal of Public Economics* (April/May).

Schwartz, A.J. (1976), 'Comments on Modigliani and Ando', in Stein, J.L. (ed.), *Monetarism* (North-Holland: Amsterdam).

Shapiro, N. (1981), 'Pricing and the growth of the firm', *Journal of Post Keynesian Economics* (Fall).

Silber, W., (1970), 'Fiscal policy in IS–LM analysis: a correction', *Journal of Money, Credit and Banking* (November).

Simon, H. (1976), *Administrative Behaviour*, second edition (Collier-Macmillan: New York).

Skouras, T. (1975), 'Government activity and private profits', *Thames Papers in Political Economy* (Summer).

Skouras, T. (1978a), 'The "intermediate regime" and industrialisation prospects', *Development and Change* (October).

Skouras, T. (1978b), 'On the analysis of the industrialisation process and the notion of the "intermediate regime": a reply to critics', *Development and Change* (October).

Smith, A. (1937), *The Wealth of Nations* (London Houses, Inc.: New York).

Smith, P.R. (1977), *Keynes' Finance Motive: Some Theory and Evidence* (unpublished PhD thesis: Adelaide).

Spence, A.M. (1977), 'Entry, capacity, investment and oligopolistic pricing', *Bell Journal of Economics* (Autumn).

Spencer, R.W. and Yohe, W.P. (1970), 'The "crowding-out" of private expenditures by fiscal policy actions', *Federal Reserve Bank of St Louis* (Monthly Review, October).

Steedman, I. (1977), *Marx after Sraffa* (New Left Books: London).

Stein, J.L. (1976a), 'The monetarist criticism of the new economics: introduction', in Stein, J.L. (ed.), *Monetarism* (North-Holland: Amsterdam).

Stein, J.L. (1976b), 'Inside the monetarist black box', in Stein, J.L. (ed.), *Monetarism* (North-Holland: Amsterdam).

Steindl, J. (1982), 'The role of household saving in the modern economy', *Banca Nazionale del Lavoro, Quarterly Review* (March).

Tanner, J.E. (1969), 'Lags in the effect of monetary policy: a statistical investigation', *American Economic Review* (December).

Tavlas, G.S. and Aschheim, J. (1981), 'The Chicago monetary growth rate rule: Friedman or Simons reconsidered', *Banca Nazionale del Lavoro, Quarterly Review* (March).

Taylor, C.T. (1979), '"Crowding-out": its meaning and significance', in Cook, S.T. and Jackson, P.M. (eds), *Current Issues in Fiscal Policy* (Martin Robertson: Oxford).

Taylor, C.T. and Threadgold, A. (1979), '"Real" national savings and its sectoral composition', *Bank of England Discussion Paper* (No. 6).

Thirlwall, A.P. (1978), 'The UK's economic problem: a balance of payments constraint?', *National Westminster Quarterly Bank Review* (February).

Tobin, J. (1971), 'Essays on the principles of debt management', in his *Essays in Economics, Vol. 1: Macroeconomics* (North-Holland: Amsterdam).

Tobin, J. (1972), 'Inflation and Unemployment', *American Economic Review* (March).

Tobin, J. (1978), 'Government deficits and capital accumulation', in Currie, D. A. and Peters, W. (eds), *Contemporary Economic Analysis, Vol. 2* (Croom Helm: London).

Tobin, J. and Buiter, W.H. (1976), 'Long-run effects of fiscal and monetary policy on aggregate demand', in Stein, J.L. (ed.), *Monetarism* (North-Holland: Amsterdam).

Treasury and Civil Service Committee (1980), *Memoranda on Monetary Policy* (HMSO: London).

Tucker, D. (1966), 'Dynamic income adjustment to money supply changes', *American Economic Review* (June).

Turnovsky, S. (1977), *Macroeconomic Analysis and Stabilization Policy* (Cambridge University Press: Cambridge).

Viner, J. (1936), 'Mr. Keynes and the causes of unemployment', *Quarterly Journal of Economics* (November).

Vrooman, J. (1979), 'Does the St Louis equation even believe in itself?', *Journal of Money, Credit and Banking* (February).

Walsh, V. and Gram, H. (1980), *Classical and Neoclassical Theories of General Equilibrium* (Oxford University Press: Oxford).

Ward, T. (1981), 'The case for an import control strategy in the UK', *Socialist Economic Review* (The Merlin Press: London).

Weintraub, S. (1966), *A Keynesian Theory of Employment, Growth and Income Distribution* (Chilton: Philadelphia).

Weintraub, S. (ed.) (1977), *Modern Economic Thought* (Basil Blackwell: Oxford).

Wilson, T. (1979), 'Crowding-out: the real issues', *Banca Nazionale del Lavoro* (September).

Wood, A. (1975), *A Theory of Profits* (Cambridge University Press: Cambridge).

Wood, A. (1978), *A Theory of Pay* (Cambridge University Press: Cambridge).

World Bank (1982), *World Development Report* (Oxford University Press: Oxford).

World Financial Markets, Morgan Guaranty Trust (various issues).

Zahn, F. (1978), 'A flow of funds analysis of crowding-out', *Southern Economic Journal* (July).

Index